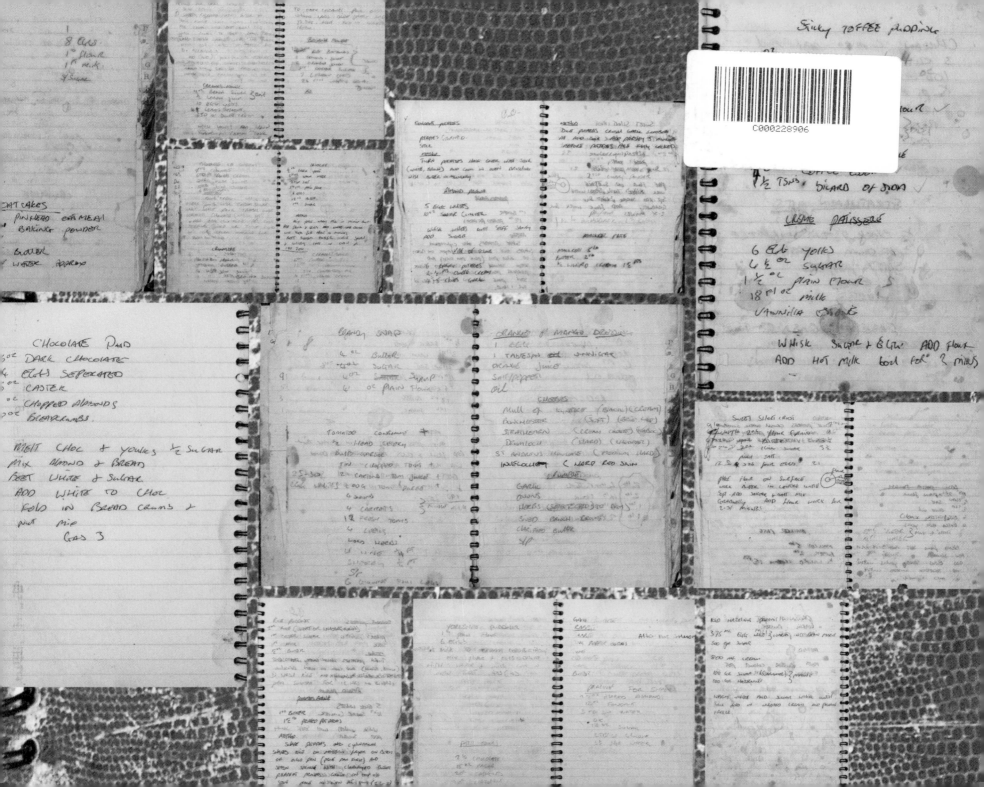

PERCEPTIONS

RECIPES FROM RESTAURANT MARK GREENAWAY

PHOTOGRAPHY BY PAUL JOHNSTON - COPPER MANGO

ISBN 978-0-9934678-2-0

Author © Mark Greenaway
Contributor Emma Louise McGettrick
Photography © Paul Johnston, 2016
Design by Vicki Brown
Edited by Paul Robertson

Printed in Slovenia on behalf of Latitude Press.

Relish Publications
Shield Green Farm
Tritlington
Morpeth
Northumberland
NE61 3DX

For cookbooks and recipes visit:
www.relishpublications.co.uk

For publishing enquiries visit:
www.relish-publishing.co.uk

Mark Greenaway

CONTENTS

Foreword By Ian Rankin

The essence of Mark Greenaway's genius in the kitchen is his seemingly endless inventiveness. He sources locally and uses only the best, most trusted suppliers, and is aware this means a menu must be seasonal. Many chefs of renown agree with this approach, both in Scotland and elsewhere, but few offer the sense of theatre accompanying Mark's dishes. This is evident not just in the combinations of flavours, but also in the colour palate of each serving.

A trip to Restaurant Mark Greenaway becomes an occasion like no other. An egg box contains a fishy surprise. 'Roks and Moss' look the part yet taste sweetly exquisite. When unsealed, flavoursome smoke rises from a glass bowl. Once, memorably, I broke open a Halloween skull to find it filled with the most gorgeous fruit dessert. Great thought has gone into every dish, from start to finish, from initial ingredient to final presentation. So yes, this is food as theatre, food as fun, fine dining that also puts a smile on your face. Having worked for the shortest of times in Mark's kitchen (for a charity video), I've seen first-hand the effort that goes in to ensure each table enjoys the most memorable of dining experiences.

This is cooking which truly challenges perceptions (and preconceptions) while heightening the senses and delighting the palate. Prepare to be amazed as Mark shares with you his story, the secrets of his kitchen and his extraordinary recipes.

How To Use This Book

Although this book has taken me a year to write, it has actually taken 24 years' worth of hard graft in kitchens all across the country and around the world. As far as Rome, London, Boston, Bangkok and Sydney, working at one off dinners or representing the UK as an ambassador, showcasing our outstanding ingredients. It is an industry that really can take you all over the world if you are focused and driven enough.

Each dish in this book is broken down into stages, with an ingredients list and method for each stage. Don't let the size of the recipe daunt you, if you're going to recreate a dish from start to finish, make sure you read the recipe through twice and check if there is any specialist equipment needed first. This way you won't get halfway through the recipe to find yourself stuck.

However, not all recipes need to be looked at this way. If tonight you fancy some beef or lamb, flick through to find my method of cooking and give it a go. You can build up your confidence that way. Or use the book as a quick pairing guide. For example, on page 088 you will see I have paired my 11 hour slow roasted pork belly with sweetcorn, but you could get an amazing pork chop from your local butcher and use that, until you have more time to try the 11 hour slow roasted version. This is now your book, you have all the recipes within it and are free to experiment as much or as little as you like. After all, it is cooking and in my mind there really isn't any right and wrong.

Shop as locally as you can afford, you will be amazed at the deals a local butcher or fishmonger can get you. They will also be on hand to help you with the preparation of the meat and fish if you ask nicely enough! The better the relationship you have with your suppliers the more they will go out of their way to help you.

At the back of the book, I have included a list of my suppliers on page 254 and also handy links for equipment. However, nowadays most specialist equipment can be found on eBay or Amazon, so it is always better to get a couple of quotes before you go ahead and spend your hard earned money.

So, there are a few points to remember: all measurements are in grams and oven temperatures are for fan assisted ovens Celsius, but worry not, there is a quick conversion chart at the back of the book for you to refer to on page 255. All the milk we use is full-fat unless otherwise stated and the sugar is caster sugar, again unless stated otherwise. All eggs are free range and medium in size, butter is unsalted.

I have included a 'Basic Recipes' at the back of the book on page 238 - a great little go to section if you are looking for a basic sauce or accompaniment for a dish that you have in mind. I have also included a section called 'Terms, Meanings, Fancy Words' page 246, for reference just in case you get stuck with any of the 'cheffy' terminology.

If you don't have a dehydrator then don't worry, you can use an oven set on its lowest setting (below 80°C) and it will work just fine, the only problem is it puts your oven out of commission until whatever you are drying is finished, so a dehydrator is a great investment.

Some recipes will make quite a few portions, one of the reasons for this is when there is a blender needed. There is a minimum amount that you can blend without spending the whole time scraping down the sides, so sometimes it's easier to make a batch and use for other things, or to freeze for another time.

All of my ice cream recipes are actually what we call frozen parfait, the recipe was developed by us due to the fact we couldn't afford an ice cream machine when we first opened, so at least you don't need to buy an ice cream machine!

A very handy piece of equipment to invest in is a Thermomix. In mainland Europe these are domestic machines, we chefs however, have really embraced their capabilities. With the dishes that require you to blend with heat, it really is in my mind the only way to do it, not only for efficiency but also consistent results.

It is also worth noting, that some dishes are designed as part of a multi course tasting menu so are smaller in size than others. Salmon, Cucumber, Saffron on page 119 is a great example of this, whereas Beef, Ash, Asparagus on page 107 is meant to be eaten as a complete main course. Right, now all you have to do is get cooking and enjoy.

My First Day As A Chef... Well Kind Of!

Why on earth I got into this trade is a question I am often asked. Was it because I spent summer holidays picking berries in the fields of Scotland or shucking oysters in the south of France, or vanilla picking in Madagascar?

Not bloody likely. I went to Butlins on holidays. I spent one summer in a caravan in Wales. I never even knew what vanilla was let alone oysters. I didn't have a clue where berries came from and, as it turns out, our back garden was full of them. I just had no interest. I was too busy climbing trees, chasing girls and trying to be cool like all of the other kids at school and this is coming from a boy who failed home economics. Unlike a lot of chefs who tell you it was an early calling or that they fell into it, it was never a decision I even thought about until I was about 14 but it has been a decision I have never regretted and wouldn't change even if I could.

I was 15 and a half years old when I started. Sitting in my bedroom, telephone stretched in from the hall, I picked up the Yellow Pages for my local area and started phoning local hotels and restaurants. I explained my want to be a great chef and that I was willing to work for whatever they were willing to pay me. On the third or fourth call my luck was in. I spoke to a very nice chef called Alistair Gillespie from the Cartland Bridge Hotel just outside Lanark in Scotland. He told me a position had unexpectedly come up. I was to start in three days and to be there at 8am ready for my first day. I ran through to the living room shouting the good news to my mum. I was going to be a chef!

Elated is not a strong enough word to describe how I felt. My mum was so proud of her little boy getting such a great job and ultimately a career in such a posh hotel. The next morning, after a very sleepless night, my mum and I jumped on a bus to go shopping for my first set of whites. After a very long and tiring trip we managed to find some. The following day was a write off, my mum was on the phone all day telling everyone about her boy and the big fancy hotel and I was too busy trying on my chef's whites a million times to do anything else.

On my first day I reported to the reception at the Cartland Bridge Hotel at 7.30am sharp - a whole half hour early - wanting to make a good impression. I spoke to the girl behind the reception desk who pointed me downstairs to the kitchen. After speaking to the chef for half an hour I was told to get into my uniform. I was then sharply pointed to the pot sink to clean the breakfast dishes and stock pots that had been on the simmer all night. Perfectly normal I thought for my first day as an apprentice. After finishing, I was sent to the still room to wash up all of the plates, cutlery and teapots which took me about an hour, after which I was swiftly sent back to the pot sink. This continued all day, getting sent from one sink in the main kitchen down the corridor to the other, until 11.30pm. **Continued on page 031.**

CANAPÉS

Rice Cracker | Halibut | Whisky
Makes 8 Canapés

Beetroot & Whisky Cured Halibut

500ml beetroot juice
100ml whisky
200g sea salt
300g caster sugar
1 lemon (juice and zest of)
1 orange (juice and zest of)
360g halibut (skinned, deboned)

(Prepare 3 days ahead)

Reduce the beetroot juice by half and allow to cool.

Mix the beetroot juice, whisky, sea salt and caster sugar with the juice and zest of the lemon and orange.

Pour this liquid over the halibut, then cover and refrigerate for 3 days, turning the halibut over twice a day.

Rinse the halibut well, pat dry with kitchen paper and dice into ½cm cubes.

Return to the fridge and chill until required.

Beetroot Pickled Pearl Onions

2 pearl onions (peeled)
50ml beetroot juice
15ml red wine vinegar
4 coriander seeds
1 star anise

Peel the pearl onions into separate layers and set aside - this is done best by cutting each onion in half and using a small knife to tease the layers apart.

In a heavy-based pot, add all of the remaining pickling ingredients and bring to the boil.

Pour the boiling liquid over the pearl onions, then set aside to cool.

Rice Cracker

50g pudding rice
300ml water
1 litre vegetable oil (for deep frying)

Boil the rice in 300ml of water for 1 hour, then blend in a high speed blender with the liquid.

Spread onto a silicone mat or lined baking tray until 3mm thick.

Place in a dehydrator on its highest setting for 4-5 hours until completely dry. Break into shards.

Deep fry at 210°C until puffed and crisp. Drain on kitchen paper to remove any excess oil.

Sweetened Capers

50g caster sugar
50ml water
100g mini capers (washed, dried)

Boil the sugar and water. Allow to cool.
Pour over the capers and marinate for 3 hours.

To Assemble

75g crème fraîche
50g cornichons
24 nasturtium leaves

Place the crème fraîche in a piping bag and chill until required.

Slice half of the cornichons, dice the remainder.

Place the rice crackers on a serving dish.

Spoon the diced halibut on top of each cracker and dot with crème fraîche.

Scatter over the sliced and diced cornichons, sprinkling 6 capers on each.

Finally garnish with 3 leaves of pickled pearl onions and 3 nasturtium leaves.

Black Haggis | Apple | Thyme
Makes 25 Bon Bons

Parsley & Thyme Mayonnaise

¼ bunch parsley (leaves picked)
1 bunch thyme (leaves picked, chopped)
500ml rapeseed oil
1 whole egg
1 egg yolk
1 tsp Dijon mustard
2 tbsp cider vinegar
sea salt (to taste)

Blanch half of the parsley in salted, boiling water and refresh in ice water. Once chilled, squeeze out any excess liquid.

Place the thyme, the blanched and fresh parsley and rapeseed oil in a blender. Blend on a high speed for 6 minutes, before passing through a fine chinois and refrigerating.

Combine the egg, egg yolk, mustard and vinegar using a food processor. Blend on a medium speed and gradually drizzle in the herb oil while blending.

When all of the oil has been added, taste and season with salt, then place in a piping bag and store in the fridge until required.

Black Haggis Bon Bons

25g butter
2 shallots (finely diced)
1 tsp thyme leaves
400g haggis
300g black pudding
1½ Granny Smith apples (peeled, cut into ½cm cubes)
80g plain flour

1 egg
100ml milk
100g panko breadcrumbs (blended until very fine)
vegetable oil (for deep frying)

Melt the butter and sweat the shallots in a pan, then add the thyme.

Meanwhile, bring the haggis and black pudding up to room temperature. Combine with the shallots, butter and thyme mixture.

Weigh the mixture into 26g balls, inserting a cube of apple into the centre of each bon bon. You should have enough mixture to make 25 bon bons. Refrigerate until required.

Coat the haggis balls evenly in the flour. Beat the egg and milk together. Cover the haggis balls evenly in egg wash, shaking off any excess mixture. To finish, roll in the panko breadcrumbs, shake off the excess mixture once again and deep fry in the oil at 180ºC until golden brown.

To Assemble

thyme (to garnish)

Serve the stacked bon bons in a bowl and top with a dot of herb mayonnaise. Garnish the bowl with a sprig of thyme.

Beef | Bread | Horseradish
Makes 12 Canapés

Beef Carpaccio

280g centre cut beef fillet
sea salt (to season)

(Prepare ahead)

Season the beef with a generous amount of salt.
Sear the beef in a smoking hot, dry pan on all
sides. Whilst still hot, wrap well in cling film.
Set aside to cool, then refrigerate for 2 hours.

Remove from the fridge and slice the beef as
thinly as possible. Place the slices between
2 pieces of silicone paper.

Using a rolling pin, roll the silicone paper so that
the beef trapped between the sheets becomes
flattened to a 1mm thickness. Freeze for 1 hour.

Once frozen, cut into 3cm x 7cm strips and
return to the freezer.

Bread Tubes

6 slices white bread (crusts removed)
50g clarified butter (see page 239)
vegetable oil (for deep frying)

In a pasta machine, pass the bread through each
size setting twice until the last setting is reached,
then cut each slice of bread into 2 rectangles.

Brush a metal tube or pipe, measuring
approximately 2cm in diameter and 20cm in
length, with a little oil. Wrap in silicone paper.

Lightly brush the bread rectangles with clarified
butter before wrapping around the pipe, 2 at a
time. Press the edges together to form a tight seal.

Keeping the bread on the pipe, deep fry in the
oil at 180°C until golden and crispy.

Slide the bread off the pipe to retain a tubular
shape and allow to cool. Repeat with the
remaining slices.

Beef Tartare

150g centre cut beef fillet (fully trimmed,
finely diced)
1 shallot (finely diced)
10 capers
3 cornichons (finely diced)
1 tsp Dijon mustard
6 drops Tabasco sauce
1 tbsp Worcestershire sauce
1 tbsp parsley (chiffonade)
sea salt (to taste)

Combine all of the ingredients and season with
salt to taste. Transfer the mixture into a piping
bag and refrigerate until ready to use.

Horseradish Cream

800ml double cream
fresh horseradish (finely grated)
sea salt (to taste)

Pour the cream into a metal bowl. Season with
horseradish and salt to taste.

Whisk to soft peaks, then spoon into a piping
bag and refrigerate until required.

To Assemble

caraway seeds (to sprinkle)
fresh horseradish (finely grated)

Remove the carpaccio from the freezer and
defrost for 5-6 minutes.

Fill half of each bread tube with horseradish
cream before piping a generous amount of beef
tartare into the centre. Fill the remaining half
with horseradish cream.

Remove the silicone paper from the carpaccio.
Wrap a slice of carpaccio around one end of
each bread tube. Garnish with caraway seeds and
finish with finely grated fresh horseradish.

Salmon | Treacle | Grapefruit
Makes 12 Canapés

Salmon

1kg treacle
1kg caster sugar
500g sea salt
100ml gin
1 grapefruit (juice of)
500g salmon fillet (deboned)

(Prepare 3 days ahead)

Blend together the treacle, sugar, salt, gin and grapefruit juice. Smother the mixture over the salmon. Cover with cling film and refrigerate for 3 days, turning the salmon twice a day.

Rinse the cure off the salmon and pat dry with kitchen paper.

Skin the salmon, discard the skin and cut into 3cm cubes.

Burnt Grapefruit Jelly

70g caster sugar
1 grapefruit (zest of)
1 vanilla pod (seeds of)
250ml fresh grapefruit juice
4 leaves gelatine (soaked in cold water)

Pour the sugar into a heavy-based pot and set over a high heat, stirring with a wooden spoon until the sugar is equally melted to a golden caramel. Once achieved, take off the heat, then add the zest and vanilla seeds.

Very slowly add in the grapefruit juice, stirring frequently until all of the liquid has been incorporated. Return to the heat and bring to the boil.

Stir the soaked gelatine in until dissolved, then pour the liquid through a fine sieve. Set aside to cool.

Pour the mixture into a tray and leave to set in the fridge for 2 hours. Once the jelly is set, cut into ¼cm cubes.

Smoked Mayonnaise

In the restaurant we cold smoke our own eggs however, you could ask your fishmonger to do some for you while they are cold smoking fish.

1 egg (smoked)
1 egg yolk (smoked)
1 tsp Dijon mustard
2 tbsp sherry vinegar
2 drops hickory smoke essence
500ml rapeseed oil
sea salt (to season)

Combine the egg, egg yolk, mustard, vinegar and hickory smoke essence in a bowl or container of a food processor.

Set the food processor on medium speed or whisk by hand and gradually drizzle in the oil while whisking or blending. When all of the oil has been added, taste and season.

Place in a small piping bag or squeezy bottle. Refrigerate until required.

To Assemble

10g salmon caviar
36 sprigs dill

Allow the salmon to come up to room temperature - this usually takes about an hour when out of the fridge.

Arrange 2 squares of grapefruit jelly on top of each salmon cube.

Dot over the mayonnaise and finish with a sprinkling of salmon caviar.

Finally, garnish each canapé with 3 sprigs of dill.

Peanut | Caramel | Shortbread
Makes 40 Lollipops

Candied Kumquats

250g kumquats (halved, deseeded)
900g caster sugar
1.8 litres water

(Prepare ahead)

Place the kumquats, sugar and water into a large pot. Simmer for 2 hours until softened.

Once softened, drain the kumquats and dice into 1cm cubes.

Peanut Base

300g condensed milk
160g peanut butter (smooth)
140g golden syrup
120g butter

Melt all of the ingredients together and bring to the boil whilst whisking continuously.

Once incorporated, remove from the heat and allow to cool.

Lollipops

400ml double cream
400g cream cheese
400g peanut base

(Prepare ahead)

Whip the cream to soft peaks.

Using a whisk, mix the cream cheese with the peanut base until broken down, then fold into the cream. Dollop the mixture into a piping bag and refrigerate for 2 hours. Once chilled, pipe into small, hemispherical moulds before freezing.

Repeat until all of the mixture is used up.

Once frozen, push the hemispheres together, then return to the freezer.

Shortbread

300g plain flour
200g butter
100g caster sugar
200g 70% dark chocolate pistoles
30g white chocolate

(Prepare ahead)

Combine the flour, butter and sugar to form a dough. Roll the dough into logs. Wrap in cling film and place in the refrigerator for 2 hours.

After 2 hours, take the logs out of the fridge and slice to 1cm in thickness.

Preheat the oven to 185°C.

Place the slices of shortbread onto a lined baking tray and bake for 12 minutes until deep brown in colour.

Add 500g of the warm, cooked shortbread to a blender with the dark chocolate and blend to a smooth paste. Reserve half of this paste and keep warm.

Roll the remaining mixture between silicone paper until 3mm thick and refrigerate. Once chilled, remove the silicone paper and cut into 3cm squares.

Melt the white chocolate over a bain-marie. Using a dessertspoon, drizzle over the squares to form fine lines. Return the shortbread squares to the fridge.

To Assemble

Remove the spheres from the freezer, insert the lollipop sticks, then return to the freezer to keep frozen as you work.

Holding the lollipop stick, dip the spheres in the reserved shortbread paste and place on a lined tray before returning to the freezer.

Turn over the chocolate shortbread squares so that the white chocolate side is face down. Using a warm plate or blow torch, slightly melt the tip of each lollipop and stick to the shortbread square.

Refrigerate for 2 hours to allow them to defrost.

To finish, place 2 cubes of kumquat on the top of each shortbread square.

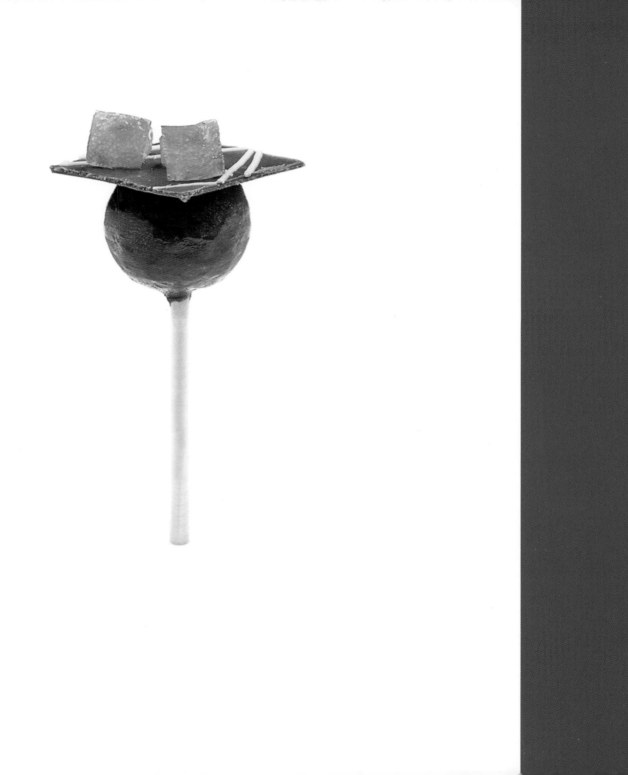

STARTERS

Crab Cannelloni | Cauliflower | Lemon
Serves 12

Herb Butter

100g chervil
100g chives
100g coriander leaves
200g flat leaf parsley
1 clove garlic
300ml milk
375g butter (softened)
sea salt

Take half of all the herbs and blanch in boiling water for 10 seconds, then refresh in ice water. Finely chop the remaining half.

Peel the garlic clove and blanch in 100ml of fresh milk 3 times. Transfer all of the herbs into a blender with the butter and garlic, blend on full until the mixture turns bright green and is completely combined. Check the seasoning, add salt accordingly.

Spread the butter mixture thinly on a sheet of acetate (53cm x 32cm) making sure it is all the same thickness (1-2mm). Place in the fridge. Repeat until all of the butter has been used up.

Crab Mayonnaise

500g fresh white picked crab meat
½ lemon (zest of)
1 tbsp mayonnaise

(Prepare ahead)

Lay the crab meat on a tray and carefully pick through the meat discarding any shell. Once picked, put the crab on a double layered muslin cloth and squeeze out all the excess liquid.

Place the crab meat, lemon zest and mayonnaise in a large bowl and mix until just combined.

Reserve 100g of the mixture in the fridge. Transfer the remainder into a piping bag and pipe onto some outstretched cling film to a thickness of 2½cm. Roll up the crab mixture tightly in the cling film to form cylinders and tie off the ends. Freeze for 2 hours until almost frozen.

Brown Crab Meat

250g fresh brown crab meat
1 lime (zest and juice of)

Pass the brown crab meat through a drum sieve.

Add the lime zest and juice, mix well and place into a piping bag. Store in the fridge.

Cauliflower Custard

¼ large onion (diced)
62g butter
sea salt
1 cauliflower (diced including the stalk)
110ml milk
110ml double cream
1 egg yolk
1 sheet gelatine (soaked in cold water)

Sweat the onion in the butter and add a generous pinch of salt. Add the cauliflower and cook until tender. Pour in the milk and cream and simmer for 8 minutes. Blend immediately, adding in the egg yolk and gelatine while it is blending. Pass through a fine sieve into a large bowl and check the seasoning.

Cover with cling film and store in the fridge.

Compressed Cucumber

1 cucumber
sea salt (pinch of)

(Prepare ahead)

Peel the cucumber, slice lengthways to 3mm thick slices and discard the seeds.

Season the cucumber slices with salt and vacuum pack on the machine's highest setting.

Trim off the end of the bag and vacuum pack once again, at the machine's highest setting. Refrigerate for 2 hours.

Remove from the vacuum pack bag, dry on a clean j-cloth and dice into 2mm cubes.

Lemon Pearls

For the calcium bath

500ml cold water
3½g calcium chloride

For the lemon pearls

100g caster sugar
6.8g sodium alginate
2g citrate
200ml water
100ml lemon juice
extra lemon juice (for storage)

To make the calcium bath, dissolve the calcium chloride in the water and place in the fridge.

To make the lemon pearls, combine the sugar, sodium alginate and citrate in a pan.

Add the water and using a stick blender, blend the ingredients together.

Bring to the boil, remove from the heat and blend again whilst adding the lemon juice. Repeat once more - return to the boil, remove from the heat and blend one last time with the stick blender.

Transfer the mixture into a squeezy bottle and refrigerate for 1 hour.

Once cooled down, slowly empty the mixture from the squeezy bottle into the calcium bath, drop by drop. When finished, take the pearls out of the liquid, rinse and reserve in a bowl of fresh lemon juice. Store in the fridge.

To Assemble

4 baby gem lettuce (shredded, washed)
24 stalks baby coriander

Cut the cylinders of white crab meat to 9cm in length, remove the cling film and return to the freezer.

Slice the herb butter, using a scalpel, into 10cm wide strips.

Remove the crab cylinders from the freezer, place one of the cylinders at the edge of a strip of herb butter. Using the acetate, wrap the butter around the crab until the edges just meet. Trim with a scalpel, then smooth the edges to encase the crab. Repeat with the remaining crab cylinders and herb butter, then return to the freezer.

Trim off both ends of each cylinder, remove the acetate and lay the cannelloni on a clean j-cloth. Allow to defrost completely in the fridge, this should take no more than 1 hour.

Using martini chillers, separate the tops from the bottoms (see photo). Pipe the brown crab meat into the bottom of each round glass, then layer 2cm of cauliflower custard and a spoonful of the reserved crab mayonnaise. Top with lemon pearls and a stalk of baby coriander.

In the bottom of the conical shaped glass, pipe in 1cm of brown crab meat and 2cm of cauliflower custard. Cover over with the shredded baby gem lettuce and compressed cucumber. Top with a cannelloni, some lemon pearls and a stalk of baby coriander.

Using a bench top smoker, fill the bottom glasses with applewood smoke using the top glasses to trap the smoke inside.

Serve immediately.

Continued from page 012

I managed to speak to chef before I finished and asked why I wasn't cooking anything and only washing up? He told me that the position I was given was for a 'KP' which is what he had originally told me on the phone. Of course I had no idea what a 'KP' was and presumed it was another name for apprentice chef. How ridiculous I must have looked standing there all day in full chef whites, a tall white hat and a long white apron, elbow deep in dishwater and sweating like a pig with the grand illusion of being a great chef. I told chef that I wouldn't be coming back unless it was to cook as I wanted to be a chef not a kitchen porter and he told me to come back the next day at 9am to start my apprenticeship. Needless to say, I got the mickey taken out of me for months following my first day and I've had full appreciation for 'KPs' ever since.

Perceptions

Writing a cookbook is something I never thought I would do. I never entered the industry to write books, be on TV or be famous. I don't believe in fame, I think it's a load of old tosh! Just because someone gets paid a little more to do a job, kicks a ball or acts in a movie better than someone else, in my mind, that doesn't make them famous.

Einstein was famous. Steve Jobs was famous. These were people who changed the way we either look at life or conduct our daily lives - they deserve to be famous. The same can't be said of chefs, footballers and actors, in my opinion. At the end of the day, all chefs put their aprons on the same way, we all stand over hot stoves and rattle pans for a living, so in my mind we are all equal. Just because some in the industry have awards, more column inches or airtime on the television doesn't make them famous.

When I started cooking in 1992 there were very few well known chefs. There was Delia Smith and Keith Floyd, I certainly didn't want to be Delia and I really didn't understand Floyd. He just didn't do it for me. However, when I watch one of his shows now I love it; he was a real pioneer and about 20-30 years before his time. We chefs like to go on about local, seasonal food. I am sat here writing a book about it, but Keith Floyd actually went to the far flung corners of the earth and cooked the local food from that region so now I completely understand what he was doing.

So why did I get into the industry? Well simple really, I thought that it would be easy. I mean how hard could it really be? You have all day to do your prep and then you are simply cooking someone's lunch and dinner...right? That's not difficult is it? So was I right? Well no. Not even close to being right; it is one of the most physically and emotionally demanding jobs out there. Not that I am comparing it to anything as I have never done anything else. Ever. I have only ever been a chef. Well that is a bit of a lie; I covered my mate Ally's paper round for two weeks when I was 13, while he was on holiday, for £4 a week. And that was hard, especially on a Sunday with all the supplements, but apart from that, my life has and still does revolve around the seasons in the kitchen and trying to perfect my craft.

Writing this book was no easy undertaking. The man hours alone putting my stories down on paper have been especially difficult due to the fact that as soon as I step foot in my restaurant, I get constantly pulled from one phone call or one question or in and out of meetings. So for a chef who already has no time to actually sit down and write, it proved particularly challenging. **Continued on page 057.**

Chicken | Potato | Damson
Serves 4

Chicken & Potato Pressé

1kg duck fat
6 chicken legs
sea salt (to season)
6 sprigs thyme (picked, finely chopped)
5 Maris Piper potatoes

(Prepare the day before)

Preheat the oven to 120°C.

Melt the duck fat and season the chicken legs with salt and chopped thyme.

Arrange the chicken legs in a casserole dish and cover them with the duck fat.

Place the chicken legs into the oven for 3 hours, until the meat is meltingly soft.

Remove from the oven, then drain the chicken legs.

Once slightly cooled, pick all of the meat, discarding the skin and bones.

Preheat the oven to 185°C.

Peel and thinly slice the potatoes.

Layer the potato slices and the confit chicken in the tray, 3 layers of potatoes for every layer of chicken, making sure to season each layer with a little salt.

Bake in the oven for 50 minutes until the potatoes are soft.

Remove from the oven and lay silicone paper over the top. Press the mixture down with a tray of equal size and refrigerate overnight.

Pickled Damsons

150g caster sugar
6 star anise
150ml water
150ml red wine vinegar
200g damson plums (stones removed)

Place the sugar in a non-stick pan and heat until it melts to a caramel. Once achieved, add the star anise, water and vinegar. Bring to the boil.

While the pickling liquor is still boiling hot, pour over the plums.

Allow the plums to cool in the liquor.

Bread Tubes

2 slices white bread (crusts removed)
50g clarified butter (see page 239)
vegetable oil (for deep frying)

In a pasta machine, pass the bread through each size setting twice until the last setting is reached. Cut each slice of bread into 2 rectangles.

Brush a metal tube measuring approximately 2cm in diameter and 20cm in length with a little oil and wrap it in silicone paper.

Lightly brush the bread rectangles with clarified butter.

Wrap 2 of the rectangles around the pipe at a time, pressing the edges together to form a tight seal. Deep fry in the oil at 180°C until golden and crispy.

Slide the bread off the pipe, retaining a tubular shape and allow to cool.

Repeat with the remaining slices.

Chicken Liver Parfait

250g chicken livers (fully prepared, sinew removed)
200ml milk
150g butter
1 shallot (peeled, finely chopped)
120g foie gras (ethically sourced)
75ml brandy
200ml double cream
sea salt

(Prepare ahead)

Cut the livers in half and soak in the milk for 2 hours. Once adequately soaked, drain the livers, rinse well and pat dry.

Melt the butter in a frying pan over a medium heat, add the shallot and sweat gently.

Turn up the heat, add the livers and foie gras. Sear for a couple of minutes until browned on the outside but pink on the inside. Add the brandy, be careful as this will flame, and then add the cream.

Blend the mixture in a food processor until smooth and lump free. Season with salt to taste.

Pass the mixture through a fine chinois into a bowl set over ice. Press cling film onto the mix to stop any discolouration and refrigerate for 3 hours.

Chicken Jelly

500ml double chicken stock (see page 239)
2 star anise
sea salt (pinch of)
1 sheet gelatine (soaked in cold water)

(Prepare ahead)

Bring the chicken stock, star anise and salt to the boil, reducing to 400ml before removing from the heat and adding the gelatine.

Pass through a fine chinois onto a cling film lined tray to a 1½cm thickness and then refrigerate for 4 hours.

Cut into 1½cm cubes.

To Assemble

20g pistachios (ground)
20 candied sea buckthorn berries (see page 239)
mixed baby herbs (handful)

Scatter the ground pistachios in a line across each of the plates.

Slice the pressé, then place onto the centre of the plates.

Place the parfait into a piping bag. Pipe into the bread tubes and rest the tubes on the pressé.

Scatter the pickled plums, mixed herbs and candied sea buckthorn berries around the plates.

Finish by scattering 3 pieces of chicken jelly on top of and around the pressé on each plate.

Squid | Squid | Squid
Serves 6

Beetroot & Chilli Gel

3g gellan gum type F
5g caster sugar
200ml beetroot juice
100ml apple juice
½ red chilli

Rub the gellan gum through the sugar.

Blend the sugar through the beetroot and apple juice in a pot with a stick blender, then add the red chilli. Place on the heat and slowly bring up to the boil, stirring continuously. Once boiled, remove from the heat and blend again with a stick blender. Pass through a fine chinois and set in a tray.

Once fully cooled, add the set gel to a blender and blend on a high speed, scraping the sides to achieve a smooth, silky gel. Decant into a squeezy bottle.

Poached & Fried Squid

300g fresh baby squid (cleaned, innards removed)
120ml fish stock (see page 240)
20g plain flour
15g coriander seeds (freshly ground)
sea salt (generous pinch of)
50g squid tentacles
vegetable oil (for deep frying)

(Prepare ahead)

Cut the squid in half and lay it out flat on silicone paper.

Wrap in cling film and freeze (freezing overnight will tenderise the squid).

Defrost the squid a little but not fully.

Using a very sharp knife, score the squid on an angle but not all the way through the flesh. Once scored, cut each side into 6 equal pieces.

Separate the squid into 2 piles, half for poaching and half for deep frying.

Bring the fish stock to a rapid boil and drop in half of the reserved squid. Bring back to the boil and remove from the heat immediately. Allow to sit in the fish stock whilst frying the other half.

Sift together the flour, ground coriander seeds and salt. Douse the remaining squid and tentacles in the flour mixture. Deep fry at 185°C for 2-3 minutes until crisp and golden. Drain on absorbent paper and season a little with sea salt.

Drain the poached squid and season a little with salt.

Candy Beetroot

2 candy beetroots

Slice the beetroots as thinly as possible using a mandoline. Cut each slice into 2cm squares, 36 squares will be required. Set aside.

Squid Lasagne

500g squid (cleaned, roughly chopped)
sea salt (generous pinch of)
2 egg whites
2 sachets squid ink
1½g carbon black

Blend the squid for 2 minutes, then add the salt and blend again for 2 minutes. Pour in the egg

whites and blend for a further 2 minutes. Add the squid ink, carbon black and blend for 2 minutes, then pass through a drum sieve.

Weigh out 45g of the mixture into 12 separate vacuum pack bags measuring 24cm x 18cm. Vacuum pack the bags on the highest setting.

Using a rolling pin, smooth the mixture out so you have an even layer of mixture inside the bags. Poach for 4 minutes. Cut the bags carefully and remove the 'lasagne'. Drain on absorbent paper immediately and plate up.

To Assemble

½ fennel bulb (finely shaved)
fennel fronds (from 1 fennel bulb)

Divide the squid 'lasagne' between 6 plates. Scatter over the fried and poached squid. Dot around the beetroot and chilli gel. Lay slices of the raw fennel and candy beetroot over the top of the squid.

Finally, garnish with some of the fennel fronds.

Trout | Cucumber | Horseradish
Serves 4

Home Smoked Trout

400g trout fillet (skin removed, deboned)
200g Demerara sugar
½ orange
1 star anise
3 peppercorns
100g sea salt

(Prepare ahead)

Blend all the ingredients together, excluding the trout. Spread the mixture over the fish on all sides. Rest in the fridge for 12 hours.

Wash off the salt and sugar mixture and pat the trout dry.

Scatter wood chips onto a baking tray and top with a wire rack. Lay the trout on the wire rack and cover in tin foil, then transfer to the hob over a medium heat. Smoke for 7-8 minutes or until the trout is medium rare. Place the trout in a smoking hot, dry pan to blacken the outside. Once blackened, remove and break into 16 pieces.

Beetroot Pickled Shallots

4 shallots (peeled)
100ml beetroot juice
25ml red wine vinegar
4 coriander seeds
1 star anise

Peel the shallots into separate layers and set aside. This is done best by cutting each shallot into quarters and using a small knife to tease the layers apart.

Add all of the pickling ingredients to a heavy-based pan and bring to the boil. Pour the boiling liquid over the shallots and set aside until cool. This will turn the shallots a crimson red colour and impart flavour.

Roasted Cucumber

1 cucumber

Peel the cucumber and char the outside with a blow torch. Whilst the cucumber is still hot, vacuum pack on the highest setting. Leave for 20 minutes so that it cooks in its own heat. Once it has cooled completely, remove from the vacuum pack bag and cut into 1cm slices, allowing 3 slices per portion.

Horseradish Panna Cotta

650ml double cream
150ml milk
sea salt (pinch of)
3 sprigs thyme
1 tbsp creamed horseradish
4 sheets gelatine (soaked in cold water)

(Prepare ahead)

Add all the ingredients to a pot and bring to a simmer.

Pass through a fine chinois onto a tray lined with cling film, then set in the fridge for 3 hours.

Semi Dried Cherry Tomatoes

40g sea salt
6 sprigs thyme
1 clove garlic (sliced)
6 cherry tomatoes (halved)

(Prepare ahead)

Scatter sea salt, thyme and garlic on a silicone paper lined tray that will fit inside a dehydrator. Place the tomatoes on top, then dehydrate for 9 hours at 85°C.

To Assemble

16 sprigs dill
4 bread tubes (see page 238, these tubes need to be made to be 3cm in length)

Arrange 3 slices of cucumber on each plate. Scatter around 4 pieces of trout and 3 tomato halves. Pipe half of the horseradish panna cotta into the bread tubes and arrange one in the centre of each dish. Spoon a rocher of the remaining horseradish panna cotta onto the plate.

To finish, sprinkle over some of the pickled shallots and dill.

Mackerel | Hibiscus | Apple
Serves 4

Hibiscus & Elderflower Pickled Shallots

4 shallots (peeled)
60ml elderflower cordial (see page 240)
90ml hibiscus syrup
100ml vegetable stock (see page 244)
25ml cider vinegar
4 coriander seeds
1 star anise

Peel the shallots into separate layers and set aside. This is done best by cutting each shallot into quarters, using a small knife to tease the layers apart.

Add the elderflower cordial, hibiscus syrup, stock, vinegar, coriander seeds and star anise to a heavy-based pot and bring to the boil. Pour the boiling liquid over the shallots and set aside until cool. Drain the cooled shallots and reserve the pickling liquor.

Candied Gooseberries

12 gooseberries
100g caster sugar
50ml water

(Prepare ahead)

Gently combine the gooseberries, sugar and water. Vacuum pack and cook at 48°C for 3 hours in a water bath.

Beetroot Cured Apple

500ml beetroot juice
100g caster sugar
¼ lemon (juice of)
1 Granny Smith apple

(Prepare ahead)

Reduce the beetroot juice and sugar down to 200ml, add the lemon juice, then leave to cool.

Using a large Parisienne scoop, scoop out the apple leaving the skin on. Allow 3 per portion.

Drop the apple balls into the beetroot juice, then leave them to infuse for a minimum of an hour.

Israeli Couscous

150g Israeli couscous
400ml vegetable stock (see page 244)
dill (sprig of)
sea salt (pinch of)

Simmer the couscous in the stock with the dill for 6-8 minutes until tender.

Drain the liquid off and season with salt before setting aside to cool.

Mackerel

4 mackerel fillets (deboned)

Blow torch the skin-sides of the mackerel fillets until blackened. This will add great flavour and also cook the fish.

To Assemble

16 sprigs affilla cress or pea shoots
edible flower petals

Sprinkle some of the Israeli couscous over each plate, then arrange a mackerel fillet in the centre. Scatter around the pickled shallots, beetroot cured apple, gooseberries, cress or pea shoots and edible petals.

To finish, drizzle over some of the reserved pickling liquor from the shallots.

Beef | Tomato | Parmesan
Serves 4

Beef Carpaccio

280g centre cut beef fillet
sea salt

(Prepare ahead)

Season the beef with a generous amount of salt and place into a smoking hot, dry pan, searing the beef fillet on all sides. Whilst the beef is still hot, wrap it well in cling film. Set aside to cool, then refrigerate for 2 hours.

Slice the beef as thinly as possible. Lay 4-5 slices, creating a rough round shape, between 2 pieces of silicone paper. With a rolling pin, roll the silicone paper so that the beef is trapped between the sheets and gets flattened to a thickness of 1mm. Repeat until you have 4 circles of beef rolled out between the pieces of silicone paper. Freeze for 1 hour.

Remove the upper layers of silicone paper and, with a 15cm round cutter, cut out 4 large rounds from the beef.

Tomato Tartare

2 plum tomatoes (skinned, seeds removed)
olive oil (drizzle of)
2 tbsp sweetened capers (see page 243)
4 gherkins (diced)
1 large shallot (diced)
½ lemon (juice of)
2 tbsp parsley (chopped)
Worcestershire sauce (dash of)
¼ tsp Dijon mustard
Tabasco sauce (splash of)

(Prepare ahead)

Finely dice the tomatoes and drizzle with olive oil before adding most of the capers (reserve some for garnish), the diced gherkins, the shallot and the lemon juice. Add a little of the chopped parsley to the mixture, reserving some for garnish.

Mix through the Worcestershire sauce, mustard and Tabasco. Refrigerate until required.

Leave this to rest out of the fridge for a good hour before serving.

Parmesan Crisps

100g Parmesan (finely grated)

Preheat the oven to 185°C.

Sprinkle the Parmesan evenly over an oven tray lined with silicone paper. Cook in the oven for approximately 7 minutes or until the Parmesan has melted and is golden brown.

Remove the tray from the oven and whilst the Parmesan is still hot, cut it into squares and reserve in an airtight container until needed.

Parmesan Snow

500g Parmesan (finely grated)
450ml water
1 leaf gelatine (soaked in cold water)
2 egg whites

Add the Parmesan and water to a pan and bring to the boil. Once it reaches the boil, remove from the heat and immediately add the gelatine. Allow to cool.

Pass the mixture through a fine chinois and discard the solids. Add the egg whites to the cooled mixture, then pour into an espuma gun and charge twice.

Empty the mixture into a frozen tray and place in the freezer. When frozen, scrape the mixture to break it up as if it was a granita.

To Assemble

reserved parsley and capers
4 gherkins (sliced)
2 tbsp celeriac (finely shredded)
12 sprigs wood sorrel
sea salt

Lay the beef carpaccio on each plate and remove the bottom layer of silicone paper. Press some of the tomato mixture into a 4cm round cutter to form a disc. Place on top of the beef.

Scatter some of the capers and sliced gherkins over the beef along with the finely shredded celeriac. Sprinkle around the remaining parsley, some wood sorrel and a little sea salt.

To finish, scatter the Parmesan snow and Parmesan crisps over the dish, allowing roughly 4 per person.

Smoked Salmon | Caviar | Sauce Gribiche
Serves 6

Sauce Gribiche

4 hard-boiled eggs (yolks discarded, whites finely diced)
100ml olive oil
½ bunch fresh chervil (chopped)
½ bunch fresh tarragon (chopped)
½ bunch fresh flat parsley (finely shredded)
100g sweetened baby capers (see page 243)
100g cornichons (drained, finely diced)
sea salt

Mix all the ingredients in a bowl and gently fold together. Season with a little salt but be careful as the capers can already be a little salty.

Smoked Salmon Cannelloni

200g smoked salmon trimmings
100g crème fraîche
50ml double cream
2 tsp chives (chopped)
sea salt (pinch of)
6 strips smoked salmon (thinly sliced)

(Prepare ahead)

Blend the smoked salmon trimmings together with the crème fraîche and cream until it forms a smooth mousse-like texture. Place the mixture into a small bowl and fold through the chives, adding a little pinch of salt. Refrigerate for approximately 1 hour.

Place the smoked salmon mousse mixture into a piping bag with a plain nozzle.

Lay out the smoked salmon on outstretched cling film to form a large strip. Pipe the smoked salmon mousse along the length of the slices and roll up tightly together to form a cylinder. Tie off the ends of the cling film and refrigerate for 1 hour.

Slow Cooked Egg Yolk

4 eggs
sea salt

(Prepare ahead)

Place the eggs in a water bath at 62°C for 4 hours.

Peel the eggs, discard the shell and the white. Place the yolks in a bowl and season with a little sea salt. Place in a piping bag and refrigerate.

Melba Toasts

2 slices white bread (crusts removed)
50g clarified butter (see page 239)
vegetable oil (to deep fry)
sea salt

In a pasta machine, pass the bread through each size setting twice until the last setting is reached. Cut each slice of bread into 16 triangles. Lightly brush the bread triangles with clarified butter. Deep fry in the oil at 180°C until golden and crispy.

Drain the triangles on kitchen paper, then season with a little sea salt.

To Assemble

1 leaf radicchio (torn into small pieces)
½ jar caviar

Cut the salmon cannelloni into 11cm lengths and remove the cling film.

Using a 14cm cookie cutter, press the gribiche around the inside to form a circle on each plate. Remove the cookie cutter and arrange the smoked salmon cannelloni in the middle of the circle. Decorate the circle of gribiche with the egg yolk, Melba toasts, caviar and radicchio.

Farm

Rob is one of those guys who you meet and instantly like. The fact he used to be a chef before he found his true passion in farming probably has a lot to do with that, however I am getting a little ahead of myself here. Who is Rob? We will get to that in a minute. First let me give you a little background on where he works.

My relationship with Cyrenians began after a chance meeting with Ewan Aitken, their chief executive, at the STV Edinburgh studios in Fountainbridge. I was there to film a cooking spot and he was there to talk about some local issues regarding his charity. I had no idea at the time how much of an impact this encounter would have on me going forward. Ewan and I chatted and I invited him into the restaurant for a coffee just to see if there was any way I could get involved in the amazing work they do. It was only during this meeting that I discovered their close connection to food and the cogs really began to turn.

For nearly 50 years, Cyrenians has served those on the edge, working with the homeless and vulnerable to transform their lives, helping them believe that they can change their lives, and working with them as they lead their own transformation.

Shortly after this meeting I headed along to their Good Food depot in Leith. The depot runs a FareShare programme where they redistribute surplus food from producers and suppliers to organisations working with vulnerable people. The depot is also home to their Food Education programme which provides practical classes that encourage healthy eating and promote social inclusion. I was honoured to be asked to teach one of these classes and spent an enjoyable afternoon in their kitchen making fishcakes, wilted spinach and poached eggs with the students.

Cyrenians also has a farm and this really peaked my interest. The farm is a social enterprise located just outside Edinburgh. It is a working farm producing fruit, vegetables and eggs; it is also home to a community of vulnerable young people, many with experiences of homelessness.

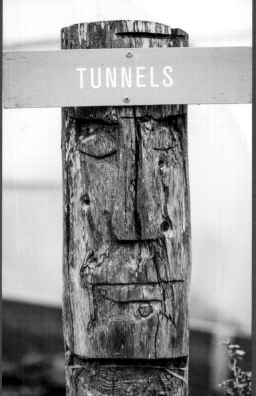

The farm grows food and helps the community to grow people, providing a range of opportunities for individuals to develop skills and confidence as a step towards a settled lifestyle.

I soon set up a visit with Rob Davidson, the farm's enterprise manager. This was the first of many trips to the farm. I couldn't believe that such an incredible space existed such a short distance from my restaurant. Rob, along with Tim Haslin, a project worker and horticulturist, gave me an extensive tour. Rob's knowledge and expertise astounded me. As it turns out, he is a 10th generation farm labourer; he was brought up on farms across Scotland. After Rob left home, he studied Environmental Biology, all the while working as a chef and he continued his cooking career after he graduated. Because of this, his knowledge of ingredients is second to none. He gave me a full tour of the eight acre holding and of the produce that they grow. I was transported back to being like a little kid in a sweet shop, everywhere I looked I could see endless pairing opportunities with the vegetables growing right in front of me and to get vegetables out of the ground and onto a plate the same day really is any chef's dream. In fact, a few lucky chefs are now buying farms and turning them into kitchen working farms. I have the luxury of not only getting amazing produce and supporting a very worthy cause but also I don't have the day to day stresses of running a farm. Believe me - running a restaurant is stressful enough.

I knew straight away that I wanted to use this local produce on the plates leaving my kitchen. Every week since then, we look forward to their fruit and vegetable delivery. As Rob and I chatted, I realised that there was a real opportunity here. I enquired as to whether they would be able to grow specific ingredients for me. In November 2015, Rob and I sat down and created a cutting and growing plan for the coming year. I requested vegetables and herbs that I never dreamed I would be able to get my hands on - whether it is parsnips picked at a specific time so that they are an exact size, kale flowers or specific herbs, it has opened up a whole range of possibilities when it comes to the food we serve.

Spring Garden
Serves 10

Pea Custard

1 large shallot (finely diced)
1 large garlic clove (crushed)
125g butter
sea salt (to taste)
500ml milk
150ml double cream
1kg fresh peas (shelled)
14 egg yolks
5 leaves gelatine (soaked)

(Prepare ahead)

Sweat the shallot and garlic in the butter with a generous pinch of salt until soft and translucent.

Pour in the milk and cream, then bring to the boil. Add the peas and return to the boil.

Remove from the heat immediately.

Blitz half of the mixture in a blender on full power for 5 minutes until smooth. Repeat for the other half. Pass through a chinois, taste and add more salt if needed.

Transfer 1½kg of the mixture to a Thermomix, blend and add in the egg yolks.

Continue to blend on setting 5 at 80°C for 10 minutes. After 5 minutes, use a thermometer to check that the temperature of the mixture has reached 80°C. Add the gelatine and blend for a further 5 minutes.

Set the bowls for serving into a tray of ice water.

Pour the custard mixture into the bowls until it comes one third of the way up. Set in the fridge.

Once cooled and set, individually wrap each bowl in cling film and store back in the fridge until required.

Carrots

10 baby carrots
rapeseed oil (to drizzle)
sea salt (pinch of)

Peel the carrots very gently, scraping away any dirt from the top, taking care not to break the head of the carrot.

Vacuum pack the carrots in a single layer with a drizzle of rapeseed oil and a pinch of salt.

Cook in a water bath set at 85°C for approximately 40 minutes, or until just tender. Refresh the pouch in ice water.

Set aside until required.

Croutons

5 slices white bread (crusts removed)
vegetable oil (for deep frying)
sea salt

Feed the slices of bread through a pasta machine until the third thinnest setting.

Dice the bread to 3mm cubes and then deep fry at 180°C for 1 minute or until crispy, but not too dark.

Season with salt, drain on kitchen paper and leave to dry out in a warm environment.

Truffle Dressing

15g wholegrain mustard
6ml cider vinegar
5ml truffle oil
200ml honey
200ml rapeseed oil
1 black truffle (roughly chopped)
sea salt

Place the mustard, vinegar and truffle oil in a food processor and blend at a low speed.

Slowly pour in half of the honey and half of the rapeseed oil. Turn up the speed slightly until it starts to emulsify, then add in the chopped truffle, the remaining honey and rapeseed oil.

Taste and season with salt.

To Assemble

10 spears of asparagus (peeled, blanched)
1 packet enoki mushrooms
150g peas (shelled, blanched)
100g broad beans (shelled, blanched)
selection of wild herbs and edible flowers

Toss the carrots, asparagus, peas and broad beans in the truffle dressing.

Top each bowl of custard with a mixture of the vegetables, wild herbs and flowers.

Finally sprinkle over the croutons to create your perfect 'Spring Garden'.

Ham Hough | Puffed Pork Skin | Piccalilli
Serves 6

Ham Hough Ballotine

3 smoked ham houghs
3 unsmoked ham houghs
1 stick celery (peeled, washed)
2 carrots (peeled, washed)
1 onion (peeled, halved)
3 cloves
2 bay leaves
8 sprigs thyme
150g walnuts
sea salt
2 shallots (diced)
20g tarragon (chopped)

(Prepare ahead)

Rinse the ham houghs under cold running water for 1 hour.

Transfer the houghs into a large pot, cover with water and bring to the boil. Drain and discard the liquid. Top the pot up with water, then add the celery, carrots, onion, cloves, bay leaves and thyme. Gently simmer for 4 hours until the ham houghs are tender. Pick the meat from the ham houghs while they are still hot, discarding any fat, sinew or skin.

Preheat the oven to 175°C.

Roast the walnuts with a generous pinch of salt for 8 minutes, add to the ham hough meat with the shallots and tarragon and mix well. Wrap the mixture in cling film to form a cylinder (5cm in diameter) tying off both ends. Refrigerate until ready to serve.

Croutons

2 slices white bread (crusts removed)
vegetable oil (for deep frying)
sea salt

Feed the slices of bread through a pasta machine until the second thickest setting. Dice the bread into 1cm cubes and deep fry at 180°C for 1 minute or until crispy, but not too dark. Season with salt.

Drain on a piece of kitchen paper and leave to dry out in a warm environment.

Salt Baked White Beetroot

250g plain flour
2 egg whites
150g rock salt
75ml water
1 white beetroot

Mix the flour, egg whites and rock salt in a mixer for 4 minutes. Slowly add the water until it becomes a tight dough. Keep mixing for a further 10 minutes.

Preheat the oven to 180°C.

Roll out the salt dough to a ½cm thickness, wrap it around the beetroot and place on an oven tray. Bake for 1½ hours.

Break open the crust, discard and allow the beetroot to cool naturally, do not cool with the crust on as the beetroot will end up too salty. Peel and dice into 1cm cubes.

Piccalilli Purée

140g silverskin onions (peeled)
100g courgette (finely diced)
½ small cauliflower (thinly sliced)
1 pear (deseeded, diced)
rapeseed oil (drizzle of)
6g sea salt
10g ginger (grated)
1 tbsp coriander seeds
1 tbsp mustard seeds
85g Demerara sugar
1 tbsp turmeric
2 tbsp English mustard powder
380ml sherry vinegar
200ml water
10g Ultratex

Gently sweat the onions, courgette, cauliflower and pear in a little rapeseed oil in a heavy-based pan. Add the salt, ginger, coriander seeds, mustard seeds, sugar, turmeric, mustard powder, vinegar and water. Bring to a simmer, then transfer to a blender and blend on a medium speed for 8 minutes.

While blending, add in the Ultratex, a little at a time, until a coating consistency is achieved, then pass through a fine chinois.

To Assemble

20g puffed pork skin (see page 242)
hairy bittercress (to garnish)

Cut the ballotine into 1cm slices and remove the cling film. Arrange the pieces on each plate. Dot around the purée, scatter the croutons, beetroot, puffed pork skin and hairy bittercress.

Salmon | Dill | Kuzu
Serves 12

Dehydrated Salmon

150g smoked salmon

(Prepare 48 hours ahead)

Shred the salmon onto a silicone mat and, using a dehydrator on the highest setting, dehydrate for 48 hours. Blend in a spice blender and store in an airtight container.

Dill Powder

100g dill

(Prepare in advance)

Place the dill on a silicone mat, dehydrate on the dehydrator's highest setting for 8 hours.

Blend in a spice blender, then store in an airtight container.

Dill & Kuzu Crackers

100g kuzu powder
1 litre fish stock (see page 240)
vegetable oil (for deep frying)
sea salt
dill powder

(Prepare 24 hours ahead)

Blend the kuzu powder with the fish stock in a heavy-based pan. Bring to the boil and cook out for 2-3 minutes. Pour out onto a silicone mat to a ½cm thickness. Dehydrate for 24 hours on the dehydrator's highest setting.

Break into irregular shaped shards and deep fry at 220°C until the crackers puff up and triple in size. Drain well on kitchen paper, season with sea salt and dill powder.

Smoked Salmon Espuma

300g smoked salmon trimmings
300ml double cream
300ml milk
4g sea salt
1 leaf gelatine (soaked in cold water)
4 drops liquid smoke essence

(Prepare ahead)

Add the salmon, cream, milk and salt to a heavy-based pan. Bring to a gentle simmer on a medium heat, then remove from the heat. Add the gelatine and liquid smoke. Cling film the pan and leave to infuse for 1 hour.

Pass the mixture through a fine chinois and discard the salmon. Pour into an espuma gun. Charge the gun twice. Refrigerate for 3 hours.

Salmon Tartare

200g salmon fillet (skinned, deboned)
1 shallot (finely diced)
1 tbsp parsley (chopped)
10g sweetened capers (see page 243)
10g gherkins (diced)
25ml lemon juice
sea salt (pinch of)

Dice the salmon into ½cm cubes and combine with all the ingredients. Refrigerate until ready to serve.

To Assemble

½ jar salmon caviar
12 ceramic egg shell moulds, or sterilised egg shells

Place a teaspoon of salmon tartare in the bottom of the egg moulds, followed by half a teaspoon of salmon caviar and a generous sprinkling of dehydrated smoked salmon. Fill up the moulds with the salmon espuma and finish with a dusting of dill powder. Serve with the crackers.

Pheasant | Truffle | Carrot
Serves 16

Pheasant Terrine

6 pheasants (legs and breasts)
40g sea salt
3 sprigs rosemary
2 oranges (zest and juice of)
3 cloves garlic (skin on, crushed)
2 litres rapeseed oil
10g tarragon (chopped)
3 shallots (diced)
extra sea salt (to season)

(Prepare 2 days ahead)

Wash the pheasant legs well and pat dry. In a large bowl, cover the legs with the 40g of sea salt, rosemary, orange zest and juice and one of the garlic cloves. Cover the bowl with cling film, then marinate in the fridge for 10 hours.

Preheat the oven to 95°C.

Wash the marinade off the pheasant legs, pat dry and place in a casserole dish. Cover with the rapeseed oil and the remaining garlic cloves, then transfer to the oven for 8 hours.

Remove from the oven and allow to cool. Reserve the confit oil.

Pick the meat from the bones, discarding the skin, bones and any sinew. Roast the pheasant breasts in a pan with a drizzle of rapeseed oil and a pinch of sea salt for 3 minutes on each side. Cut the breasts in half lengthways, discarding the ends to form 2 rectangles from each. Mix the picked leg meat with 80g of the confit oil, the tarragon and shallots. Season with sea salt to taste.

Line a terrine mould with cling film. Add half of the leg meat mixture into the mould and press down firmly.

Top lengthways with the pheasant breasts, pushing down to secure the meat. Add the remaining leg meat mixture, again pushing down firmly to secure and remove any excess air trapped within. Fold the cling film over the top to seal the terrine.

Place a mould of equal size on top, weigh it down so it presses the terrine, then refrigerate for 24 hours.

Remove the terrine from its mould and discard the cling film. Wrap fresh cling film tightly around the terrine 8-10 times, refrigerate until required.

Boudin

250g pheasant breast
sea salt
1 egg
570ml double cream
10ml black truffle oil

Blend the pheasant breast with a pinch of sea salt, then pass the mixture through a fine drum sieve. Using a spatula, incorporate the egg fully until smooth. Slowly add in the cream while stirring with the spatula, followed by the truffle oil.

Bring a pan of water to a simmer. Firstly, test with a small amount of the pheasant boudin mixture. Wrap a small amount in cling film, tie off at the ends and poach for 6 minutes. Remove the cling film, taste and season with sea salt accordingly.

Divide the rest of the mixture into 4 and wrap each quarter in cling film, creating a cylinder measuring approximately 2cm in diameter and 18cm in length. Tie off both ends of the cling film and poach in the simmering water for 6 minutes. Once poached, rest in ice water until cool.

Continued: Pheasant | Truffle | Carrot

Star Anise Jelly

4g gellan gum
sea salt (pinch of)
500ml chicken stock (see page 239)
6 star anise
1 tsp thyme leaves (chopped)

Rub the gellan gum and salt together. Blend through the cold chicken stock with a stick blender. Add the star anise and thyme. Bring to the boil, then simmer for 3 minutes. Pass the mixture through a fine chinois before pouring into a 18cm square tray lined with cling film. Set in the fridge for 1 hour.

Once set, cut into 2cm cubes and store in the fridge.

Carrot Gel

500ml carrot juice
40g stem ginger
30ml stem ginger syrup
35-45g Ultratex

Blend the carrot juice, stem ginger and syrup on a medium setting for 8 minutes. While blending, add the Ultratex, a spoonful at a time, until a coating consistency is achieved. Pass the mixture through a fine chinois, then pour it into a squeezy bottle and refrigerate until required.

Bread Tuiles

8 slices white bread (crusts removed)
60ml clarified butter

Preheat the oven to 160°C.

Roll the slices of bread through a pasta machine until the thinnest setting. Cut 2 rectangles measuring 10cm x 6cm out of each slice of bread. Using a selection of round cutters, cut holes out of each rectangle. Brush the rectangles with clarified butter, then place in a single layer between 2 silicone baking mats. Bake for 20 minutes.

To Assemble

1 purple carrot
butter (knob of)
sea salt (pinch of)
48 thin slices black winter truffle
40ml parsley oil (see page 241)

Using a peeler, thinly slice the carrot lengthways into ribbons. Plunge the ribbons into ice water then drain.

Slice the terrine into 1½-2cm thick slices, make sure there are 16 pieces, and remove the cling film.

Remove the cling film from the boudin. Slice each boudin cylinder into 4 equal pieces, roast in a pan with the butter and a pinch of sea salt to create a golden brown colour. Remove from the pan and cut each piece in half.

Preheat the oven to 140°C.

Warm the jelly cubes through in the oven for 5-6 minutes.

Position a slice of terrine on every plate and rest a bread tuile against each piece. Dot the parsley oil and carrot gel around the front of the dishes. Add 2 cylinders of boudin, one lying down and one standing up.

Scatter 3 slices of the truffle and 4 cubes of jelly on each plate before finishing with 2 carrot ribbons.

Continued From Page 031

But why did I even decide to write a book in the first place? The driving force began four years ago on a trip to Bangkok as an ambassador for the Visit Britain 'great' campaign. I was to give five talks to journalists on the perception of British food abroad. I obviously focused quite heavily on Scottish food as I am Scottish and it's a sector I happen to know most about. What can I say? The perception shocked me even more than I thought it would. Here I was, in the middle of a conference room at the Shangri-La Hotel in Bangkok, giving my speech and the first question I asked was "what is the perception of British food?" Hands shot up immediately and, one by one, they all started naming the classics from about 1970 - so prawn cocktail, shepherd's pie, roast beef, fish and chips and there was even a mention of the deep fried Mars bar. Now don't get me wrong. There is nothing wrong with 99% of these dishes and a whole lot wrong with deep frying a chocolate bar! But had none of these people heard of Marco, Gordon or Heston? Of course they had. The mere fact that these chefs are recognisable by their first names would say that they have had a huge impact on the industry globally but, for some reason, it's not their food or signature dishes that people think about when they think of British cuisine, never mind Scottish cuisine.

Whether it's langoustines, lobsters, cockles, scallops, soft berries, venison, game birds, Aberdeen Angus beef, Hebridean Sea Salt... I could wax lyrical all day long. These things are exported all over the world but the other countries think they cook them far better than we can. Hopefully this book goes a little way to dispel that myth, change the perception of Scottish food and hopefully inspire the next generation of Scottish chefs to shout from the rooftops about how amazing our products and chefs really are.

My Journey So Far... To The Other Side Of The World And Back

I was 23 when I packed my rucksack to move to the other side of the world, a trip that would definitely change my life and very nearly end it.

Moving to Australia was one of the most career defining moments of my life so far. I moved to Australia originally on a promise from every Australian back packer I had met, that once there I would never want to return. They were almost right.

Two years previous to this, whilst working at Auchterarder House Hotel, I won the Plated Restaurant Dessert of the Year for Great Britain. The competition was run by the Association of Pastry Chefs and the awards were held in a prestigious hotel in London. Travelling down on the train I had no idea that I had won and really didn't expect to at such a young age. After only doing pastry for about a year, it was then that I decided I would focus on being a pastry chef and dedicated every waking moment to being better at it. This was one of the reasons I wanted to travel, to perfect my skills and learn from some world class chefs.

I moved to Sydney in April 1999, a year before the 2000 Olympic Games. I wanted to spend the Millennium celebrations at the Opera House and Harbour Bridge and to be there for the Olympics. It is safe to say that all my huge expectations were exceeded during my time there.

I arrived at Sydney airport at 6am on a very warm April morning, nowhere to stay, no job and really no idea what I was going to do. But I had my chef knives and whites in my rucksack so somehow I knew I would be ok. **Continued on page 071.**

Scallop | Dashi | Sea Vegetables
Serves 8

Dashi Broth

½ red chilli
1 sheet dashi kombu
1½ sheets nori seaweed
250g white miso
250g brown miso
3 litres water
1 bunch lemongrass (crushed)
100g ginger (peeled, sliced)
250ml soy sauce
50g honey
75g coriander

Place all ingredients, except the coriander, into a large, tall pot and bring to the boil. Simmer gently for approximately 1½ hours. Bring back to the boil and add the coriander. Remove from the heat immediately and cover the top of the pot with cling film. Allow to steep for 1 hour.

Remove the cling film, pass through a fine chinois and leave to separate. Pour the separated liquid through a muslin cloth and discard the sediment at the bottom.

Rice Wine Vinegar Jelly

200ml rice wine vinegar
150ml soy sauce
150g caster sugar
5 leaves gelatine (soaked in cold water)

Place the vinegar, soy sauce and sugar into a pan and bring to the boil. Dissolve the gelatine into the mixture, then pass through a fine chinois into a container. Set in the fridge for 2 hours.

Pork Crackling

20g pork rind crumble
vegetable oil (for deep frying)
sea salt

Deep fry the pork rind crumble at 210°C until puffed up, this should take approximately 15 seconds. Transfer to a clean j-cloth, season with salt and allow to dry out in a warm environment.

Soy Caramel

200g caster sugar
200ml soy sauce

Heat the sugar to create a dry, golden brown caramel, slowly adding in the soy sauce. Bring to a rapid boil for 2 minutes before removing from the heat and passing through a fine chinois.

Scallops

16 scallops
sea salt
rapeseed oil (drizzle of)
selection of picked sea vegetables (depending on the season these could include channel wrack, beach coriander, sea aster, sea plantain, sea purslane or samphire)

(Prepare ahead)

Remove the scallops from the shell, wash thoroughly removing all of the skirt and roe. Reserve the roe and store the scallops in the fridge. Dehydrate the roe for 24 hours on the dehydrator's highest setting.

Once dry, blend to a fine powder, season with salt and pass through a fine chinois. Wash the shells and dry well.

Finely slice 8 of the scallops, and rest them in 8 of the clean shells. Season with a little salt and top with a teaspoon of the jelly, some sea vegetables and puffed pork crackling.

Heat up the dashi broth.

Meanwhile, heat a non-stick frying pan with a drizzle of rapeseed oil. Dip one side of each of the full scallops into the dehydrated roe and place in the non-stick pan roe-side down. Cook for 2 minutes. Turn over and cook for a further 2 minutes, then season with a little salt. Remove the scallop pan from the heat and rest for about 2 minutes.

To Assemble

Dot the soy caramel on each plate, top with a roasted scallop alongside a shell containing the raw scallop, pork crackling and seasonal sea vegetables, as pictured. Each guest should be served a raw scallop, a cooked scallop and a jug of piping hot dashi broth.

Instruct guests to pour the dashi broth over the raw scallop and to eat the pan roasted one while the other scallop cooks.

Cullen Skink

Serves 4

Cullen Skink

4 fillets smoked haddock (skinned, deboned)
2 large Maris Piper potatoes (peeled)
2 leeks
12 pearl onions (peeled)
2 litres milk
sea salt
1 tsp rapeseed oil

Cut 4 large diamond shapes from the haddock fillets and set aside. Chop the remaining haddock into small pieces. Cut 4 large rectangle shapes from the potatoes, big enough to sit the diamond of haddock on top. Chop the rest of the potatoes into small dice.

Slice the whites of the leeks into 12 rounds, dice the remainder of the leek and set aside. Simmer the peeled pearl onions in a little salted water for 2-3 minutes until they are just cooked and keep warm. Boil the large rectangles of potato in boiling, salted water for 7-8 minutes until tender and keep warm.

Add the milk, diced leeks, chopped haddock and small diced potatoes to a heavy-based pot. Simmer for about 10 minutes or until tender. Using a hand blender, blend to a smooth soup, season to taste with sea salt and keep warm.

Meanwhile, heat the rapeseed oil in a non-stick pan and cook the haddock diamonds on the nicer looking side until cooked halfway through. Add the leek rounds to the pan and heat until the leeks are coloured. Remove the pan from the heat and turn the fish over, allowing it to finish cooking in the residual heat.

To Assemble

4 sprigs dill (to garnish)
4 tsp caviar

Place a potato rectangle in each bowl and top with a diamond of haddock. Add a spoonful of caviar and a sprig of dill. Position 3 leek rounds alongside the fish and top each with a pearl onion.

Pour the soup into jugs for guests to pour themselves.

Pacific Oyster | Apple | Beetroot
Serves 2

Calcium Bath

500ml cold water
3.2g calcium chloride

Dissolve the calcium chloride in the water and store in the fridge.

Beetroot Caviar

100g caster sugar
6½g sodium alginate
300ml beetroot juice
extra beetroot juice (to cover, for storage)

Rub together the sugar and sodium alginate, then add to a pan with the beetroot juice. Using a stick blender, blend the ingredients together and bring to the boil. Take away from the heat and blend again. Bring back up to the boil, remove from the heat and blend one final time. Pour the mixture into a squeezy bottle and refrigerate for 1 hour.

Once cool, slowly empty the sauce bottle into the calcium bath drop by drop.

Take the caviar out of the calcium bath, rinse under cold running water and place in the reserved beetroot juice. Store in the fridge until required.

Oysters

12 oysters
½ cucumber (cut into ½cm dice)
1 Granny Smith apple (skin on, cut into batons 3cm x ¼cm)
2 sprigs sea purslane (leaves picked)

Shuck the oysters and rinse to remove any broken shell or grit. Top each oyster with a generous spoonful of beetroot caviar. Sprinkle with cucumber, apple and sea purslane leaves.

Red Apple Foam

2 litres red apple juice
100ml milk
½ tsp lecithin

Reduce the apple juice to 700ml. Add the milk and lecithin, then blend with a stick blender to a foam consistency. If this needs reheating, be careful not to heat over 60ºC.

To Serve

Top one side of each oyster with a spoonful of red apple foam. Blend the mixture again to create more foam, if required.

Yonderfield farm
West Kilbride
Ayrshire KA23 9PY
Scotland
Pacific Oyster - Crassostrea Gigas

Date of packing: 08/02/2016 Weight/Quantity 20

Country of origin: UK
These molluscs must be alive when sold.

Prawn Cocktail
Serves 4

Marie Rose Sauce

1 egg
1 egg yolk
1 tbsp Dijon mustard
1 lemon (juice and zest of)
500ml rapeseed oil
50ml brandy
100g homemade tomato ketchup (see page 243)
½ tsp smoked paprika
sea salt

Combine the egg, egg yolk, mustard, lemon juice and zest in the bowl or container of a food processor. Set the food processor on medium speed and gradually drizzle in the oil while blending. Blend until fully emulsified. Transfer the mayonnaise mixture to a bowl, add in the brandy, ketchup and paprika.

Taste and season with sea salt as required.

Langoustines

6 litres water (to boil)
sea salt (generous pinch of)
20 langoustines

Bring the water to the boil with the salt. Drop the langoustines into the water and poach for 2 minutes, no longer. Remove the langoustines from the water and rest them on a tray - do not cool them in cold water as they will lose flavour. Once cool enough to handle, peel the langoustines and discard the shells.

Dehydrated Tomatoes

8 cherry tomatoes (halved)
sea salt
1 clove garlic (peeled, sliced)
4 sprigs thyme

(Prepare ahead)

Place the tomatoes on an ovenproof tray, season generously with sea salt, then top with the garlic and thyme. Transfer to a dehydrator on the highest setting for 8 hours.

Remove the tray from the dehydrator and discard the garlic and thyme.

Burnt Cucumber

1 cucumber (peeled)

Char the outside of the cucumber with a blow torch. Whilst the cucumber is still hot, vacuum pack on the vacuum pack machine's highest setting. Leave for 20 minutes so that it cooks in its own heat. Once it has cooled down completely, remove from the vacuum pack bag and slice into 1cm slices.

To Make The Ice Bowl

4 litres water (boiled, cooled - boiled water gives a very clear ice)

(Prepare ahead)

Pour the water into a tall, 4 litre container. Place the container into the freezer and leave for 24 hours; this will create a natural air pocket in the centre. Break the ice block into 4 pieces to create 4 bowls.

To Assemble

smoked paprika (to garnish)
2 baby gem lettuces (washed, finely shredded)
baby basil (to garnish)

Sprinkle some smoked paprika on the surface under each ice bowl. Arrange 5 langoustines in each ice bowl.

Scatter around the dehydrated tomatoes, cucumber and lettuce. Dot the Marie Rose sauce around and finish with some baby basil.

Quail | Egg | Bacon
Serves 4

Homemade Tomato Ketchup

12 very ripe plum tomatoes (halved)
sea salt
1 clove garlic (peeled, sliced)
6 sprigs thyme
120g caster sugar
3 shallots (peeled, sliced)
400ml tomato juice
100ml cider vinegar

(Prepare ahead)

Place the tomatoes on an ovenproof tray and season generously with sea salt. Top with the garlic and thyme, then transfer to a dehydrator on the highest setting for 12 hours.

Pour the caster sugar into a saucepan over a medium heat to make a dry caramel. This should be a light, golden brown colour.

Remove the garlic and thyme from the tomatoes. Add the tomatoes and shallots to the dry caramel, but do be cautious as this will spit. Pour in the tomato juice and vinegar, simmer for 10 minutes. Blend until a smooth consistency is achieved. Check the seasoning and pass the mixture through a fine chinois. Refrigerate until required.

Quince Jelly

1kg quinces (peeled)
2 litres water
400g caster sugar

(Prepare ahead)

Simmer all of the ingredients together for 4 hours.

Drain the quinces and discard the liquid. Halve and remove the seeds, then blend until smooth.

Hang the mixture in a muslin cloth for 12 hours. Once the mixture is set, dice into 1cm cubes and keep in the fridge until required.

Filo Discs

2 sheets filo pastry
1 egg yolk
30g Parmesan (grated)

Preheat the oven to 185°C.

Brush one of the filo sheets with some egg yolk, sprinkle over half of the Parmesan, then place the other sheet on top. Brush with the rest of the egg yolk and sprinkle over the remaining Parmesan. Using a 10cm cutter, cut out 4 rounds from the pastry. Place the rounds in a single layer between 2 sheets of silicone paper. Position between 2 baking trays and bake for 8 minutes.

Mushrooms

4 button mushrooms
20g mushroom powder (see page 241)

Cut the button mushrooms into a selection of squares and circles and dust with the mushroom powder.

Pancetta

4 slices pancetta

Preheat the oven to 170°C.

Lay the slices of pancetta between 2 sheets of silicone paper, position between 2 baking trays and put in the oven for 10-12 minutes until the pancetta is golden brown and crispy.

Quail

rapeseed oil (drizzle of)
4 quails
60g butter
1 sprig thyme
1 clove garlic (skin on, crushed)

Preheat the oven to 185°C.

Heat up a non-stick, ovenproof pan with a drizzle of rapeseed oil. Place the quails in the pan. Brown on all sides, turning every 1-2 minutes to create an even colour. Roast in the oven for 7 minutes.

Once roasted, add the butter, thyme and garlic, then baste the birds in the foaming butter. Allow to rest on a cooling rack for at least 10 minutes. Remove the breasts and legs from the quails, and clean up the wing bones for presentation. Set the legs aside to be used in another dish.

To Assemble

15g butter
4 quail eggs
rapeseed oil (drizzle of)
4 stalks baby parsley

Preheat the oven to 185°C.

Cover the quail breasts in buttered silicone paper and place in the oven for 3-4 minutes. Fry the quail eggs in a non-stick pan with a drizzle of rapeseed oil over a medium heat. Lay a filo disc in the bottom of each bowl and place 2 quail breasts on top and 1 quail egg to the side. Top the quail with a slice of pancetta. Scatter over the mushrooms, quince jelly cubes and dot around the tomato ketchup. Finish each bowl with a stalk of baby parsley.

Oxtail Broth
Serves 4

Beef Broth

Stock 1

500g oxtail
1½kg beef shin bones
200g flat pancetta
½ bottle red wine
1 carrot (chopped)
½ onion (chopped)
1 stick celery (chopped)
1 leek (chopped)
2 star anise

Stock 2

500g oxtail
1½kg beef shin bones
½ bottle red wine
sea salt

Stock 1

(Prepare ahead)

Preheat the oven to 200°C.

Roast the oxtail and beef bones together in a large tray until golden brown. Remove from the oven and, using a set of tongs, lift out the bones and oxtail into a very large pot.

Add the pancetta, wine, vegetables and star anise to the tray to deglaze and cook down until the wine reduces by half. Pour this over the bones and oxtail.

Add 10 litres of water, or just enough to cover the bones, and simmer for 4 hours.

Remove the oxtail, pick the meat off the bones and set aside. Place the bones back in the pot and simmer for a further 3 hours. Pass the mixture through a fine muslin cloth and place the liquid back in the pot.

Stock 2

(Prepare ahead)

Preheat the oven to 200°C.

Roast the oxtail and beef bones in a large tray until golden brown.

Remove from the oven and, using tongs, lift out the bones and oxtail and place into stock 1.

Deglaze the roasting tray with the red wine and pour into the stock. Simmer for a further 6-8 hours. Strain through muslin and discard the oxtail and bones. Check the seasoning and add a little salt if required.

Oxtail Ballotine

1 shallot (cut into fine brunoise)
20g butter
1 tsp thyme leaves (chopped)
1 carrot (cut into fine brunoise)
200g reserved oxtail meat
40g veal jus (see page 244)
sea salt (pinch of)

Gently sweat off the shallot in the butter. Add the thyme leaves and the carrot and continue to sweat for 2-3 minutes. Stir in the oxtail and veal jus, combining well.

Spoon the mixture onto cling film and roll up to a 4cm width. Continue rolling the mixture to a very tight ballotine. Tie off the ends and refrigerate for 4 hours. Once cold, slice into ½cm rounds.

Black Onion Gel

3 onions
700ml vegetable stock (see page 244)
20g-30g Ultratex
smoked sea salt

Cut the onions in half and remove the skins.

Blacken the onions all over in a non-stick pan on a medium heat, turning every 3-4 minutes. This step should take a good 30 minutes.

Place the onions in a heavy-based pan and pour over the vegetable stock. Simmer for 30 minutes until the stock has almost evaporated.

Blend in a high speed blender for 10 minutes, scraping down the sides halfway through.

Add the Ultratex, a spoonful at a time, until a glossy, smooth purée is achieved. Season with smoked sea salt, to taste. Pass through a fine chinois and decant into a squeezy bottle until required.

Tomato Butter

sea salt
5 sprigs thyme
3 sprigs rosemary
3 cloves garlic (thinly sliced)
10 very ripe large plum tomatoes (halved)
60g caster sugar
50ml cider vinegar
250g butter

Preheat the oven to 100°C.

Sprinkle a layer of salt in a roasting tray.

Scatter the thyme, rosemary and garlic over the salt. Place the tomatoes on the salt, open-side up, and bake for 4 hours.

Carefully remove the tomatoes from the salt and brush off any salt that is stuck to the bottom of each tomato. Blend the tomatoes to a fine purée and pass through a fine chinois.

Melt the sugar over a medium heat until it becomes a light golden caramel. Add the vinegar, being careful as it will spit, then stir the tomato mixture into the caramel. Cook the tomato mixture for 30 minutes until it has halved in volume; it should be a deep crimson red colour.

Chill the tomato mixture in the fridge for at least an hour.

Whip the butter until it is light and fluffy in an electric mixer. Slowly add the tomato mixture to the whipping butter until all of the tomato is incorporated. Season with a pinch of salt, to taste.

Using boiling water and a teaspoon, rocher the butter onto a silicone paper lined tray, allowing one rocher per person.

There will be plenty butter left over; either store in the fridge or freezer for another time.

Continued: Oxtail Broth

Bone Marrow Crumble

200g bone marrow
1 shallot (peeled, finely diced)
120g panko breadcrumbs
½ tsp sea salt
1 tbsp parsley (chopped)
1 tsp tarragon (chopped)
1 tsp rosemary (chopped)

Melt the bone marrow in a non-stick pan. Once completely melted, pass through a fine sieve and return to the pan. Add the shallot and cook out for 2-3 minutes. Stir in the breadcrumbs and salt and toast in the bone marrow for 4-6 minutes until the breadcrumbs begin to turn golden brown. Add the herbs to the breadcrumbs and continue to cook for 2-3 minutes.

To Assemble

1 sprig thyme
1 sprig rosemary
50g flat pancetta

Add the thyme, rosemary and pancetta to the top of a Cona coffee machine. Place the broth in the bottom of the Cona, then light the Cona and allow to infuse.

Heat the slices of oxtail ballotine under a hot grill for 2-3 minutes.

Whilst the broth is infusing in the Cona, place one round of the warmed oxtail just off the centre of each bowl. Dot the black onion gel above the oxtail. Arrange the bone marrow crumble to one side of the oxtail and top with the rocher of tomato butter. Pour the broth over the dishes at the table. When the broth is poured over the garnish, it should melt the butter and enrich the broth.

My first stop, once I found accommodation in a hostel via a free bus from the airport, was to buy a Sydney Morning Herald Good Food Guide. In Australia they don't have AA Rosettes or Michelin stars, restaurants in Sydney are awarded Chef's Hats from the Sydney Morning Herald. I then bought all the local papers with job listings and my very first mobile phone; it was 1999 remember, mobiles were still very new. Each job in the papers which appealed to me, I cross referenced with the Good Food Guide. If it didn't have any 'Hats' I didn't even phone them, no point. I didn't travel to the other side of the world to not work in the best places. I came across a listing for a pastry chef in a little suburb called Balmain. The restaurant was called Gotham and the chef had just been awarded a Hat not long before I joined. The interview was a very quick, "tell me about you, when can you start?" sort of interview. The chef's name was Matt Brown, ex Marco Pierre White, and after he had spent 10 years with Marco I can tell you, he was not only an amazing chef but also a very tough taskmaster. I only stayed in the job for three months as that's all my visa allowed. I was offered 'cash in hand' but I really wanted the chance to stay in the country, so to cheat the system was probably not the wisest move.

My next position was again as a pastry chef. This time it was to open a restaurant for the soccer player Christian Vieri. He had just signed for Inter Milan for 70 million Australian dollars, making him the most expensive soccer player in the world at the time (to this day that record has only been broken six times) so the buzz surrounding the restaurant opening was huge. The food was to be modern Australian with European influence, something I hadn't really done as a chef so it was another very exciting opportunity. Again, due to visa restrictions, I could only stay for three months, so just enough time to open up and get the team settled.

From there, I went on to work at GPO for a chef who I think has probably had the most impact on my career so far, Darrel Felstead. His ambition and drive really was something to witness. Every plate leaving the kitchen had to reach absolute perfection 100% of the time, so although it was a very tough kitchen to work in, the two years I spent working there were also very rewarding. The food at the time was probably some of the best not only in Sydney but in Australia. We pushed ourselves and each other every day, and trust me they were long days - 7am starts until midnight. We got into the routine of arriving at 6.30am so we could have a coffee in the espresso bar before we started.

All in all, I spent five amazing years in Sydney, with some real highs and lows. I felt so lucky with the jobs and experience I attained during my time there but that luck faltered after a near death experience left me in intensive care. I will forgo all the gory details but a fall from a third floor balcony left me in an extremely bad way, so much so that I technically died twice as a result. I was devastated but the accident actually gave me a whole new perspective on life and it reinforced my drive to succeed. Life is short and delicate and not to be wasted.

I returned to Scotland a changed person. I had developed as a chef but also gained so much valuable life experience. I was enthusiastic to put the new techniques and skills I had acquired into practice but, this time, using the outstanding Scottish produce which I had missed during my time away.

'Tick Tock' - What Makes Me Tick

Time is such a rare commodity these days. Trying to grab inspiration where I can, or indeed when I can, is something I have never really had a problem with. Time on the other hand, as a chef, is something which I never have.

So what makes me 'tick'? As is the case with most chefs, my inspiration comes from numerous sources. It seems to me that inspiration often physically arrives into my kitchen. **Continued on page 079.**

Ochil Foods

I have Ochil Foods to thank for introducing me to a number of the products which get used in my kitchen on a daily basis. Ochil Foods is a third generation family food service business supplying Scottish produce to businesses across the country.

As a young, fresh faced 19-year-old chef, I was working at the Duchally House Hotel just outside Auchterarder. It was during my time here that I first encountered Neil Dixon of Ochil Foods and his then very young son Jeremy. It is quite funny looking back as Jeremy used to help his dad with the deliveries and as a young 12-13-year-old, some of the deliveries were obviously quite a lot for such a young boy to manage. Whenever Neil used to deliver, the first thing I would normally do is throw the kettle on and leave Jeremy to carry all the deliveries in on his own, whilst I chatted with his dad. Ochil Foods at the time, and even now in a way, was a very small family business with quite an extensive portfolio of some of Scotland's best produce.

I remember a phone call between Neil and me almost 20 years ago. I was looking for a full saddle of venison to put on as a special for the coming weekend. He offered to break the whole saddle down and fully prep it for free as long as he could keep the fillets for his dinner. As I had no need for them at the time and was short staffed, I thought this was a great idea. My special sold out in one night and it was probably the first full dish that I was ever allowed to create for the menu. I was only 19 at the time and we ended up putting the dish on the full à la carte menu.

It was Ochil Foods that first inspired me to include some of the producers throughout this book, as it is through Neil and Jeremy that most of the specialist Scottish produce gets to me. They are also a great sounding board if I hear of any new products on the market. It is a quick call to Jeremy to see if they can stock it and deliver it to me. Scotland is a treasure trove of small, artisanal producers. As chefs, we hear about these producers in so many different ways; sometimes someone will show up at the kitchen door with samples, other times we will hear about products from other chefs.

Ochil Food's vast knowledge of fine food and where it comes from makes them stand out. Provenance is everything and they therefore go out of their way to share this with their customers.

In the winter months when the game season is in full swing, it is Ochil Foods whom I turn to for the best game birds shot in Scotland. They have such a great relationship with the estates; they know the name of not only the gamekeeper but also the people that shoot the birds.

Twenty years on and the relationship with Neil and his family at Ochil Foods is now stronger than ever, although they now have delivery drivers and it is Jeremy whom I meet for coffee.

PIGEON | BEETROOT | HAZELNUT

Pigeon | Beetroot | Hazelnut
Serves 8

Pickled Beetroot

200g beetroot
1 shallot (diced)
150g caster sugar
130ml vinegar
50ml water
1 star anise
½ tbsp coriander seeds
2 sprigs thyme

Cook the beetroot in simmering water until tender. Cool naturally, then rub gently between fingertips to peel the skin off. Dice into 1cm cubes.

Add all the remaining ingredients to a pot and bring to the boil. Pass through a chinois over the beetroot and allow to cool naturally.

Roasted Hazelnuts

100g hazelnuts (skins removed)
hazelnut oil (drizzle of)
sea salt (pinch of)

Preheat oven to 175°C.

Place the hazelnuts on a tray and roast for 13 minutes. Remove from the oven and coat in hazelnut oil and salt. Allow to cool. Halve the hazelnuts to serve.

Beetroot Fluid Gel

3g gellan gum type F
5g caster sugar
300ml beetroot juice

Rub the gellan gum through the sugar.

Blend the sugar through the beetroot juice in a pot with a stick blender. Place on the heat and slowly bring to the boil, stirring continuously. Once boiled, remove from the heat and blend again with a stick blender. Pass through a fine chinois and set in a tray.

Once fully cooled, add the set gel to a blender and blend on a high speed, scraping the sides to achieve a smooth, silky gel. Decant into a squeezy bottle.

Candy Beetroot

1 large candy stripe beetroot
75ml water
50g caster sugar

Slice the beetroot as thinly as possible using a mandoline.

Cut out circles from the beetroot slices using a 1½cm diameter ring cutter and place in a vacuum pack bag.

Combine the sugar and water in a pot and bring to the boil, dissolving the sugar. Allow to cool completely.

Pour the syrup over the beetroot and vacuum pack on full power. Refrigerate until ready to use.

Pigeon Breasts

4 pigeons
20g butter
sea salt (pinch of)
3 sprigs thyme
1 clove garlic (crushed)

Remove the legs and breasts from the birds and set aside the legs and carcasses.

Remove the small fillet from the breasts and set aside.

Vacuum pack the breasts with butter, salt, thyme and garlic. Cook in a water bath set at 58°C for 20 minutes, then refresh in ice water.

Pigeon Legs

8 pigeon legs (reserved from earlier)
8 pigeon breast small fillets (reserved from earlier)
½ banana shallot (peeled, diced)
25g butter
sea salt (pinch of)
1 sprig thyme (leaves picked, finely chopped)
1 sprig tarragon (leaves picked, finely chopped)
50g plain flour
2 eggs (beaten)
60g very fine panko breadcrumbs
vegetable oil (for deep frying)

Remove the skin from the legs and remove the thigh bone. Butterfly the meat, keeping it attached to the top part of the leg. Clean the legs with a sharp knife, scraping excess meat off the bone.

Brunoise the small fillets from the pigeon breast, keep aside.

Sweat off the shallots in the butter with the salt and allow to cool.

Mix the shallot and butter with the herbs and brunoised fillets. Place into a piping bag and pipe a small amount of mix into the butterflied leg meat. Roll the meat up to enclose the brunoised fillets and roll tightly in cling film. Vacuum pack the legs and cook in a water bath at 68°C for 4 hours, then refresh in ice water.

Remove the legs from the vacuum pack bag and unroll the cling film. Pane the legs in the flour, eggs and breadcrumbs. Deep fry at 180°C for 3-4 minutes until golden and crisp.

Chicken Liver & Foie Gras Parfait

1 shallot (brunoised)
250g butter (diced)
125ml double cream
500g chicken livers
25ml brandy
sea salt
½ lobe ethically sourced foie gras (deveined)

Sweat the shallot in 125g of the butter, add the cream and reduce by half. Stir in the chicken livers and cook for 3-4 minutes.

Place the chicken liver mixture into a Thermomix with the brandy and salt and blend on speed 7, scraping down the sides from time to time. Bring the Thermomix up to 62.5°C and slowly add the remaining butter.

Finally, add in the foie gras whilst blending. When the temperature is at 62.5°C, remove from the heat and cool in a bowl set over ice.

To Assemble

sea salt
24 leaves baby mizuna
24 leaves baby red chard

Roast the pigeon breasts in a non-stick pan for 1½ minutes on each side and season with a little sea salt.

Drag a swipe of beetroot gel through the middle of the plate. Place the leg at one end and the breast at the other.

Scatter 5 pieces of the diced beetroot around the pigeon and lay 3 slices of the candy beetroot across the pigeon. Rocher a teaspoon of the parfait and place between the leg and breast. Scatter over the hazelnuts and garnish with the baby leaves.

My fantastic local suppliers show up on a regular basis with exciting ingredients, whether it is Ben my forager showing me a wonderful herb or mushroom or my fishmonger phoning me early in the morning to tell me that he has some fantastic line caught halibut just landed from the boat. The close relationship I maintain with my suppliers means they are never shy in coming forward to show me an array of ingredients that might just capture my imagination.

So ingredients definitely make me tick and, in my opinion, I work in one of the best, most inspiring environments in the world. Scotland is a constant source of inspiration. The seasons we get here are wonderful and supply us with an abundance of local ingredients which us native Scots have every right to be proud of. For such a small country, we really do punch well above our weight in this department.

One thing that Scotland is famous for is its rainfall so we have very rich, damp soils where we can gather wild herbs and mushrooms. The cooler climate means everything grows that little bit slower and has the time to develop a rich flavour - the Scottish berries are proof of this. The rich green pastures that our beef graze on most of the year means a superior flavour and our waters produce a wonderfully rich supply of wild fresh fish, from the world renowned Scottish langoustine to the humble mackerel fillet - not to mention scallops, lobsters and wild Scottish salmon, the list really is endless.

The seasons in Scotland mean kitchens are always filled with excitement for the 'firsts' - the first rhubarb of the season, the first asparagus, the first strawberries and so on. The definitive seasons ensure work in the kitchen never becomes stale. We are constantly thinking ahead and preparing for the arrival of new ingredients. Once an ingredient goes out of season, that entire dish comes off the menu, making space for a new seasonal creation. Then comes the glorious 12th. The date in August when the game season bursts into action - this is a date chefs up and down the country celebrate. Grouse is the first of the game birds to make it onto the dinner plate, closely followed by partridge and then pheasant.

I would love to say 100% of the produce we use in the dishes is Scottish but I can't, no chef can really, no matter their mantra. Our rhubarb for example, comes from Robert Tomlinson down in Yorkshire. His indoor forced rhubarb is so sweet and crimson red, ready way before the outdoor stuff in my mother-in-law Marianne's garden. So come January, we get it from Robert, as it moves into April it is Marianne's that keeps us going.

But my inspiration really does come from the land, sea and air of Scotland. It is a treasure trove of amazing produce and something which we should all be immensely proud of. The plates of food leaving my kitchen can only be as good as the ingredients which go on them and it is why Scottish chefs spend so much time building up close relationships with suppliers and producers. Scotland's natural larder is a bit of a dream for us chefs and the produce emerging from such a small area is truly inspirational - so I guess you could say that I am never short of inspiration.

It is because of this I have decided to share some of my amazing suppliers with you. These guys really do deserve the credit for the fantastic produce they provide us with on a daily basis, and I think I have chosen the suppliers that give a true reflection of what is available here in Scotland.

A Brand New Dish...

I am often asked how I come up with new dishes. Where do I start? What makes me think of the ingredients or techniques to use? The honest answer is chefs are hybrids, magpies if you like. We take inspiration from every chef we have worked for, every book we have read and every internet page we happen to stumble upon. We have the incredible ability to pool the information or spark an idea, sometimes when we are looking for it or even when we aren't. It is not uncommon for me to wake up at 5.30am with an idea or spark of inspiration and to quickly scribble it down or email it to myself from my phone. I then bring the idea to the kitchen and discuss it with the team. **Continued on page 091.**

Truffles

Often it takes something very small to elevate a dish to the next level. For me, truffles are something that can work this magic. I first met Gianpaolo La Greca of Sapori Truffles when he popped his head around the door of the restaurant just days after we opened and proceeded to show me the most amazing selection of truffles - the aroma when he opens up his wicker basket really is something to behold and he has been a weekly visitor ever since. Truffles are the rarest and most sought after of all food ingredients. The white truffle cannot be harvested artificially and is unique to Italy. It requires a great deal of knowledge and trust to deliver this product and Gianpaolo is the one I trust when it comes to sourcing this exceptional ingredient.

There are some jokes amongst the team at the restaurant about Gianpaolo's arrival each week. He arrives with a small, black cool bag, a small weighing scale and proceeds to weigh out the goods - it would look somewhat ominous if you didn't know what he was up to! The aroma of the truffles fills the restaurant even before I see him, so we always know when he is in the building.

Gianpaolo became a truffle supplier very much by accident; he was working in Edinburgh for a London based importer of fine Italian food and wine. Shortly after starting he was sent a selection of fresh truffles. "These are black summer truffles" the sales manager said "see if the Scots fancy some!" Before then he had never actually seen a fresh truffle, only preserved truffles in jars. The truffles looked nice and Gianpaolo was amazed by their particular aroma. He brought them along with him while he was making his usual deliveries and within a day he had sold out! This was the moment of realisation. He soon set up Sapori Truffles and his love and knowledge of truffles grew. He quickly became known as having the best selection of truffles available in Scotland. Gianpaolo has personally taken the time to visit all the fresh truffle suppliers that he deals with and can personally guarantee their integrity for this rare and much sought after ingredient.

Although truffle hunting is steeped in tradition and synonymous with pigs and cigarette smoking French or Italians, as the demand has grown, so has the professionalism and proficiency. It's now very tightly controlled where 'farmers' have their own patch and mostly use well trained dogs. Although a very expensive ingredient, as the saying goes 'a little goes a long way'. In the form of a truffle this is certainly true, so a light shaving over a fish dish or a robust beef dish can really take the dish to a whole new level.

Obviously quality truffles are not something which can be grown in Scotland. While I am all about using locally sourced as much as I can, this is not always possible. I never claim to be a chef who cooks with only Scottish produce but I would say that at least 90% of what goes on my plates is Scottish. For me flavour comes first. Luckily some of the best ingredients in the world can be found on my doorstep but I feel that some of my dishes would suffer if I imposed a strict tie to provenance on my cooking so, in some instances, I look further afield. If I think that a dish would be elevated to the next level by the inclusion of truffles, then only the best will do and fortunately, one of the best truffle suppliers in Scotland is willing to personally visit my restaurant each week.

Gianpaolo has a Scottish truffle hunt coming up in the autumn which he is hopeful about, so who knows? He might just find enough Scottish truffles to supply me!

Guinea Fowl | Truffle | Milk
Serves 4

Red Cabbage Meringues

Part 1

3g Methylcellulose
200ml boiling water

Part 2

260ml red cabbage juice
45g Methylcellulose purée
1.2g xanthan gum
40g Isomalt (blended to a fine powder)
8g caster sugar

(Prepare 2 days in advance)

Part 1

First make the Methylcellulose purée.

Using a stick blender, add the Methylcellulose to the boiling water, blending until fully incorporated. Very quickly, set the pot over a bath of ice water and continue to blend until thickened. Place the purée into a container and refrigerate overnight.

Part 2

Add the red cabbage juice and Methylcellulose purée into a stand-up mixer bowl. Blend them together using a stick blender. Add the xanthan gum and continue blending until thickened.

Place the bowl onto the stand-up mixer and whisk on full speed (treat this like a French meringue). Slowly add the Isomalt and sugar until all incorporated. Whisk for a further 5 minutes; the mixture should be stiff and hold shape.

Using a cranked palate knife, spread the meringue no thicker than ½mm onto silicone paper. Dehydrate at 58°C for 24 hours. Break into random shards and store in an airtight container.

Beurre Noisette Crumble

200g butter
150g milk powder
10ml lemon Juice
sea salt

(Prepare ahead)

Place the butter into a pan and melt. Bring to a steady boil, then add the milk powder. Cook until the milk powder starts to change colour to a golden brown, then add the lemon juice.

Take off the heat, strain the milk powder and squeeze out as much of the butter as possible, discarding the butter.

Place onto a j-cloth and dehydrate for 12 hours at 58°C. Season with salt to taste.

Guinea Fowl

4 guinea fowl legs
60g sea salt
200ml vegetable oil
5 sprigs thyme
3 cloves garlic (crushed)

(Prepare ahead)

Lightly coat the legs in salt and cure for 45 minutes.

Wash the salt off the legs and place into a vacuum pack bag with the oil, thyme and garlic. Vacuum pack on full power, then place into a water bath set at 80°C for 12 hours.

Remove the legs from the bag and very gently remove the bones, keeping the whole leg intact.

Place between silicone paper and very gently press for at least 4 hours. When cooled and pressed, trim up the legs to make rectangles of meat. Reserve the excess skin from the trimmings and set aside.

Confit Yellow Carrots

4 baby yellow carrots
20g duck fat
sea salt (pinch of)

Vacuum pack the carrots with the duck fat and salt. Cook the carrots in a water bath at 80°C for 2 hours. Drain on absorbent paper and season with a little salt.

Truffle Mayonnaise

50g pasteurised egg yolk
20g winter truffle (finely diced)
30ml sherry vinegar
500ml rapeseed oil
6g sea salt
7ml black truffle oil

Blend the egg yolks in a blender on a medium speed. Add the truffle and the vinegar. Drizzle in the rapeseed oil slowly whilst blending. Once all of the oil is incorporated, add the salt. Blend for a further 2-3 minutes, add the truffle oil and blend for a further 2 minutes. Decant into a squeezy bottle or piping bag.

To Assemble

2 baby turnips (sliced as thinly as possible)
baby mizuna leaves
sea salt

To reheat the legs, place them skin-side down in a dry, non-stick pan. Bring up to a medium heat and cook for 3 minutes. Turn the legs over and cook for a further 3 minutes on the other side. Season with a little salt.

Shred the reserved excess skin from the trimmings and scatter over a non-stick pan. Cook on a medium heat until they all stick together and become crisp.

Drag a fine line of the milk crumbs just off centre of each plate and place a guinea fowl leg in the centre of each plate. Lay 4 slices of raw turnip to the side of the leg and rest 4 shards of the meringue against the leg. Dot the mayonnaise around the leg, place the carrot on top of the leg and top with some of the crispy skin. Garnish with baby mizuna leaves.

Rabbit | Granola | Sea Buckthorn
Serves 8

Rabbit Ballotine

1 rabbit (legs removed and reserved - ask
your butcher to debone the rest but keep it
in one piece)
2 litres rapeseed oil
1 shallot (finely diced)
small handful tarragon leaves (chopped)
sea salt (pinch of)

(Prepare ahead)

Preheat the oven to 120°C.

Place the rabbit legs in a deep tray and cover
them with rapeseed oil. Transfer to the oven for
1½ hours. Once the legs have cooled, pick off
the meat and discard the bones. Mix this meat
with the shallot and tarragon, season with a
little salt.

Equally distribute this mixture down the middle
of the whole piece of rabbit, roll up the meat
tightly and wrap well in cling film, tying off both
ends. Place the ballotine in a water bath at 62°C
for 2¼ hours. Remove from the water bath and
plunge straight into ice water for 40 minutes.

Remove the cling film and rewrap in a fresh layer,
tying off both ends. Refrigerate until required.

Hazelnut & Oatmeal Granola

45g pine nuts
45g puffed millet
60g hazelnuts (skins removed)
135g rolled oats
135g pinhead oats
70g pumpkin seeds
2 cloves garlic (chopped)
110ml liquid glucose
85g duck fat
135g Parmesan (grated)
180g basil leaves
vegetable oil (for deep frying)
sea salt (pinch of)

Preheat the oven to 180°C.

Thoroughly combine the pine nuts, puffed millet,
hazelnuts, oats, pumpkin seeds, garlic, liquid
glucose and duck fat in a large baking tray.
Transfer to the oven for 25 minutes and mix
every 7-8 minutes.

Spread the Parmesan on a silicone mat and bake
for 7-8 minutes until melted together and golden.
Allow to cool before breaking into crumbs.

Deep fry the basil at 180°C until crispy, then drain
on kitchen paper. Mix the Parmesan and basil
with the other ingredients and season with a little
sea salt. Be careful as Parmesan can be salty.

Sea Buckthorn Gel

100g sea buckthorn berries
100g caster sugar
50ml water
16-20g Ultratex

(Prepare ahead)

Gently mix together the sea buckthorn berries,
sugar and water in a vacuum pack bag and seal
on the machine's highest setting. Place in a
water bath at 48°C for 3 hours. Remove from the
vacuum pack bag and transfer to a blender and
blend on a medium speed for 8 minutes.

Add the Ultratex, a teaspoon at a time, until a
coating consistency is achieved, then pass
through a fine chinois and chill over ice. Pour
into a squeezy bottle and reserve.

Hazelnut Milk

100g hazelnuts (skins removed)
30ml hazelnut oil
sea salt (generous pinch of)
250ml milk

Roast the hazelnuts in the oil and salt at 190°C
for 10-15 minutes until golden. Be careful not to
leave for too long as they will become bitter.

Whilst still hot, add the hazelnuts and the milk to
a blender. Blend on medium speed for 10 minutes.
Pass through a fine chinois and refrigerate.

To Assemble

baby violet flowers (to garnish)

Slice the rabbit ballotine into 3cm slices and
remove the cling film. Draw a line with the gel
down the length of each plate a third of the way
over. Dot the gel around one edge of the plate,
position the rabbit ballotine on the left and some
granola to the right. Garnish with baby violet
flowers and serve the hazelnut milk separately, so
that it can be poured over the granola at the table.

MAINS

Pork & Sweetcorn
Serves 6

Pork Belly

1½kg pork belly
2 litres water
sea salt

(Prepare the day before)

Preheat the oven to 120°C.

Place the pork belly skin-side down in an oven tray. Pour the water onto the belly until it reaches halfway and season with salt. Cover in tin foil and cook in the oven for 11 hours.

Remove from the oven and discard half of the cooking liquor.

Cover the pork belly with a tray of equal size and place a weight on top to press the meat down. Refrigerate for 8 hours.

Once cooled and pressed, cut into 6cm squared portions. Store in the fridge until ready to use.

Sweetcorn Powder

165g sweetcorn
sea salt

(Prepare ahead)

Drain the liquid from the sweetcorn but do not wash. Spread out the corn on a silicone mat and sprinkle with a little sea salt. Transfer the sweetcorn to a dehydrator and leave on the highest setting for 12 hours.

Once completely dry, blend in a spice blender to create a fine powder.

Braised Pork Cheeks

4 pork cheeks
½ carrot (peeled)
1 celery (stick of)
2 shallots (peeled, halved)
1 leek (white of)
2 cloves garlic (skin on)
1 bay leaf
4 sprigs thyme
200ml red wine
rapeseed oil (drizzle of)
1 litre chicken stock

(Prepare ahead)

Marinate the pork cheeks with the vegetables, garlic, bay leaf and thyme in the red wine for 3 hours. Drain off the marinade and reserve.

Preheat the oven to 140°C.

Fry the pork cheeks in a hot, non-stick pan, with a drizzle of rapeseed oil for 2-3 minutes on each side. Remove the pork cheeks from the pan and place in an ovenproof dish.

Deglaze the pan with the reserved red wine, vegetables, garlic, bay leaf and thyme, then reduce by half.

Add the wine, vegetables, garlic, bay leaf and thyme to the pork cheeks, then pour over the chicken stock. Cover and braise in the oven for 4 hours.

Once the pork cheeks are tender, remove from the oven, reserve the liquid and dice the pork into 1cm cubes. Keep warm until needed.

Pass the liquid through a fine chinois and reduce by three-quarters. When reduced, pass through a fine chinois into a clean pot.

Pomme Purée

4 large potatoes
175g butter
75ml milk
sea salt

(Prepare ahead)

Preheat the oven to 185°C.

Prick the potatoes all over with a fork. Place them on a layer of salt on a baking tray. Bake for 2 hours.

Cut the potatoes in half and scoop out the flesh. Weigh out the flesh to 400g, then mash or pass through a drum sieve and transfer to a pan.

In another pan, melt the butter into the milk, then pour slowly into the mashed potatoes while stirring.

Season with salt and place in a piping bag. Keep warm.

Roasted Sweetcorn

1 corn on the cob
15g butter
sea salt (pinch of)

Add the corn on the cob, butter and salt to a vacuum pack bag. Seal the bag and cook in boiling water for 1 hour. Plunge into ice water. Alternatively, buy precooked corn on the cob in a vacuum pouch.

Remove the corn from the bag, cut 6 strips off the sweetcorn, end to end, and trim to strips, 2 kernels wide.

Potato Tubes

1 large potato (peeled)
rapeseed oil (drizzle of)
sea salt
1 litre vegetable oil (for deep frying)

Using a spiralizer, spiralize the potato. Pick out 6 of the longest strands; they will need to be approximately 2 metres long. Douse each strand in a little rapeseed oil and sprinkle with salt.

Take a metal tube 9cm long, 5cm in diameter and wrap with oil and silicone paper. Wrap a strand of the potato around the tube from one end to the other ensuring there are no gaps. Secure both ends with steel paperclips. Deep fry at 160°C until golden brown.

Allow to cool slightly and remove from the tube. Repeat with the remaining potato strands.

Sweetcorn Purée

100g butter
1 shallot (peeled, diced)
250g sweetcorn
200ml milk
200ml double cream
sea salt (pinch of)

Melt the butter, then sweat the shallot and sweetcorn for 5 minutes. Add the milk and cream, then bring to a simmer for 5 minutes. Drain the liquid off and reserve.

Blend the sweetcorn, adding the liquid back in as required, with a pinch of salt. Pass through a fine chinois, then add the purée into a squeezy bottle and keep warm.

Pork Fillet

150g pork fillet (fully trimmed)
4 slices Parma ham

Quarter the pork fillet lengthways.

Lay a slice of Parma ham on some outstretched cling film. Place a piece of pork fillet in the centre. Using the cling film, wrap the Parma ham around the pork into a cylinder shape and tie off the ends. Repeat with the remaining Parma ham and pork fillet.

Poach in just simmering water for 9 minutes.

Remove from the water, cut one end of the cling film and use the other end to squeeze out the pork fillet. Trim both ends and cut the pork fillet in half. Repeat with each piece of pork fillet.

Savoy Cabbage

20g butter
½ Savoy cabbage (thinly sliced)
sea salt (pinch of)

Melt the butter in a pan, add the cabbage and wilt. Season with a pinch of sea salt.

Pancetta

1 clove garlic (skin on)
1 sprig thyme
50g pancetta (cut into lardons)
rapeseed oil (drizzle of)

In a cold, non-stick pan, place the garlic, thyme, pancetta and rapeseed oil. Bring to a medium heat to draw out all the fat and crisp up the lardons. Drain on kitchen paper and reserve.

To Assemble

rapeseed oil (drizzle of)
6 popcorn shoots

Preheat the oven to 200°C.

Drizzle rapeseed oil in a non-stick pan and add the pork belly, skin-side down. Put the pan in the oven for 12 minutes or until the skin has turned golden and crisp.

To plate, sprinkle the sweetcorn powder over the base of the dish and position a potato tube to one side. Scoop a generous spoon of cabbage into the bottom of each tube. Mix the pancetta and pork cheek with some of the jus and reduce until sticky, then spoon this on top of the cabbage. Pipe the pomme purée on top of each pie and arrange the pork belly to the side.

Blow torch the sweetcorn or blacken under an extremely hot grill and lay across the centre of the plate. Using the sweetcorn as a barrier, position the pork fillet on the opposite side, topping with a popcorn shoot.

To finish, decorate each plate with 9 dots of the sweetcorn purée.

Continued From Page 079

Every dish that goes on our menu is a team effort. I might have the initial idea or spark of inspiration but then I gather the chefs and we talk it through, bounce ideas off each other and then as a team we prep everything. Next comes my very bad drawing of how I would like the dish to look and I make some rough notes. I have been doing this since I was 15-years-old. The inside cover of this book is a collection of the pages of my notebooks built up over the past 24 years. Every time I was given a recipe or a particular technique, I would scribble it down and I still use them as a point of reference to this day. It is why they are part of my very first actual cookbook.

My notebooks are also filled with little doodles of the initial ideas for so many of my dishes. Samples of these sketches are scattered throughout this book. Now remember, these are my drawings and I have never been the best at art or drawing so please forgive my scribbles, but I think it gives a great insight into the workings of the dish, from concept through to finish. They really help me to visualise my food from the very early stages.

Next comes the plating up of the dish. We taste it as a team, pull it apart and try to be as critical as we can. It then gets tweaked or re-worked entirely and plated up again, tasted again and pulled apart, critiqued and so on. This process might happen four, five or even six times until we are content. Some dishes take days to complete while others take weeks. Sometimes we scrap an idea altogether, move on to the next one and only come back to the original idea a few months later. They won't appear on the menu until we are completely satisfied. The recipe is then typed up and placed in the folder for whatever section it attains to.

Because all the chefs are involved in the process, they have a sense of ownership of the dish and become extremely proud of and connected to the food they are cooking and plating up.

I am a truly impatient chef when creating a new dish, so I always want to work on them straightaway just in case I forget the idea. It means that in the kitchen we are normally working on about two new dishes at any given time.

We start with one element we want to use. It could be a particular piece of crockery or even a specific herb; it doesn't always start with the meat and fish. We then write lists of flavours which would marry well with the ingredient and whittle it down to maybe three or four main flavours per dish. The number of techniques we then put those ingredients through will depend on the dish or ingredient we are looking at.

The crab cannelloni dish on page 028 is a prime example of what I am talking about. I was clearing out one of the cupboards when I came across a branded Martini chiller and the two-part glass dish intrigued me. At around the same time, Great British Menu was in touch to ask me if I would like to be on the show. The theme was based around the Olympics so they wanted the competing chefs to push boundaries and strive to do what no other chef had done before - to think outside the box and compete as hard as Olympians do. It was then that I really got fired up. How could I use this two-part glass dish to create something no one has seen before? So I had to get Will, an artist friend of mine, to make a wooden board for the dish to sit on. Otherwise, when you lifted the lid off the glass bowl, there would be nowhere to put it and I had the novel idea of cutting grooves into the board to hold the cutlery. I had to, of course, try to get my hands on unbranded glasses also. This was all before I had any idea of what was going to go in the dish. I just knew I wanted to use it for one of the courses, it was just about figuring out which one. **Continued on page 101.**

Trout

My love of 'all things seafood' didn't come as naturally as you may think. When growing up, my experience of eating fish probably amounted to dodgy prawn cocktails and fish from the local fish and chip shop. As a 15-year-old chef starting in an industry I knew very little about, the first time I saw lobsters or fresh langoustines I was genuinely shocked. I mean, how on earth are you meant to eat something with such a hard shell? Easy answer is, peel it, of course. However, as a 15-year-old, I had no idea these creatures existed, never mind that they were edible. Imagine the shock when the chef de partie at the time, Robert Newell or 'Jock' as he was affectionately known, cut open the first sea trout I had even seen. The vibrant almost red flesh looked astonishing. I had never seen anything quite like it. I was used to breaking open batter with pearly white haddock sandwiched between the crisp exterior.

Scottish seafood is celebrated across the globe and is a source of pride for so many Scottish chefs. I feel so lucky to work with the amazing seafood in this country. So much so that my menus are almost 50/50 when it comes to meat versus fish. Scottish trout is a regular on my menu and when it comes to sourcing this ingredient, I use RR Spink. They trace their roots back to fishing in Auchmithie in 1715.

Their loch trout is raised in Loch Etive, a stunning tidal loch near Oban on Scotland's west coast. Their fish are grown in cool brackish waters, swimming against a strong tide, in an area of outstanding natural beauty and is reared to the highest welfare standards in the stunning natural surroundings of the loch.

This includes not using live bait at any time - in order to eliminate the risk of parasites - or antibiotics as a preventative treatment. Their team of skilled aquaculturists works collaboratively with organisations like the Scottish Environment Protection Agency to ensure Loch Etive remains the leader in natural fish farming. A low carbon footprint, coupled with the highest welfare standards in the UK, means Loch Etive trout really is the superior choice. Deep red in colour, their trout makes for stunning visual presentation combined with amazing flavour.

The best trout are selected for the RR Spink & Sons brand, hand cured, then mildly smoked in Arbroath, home of smoking in Scotland. This mild smoke enhances rather than hides the natural flavour of the loch trout and is coupled with a melt in the mouth texture.

TROUT | ALMOND | RAZOR CLAM

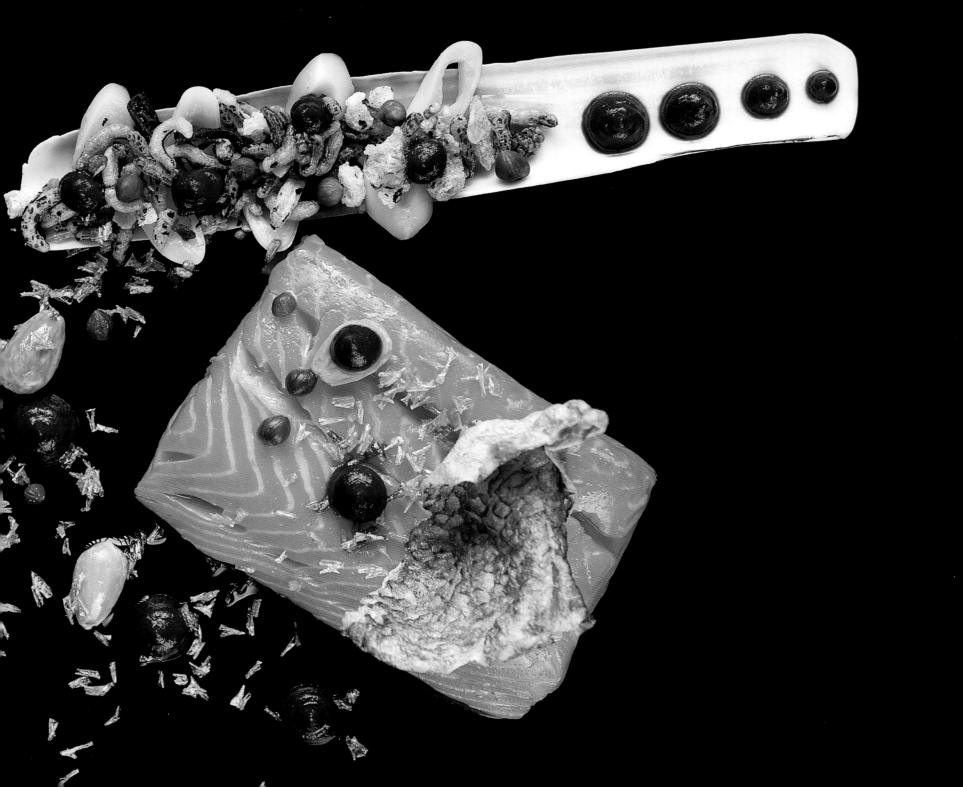

Trout | Almond | Razor Clam
Serves 4

Puffed Pork Rind

200g pork skin (excess fat removed)
vegetable oil (for deep frying)
sea salt

(Prepare ahead)

Preheat the oven to 110°C.

Place the pork skin in a deep oven tray and cover with water. Roast in the oven for 7 hours.

Drain the water and pat the pork skin dry. Dehydrate the pork skin at 54°C for 24 hours.

When the skin is completely dry, blend in a food processor to make a crumb.

Heat a pot of oil to 210°C and deep fry the pork crumble.

Drain on absorbent paper and season with sea salt.

Puffed Quinoa

100g quinoa
vegetable oil (for deep frying)
sea salt

(Prepare ahead)

Cook the quinoa in simmering water for 10-15 minutes, strain and leave to cool.

Place the quinoa onto a tray lined with silicone paper and dehydrate at 54°C for 24 hours.

Place a pan of oil on the stove and bring the temperature up to 190°C.

Using a fine mesh strainer, very quickly fry the quinoa until puffed.

Drain on absorbent paper and season with sea salt.

Curry Granola

27g butter
90g caster sugar
7g liquid glucose
80g hazelnuts (skins removed, toasted, roughly chopped)
37g almonds (toasted, roughly chopped)
¼ tsp baking powder
4g sea salt
¼ tsp Madras curry powder

Place the butter, sugar and glucose into a heavy-based pan and set over a medium heat. Take to a dark caramel and leave to cool slightly.

Add in the hazelnuts, almonds, baking powder and salt whilst stirring until the mixture breaks down. Leave to cool completely. Stir in the curry powder.

Puffed Wild Rice

vegetable oil (for deep frying)
100g wild rice
sea salt

Place a pan of oil on the stove and bring the temperature up to 210°C.

Very quickly dip the wild rice into the oil. Drain on absorbent paper and season with sea salt.

Crispy Shallots

2 banana shallots
vegetable oil (for deep frying)
sea salt

Peel the banana shallots and cut in half lengthways.

Very thinly slice them lengthways and place in a heavy-based pot.

Cover with vegetable oil and place on a low heat. Stirring occasionally, bring the oil up to a slow simmer. When the onions start to turn to a dark golden colour, remove them from the oil using a slotted spoon.

Drain on absorbent paper and season with sea salt.

Crispy Garlic

2 cloves garlic
300ml milk
40g flour
vegetable oil (for deep frying)

Peel and very thinly slice the garlic using a mandoline.

Place into a small pot with 100ml of milk and bring to the boil. Drain the garlic and repeat the process twice more. On the last time, drain the garlic and dust with flour.

Deep fry in oil at 160°C, stirring the garlic frequently. Drain on absorbent paper and season with sea salt.

To Assemble The Wild Rice, Curry & Quinoa Granola

10g black onion ash (see page 238)

Mix together the puffed pork rind, puffed quinoa, curry granola, puffed wild rice, crispy shallots, crispy garlic and black onion ash. Store in an airtight container until required.

Purple Carrot Purée

1kg purple carrots
1 banana shallot (finely diced)
250g butter
100ml milk
¼ tsp xanthan gum
sea salt (pinch of)

(Prepare ahead)

Peel the carrots, keeping the skin, and set aside. Slice the carrots very thinly and place into a vacuum pack bag with the shallot.

Melt the butter and pour in the milk. Place the skins into the mixture and leave to steep for 20 minutes.

Strain the milk and butter into the vacuum pack bag, discarding the skins. Add salt to the bag and vacuum on full power. Place the bag in boiling water and cook for 30 minutes until the carrots are tender. Take the bag out of the water and leave to cool naturally. Once cooled, keep in the fridge overnight.

Place the vacuum bag into boiling water and bring the carrots up to temperature.

Add the contents of the bag into a blender with the xanthan gum and blend on a high speed for 10 minutes. Check the seasoning and add salt as required. Pass the mixture through a fine chinois into a container and cover with contact cling film.

Crispy Scales

scales from 2 trout fillets or 1 whole fish
(a fishmonger can supply these)
vegetable oil (for deep frying)
sea salt

(Prepare ahead)

Boil the scales in lightly salted water for 2 minutes, then dry out the scales on absorbent paper.

Dehydrate for 24 hours on the machine's highest setting.

Deep fry at 185°C for 2 minutes, then drain on absorbent paper. Season with salt.

Puffed Trout Skin

1 trout skin
vegetable oil (for deep frying)
sea salt

Remove all fish and scales from the skin.

Wash the skin well in cold water, then cut into 4 equal size pieces. Dehydrate on the machine's highest setting for 24 hours.

Break the skin into random size pieces.

Deep fry the skin at 220°C, then drain on absorbent paper and season lightly.

Store in an airtight container until required.

Razor Clams

4 razor clams
100ml white wine

Freeze the razor clams straight after purchase; this will tenderise the muscle and give very tender meat.

Heat up a pan on a very high heat.

Douse the frozen razor clams in the white wine. Put the clams and wine mixture into the extremely hot pan and cook for 5 minutes.

Once cooked, drain off the wine and reserve to heat up the razor clams before serving.

Pull the meat from the shells and discard the innards, keeping only the meaty part. Cut each piece of meat into 7 slices, slightly on the angle.

Wash and clean the shells and reserve for plating up.

When ready to serve, gently warm the sliced razor clams in the wine mixture. Do not boil the razor clams as this will toughen them up.

Trout

4 x 180g trout fillets (skin removed, deboned)
sea salt (pinch of)
½ lemon (juice)

Vacuum pack each trout fillet individually. Cook in a water bath at 48°C for half an hour. Remove the trout from the bag and dry with absorbent paper. Season with a little salt and a squeeze of lemon juice.

To Assemble

12 almonds (toasted)
2 tbsp sweetened capers (see page 243)

Place the trout just off centre of each plate. Lay the razor clam shell at an angle coming away from the trout and place in the slices of razor clam.

Top with granola mixture. Pipe on the purple carrot purée. Dot more carrot purée around the trout and scatter the crispy scales, capers and almonds around the plate. Top the trout with the puffed trout skin.

Partridge | Spelt | Romanesco
Serves 4

Spelt Risotto

2 banana shallots (peeled, finely diced)
1 clove garlic (crushed)
25g butter
200g spelt
1 litre chicken stock (see page 239)

(Prepare ahead)

Sweat the shallot and garlic in the butter until translucent and soft. Add the spelt and cook in the butter for 3 minutes. Pour in all of the chicken stock and turn down the heat. Simmer for 2-3 hours until the spelt becomes swollen and has absorbed all the liquid. Cling film the pot well after removing from the heat.

Place the tube of a bench top smoker inside the cling film and, using apple wood chips, smoke the risotto for 90 seconds. Keep the cling film on the pot, allowing the smoke to infuse for 5 minutes. Once infused, spread the risotto onto a large tray to cool down as quickly as possible.

Roasted Partridge

4 partridges (fully prepared, feet and innards removed)
8 rashers pancetta
40g butter
rapeseed oil (drizzle of)
sea salt
3 sprigs thyme
2 cloves garlic (skin on, crushed)

(Prepare ahead)

Remove the legs from the partridge, take out the thigh bone and any tendons. Wrap each leg in a rasher of the pancetta, cling film the leg tightly to form a roulade shape and set in the fridge for 1 hour. Remove from the fridge and put the legs in a water bath at 58°C for 1½ hours. Remove the cling film.

Preheat the oven to 185°C.

Melt the butter with the oil in a pan, then add the partridge crowns. Season liberally with salt and brown all over before transferring the pan to the oven. Cook for 8-10 minutes. Take the pan from the oven, add the thyme and garlic. Baste the buttery garlic and thyme mixture over the bird, making sure you coat each side evenly. Rest the bird.

Remove the breasts from the carcasses, cleaning up the wing bone as you would a chicken. Cover the meat with foil and set aside. Reserve the trimmings.

Damson Jus

300ml red wine
trimmings (from the partridge)
800ml chicken stock (see page 239)
100g damsons (halved, destoned)

Reduce the red wine in a pan with the partridge trimmings, add the chicken stock and reduce again by half. Strain the partridge out otherwise the sauce will become too 'gamey'. Continue to reduce the sauce until it coats the back of a spoon or is the consistency of single cream.

Stir in the damsons. Allow to infuse for 10-15 minutes before serving.

Chervil Root Purée

500g chervil root (washed, peeled)
75ml milk
2 sprigs thyme
100g butter
sea salt

(Prepare ahead)

Set the water bath to 90°C.

Dice the chervil root into 1cm cubes.

Add the milk, thyme, butter and diced chervil root to a vacuum pack bag, seal on the highest setting. Cook in the water bath for approximately 1½ hours until the chervil root is tender. Blend in a high speed blender until the purée is silky smooth, adjusting the seasoning as required.

Romanesco & Brussels Sprouts

100ml chicken stock (see page 239)
20g butter
20 Romanesco florets
20 Brussels sprouts (outer leaves of)
sea salt

Bring the chicken stock and butter to a simmer. Add in the Romanesco florets and sprout leaves, cook for no longer than 2 minutes, then drain on a j-cloth. Season with a little salt.

Cep Croutons

3 slices white bread (crusts removed)
50g clarified butter
10g cep powder (see page 239)

Preheat the oven to 160°C.

Roll the slices of bread through a pasta machine until the thinnest setting is reached. Cut 16 rings out from the bread using a 4cm and a 2cm round cutter. Brush the rings with clarified butter and place in a single layer between 2 silicone baking mats. Bake for 20 minutes. Dust with cep powder.

Burnt Cream

200ml double cream

Cook the cream in a heavy-based pan, stirring continuously with a spatula until it starts to reduce and colour. Continue until the natural sugars start to brown, giving a nutty brown finish.

Celeriac

¼ celeriac (sliced on a mandoline)
sea salt

Cut out rounds from the celeriac with a 3cm cutter, season the rounds with a little salt.

To Assemble

chicken stock (splash of)
5g butter
sea salt

To reheat the risotto, add a splash of chicken stock to a pan with the butter. Add the risotto and warm through. Season with salt to taste.

Spoon the risotto onto the centre of each plate. Rest 2 partridge breasts on top of the risotto and arrange the 2 legs around them.

Dot around the Brussels sprout leaves, Romanesco, cep croutons, celeriac slices and damsons.

Drizzle over the damson jus to finish.

Continued From Page 091

I then had the idea of using crab. I really wanted to showcase some amazing Scottish produce, and the brown crabs we get with the sweet claw meat are really quite special. So I thought about a very modern crab salad with cauliflower custard and lemon pearls; the sweetness of the cauliflower marries amazingly well with the sweetness of the crab and the lemon pearls just cut through to add a sharpness to the dish. I also wanted to introduce a smoky element, to add a little theatre and give it the slightest back note of smoke. Using the two-part glass dish was the perfect vessel for it. It bombed on the show. I had used bought-in mayonnaise (very expensive French mayonnaise I have to add) to bind the crab before I froze it slightly, to allow me to wrap it in herb butter. My reasoning being if I had used fresh homemade mayonnaise, when it defrosts it splits, but because of the emulsifiers in the very expensive French mayonnaise this doesn't happen - it holds it together perfectly. I never had a chance to explain myself on the show to the judge Jeremy Lee and he crucified me for it. I got either a 4 or a 5 out of 10. It was the lowest score of the week and I was devastated. All that thought, all that work, and to be given such a low score, my heart just sank. If only he knew the work, research, testing and development I had put into the dish, maybe he would have been a little more understanding. I had put it on my menu about a month before the show so I could get plenty practice and the feedback was always amazing. Because the dish was new and exciting, all our customers loved it. The crab cannelloni has been on the menu ever since and it is our biggest selling dish by a mile.

So it just goes to show how subjective food is, someone's 4 or 5 out of 10 is someone else's 10 out of 10.

There Is No 'I' In Team

Well you hear this so often, but I do believe every team needs a good leader. Without a leader there is no direction or discipline. The team works in so many ways. It is more like a chain made up of links, one weak link and the whole chain has no strength. I would like to think of myself as the strongest link but there are areas of the business where I am not strong, like finance for example. That is where Nicola, my fiancée of 10 years, comes into it; she does all the hard work. I often say that I just peel the tatties and rattle some pans. Nicola does everything financial, from paying suppliers to paying staff and everything in-between. She looks after budgets and projections. She also runs front of house in the restaurant along with our current restaurant manager, Andy, so I would say the 'I' in the team would be Nicola because without that side of things being carefully monitored and looked after, there would be no business or 'team'.

When it comes to leadership in the kitchen, there is such a fine line between discipline and dictatorship. No one would like to work for a dictator as much as they wouldn't work anywhere without discipline. If there are no rules, there is no consistency. We encourage involvement in every area of the business, whether it is changing service in a certain way to give the guests a better experience or changing a dish on the menu. However, once that change has been made, everyone in the team must follow the change to the letter otherwise we wouldn't be consistent in what we do. Of course hierarchy comes into the business in a big way. My second in command, my sous chef Cameron, leads the team probably more than I do. I set the standards and agree to any changes and obviously have the final say, but it is my sous chef's job to make sure the change is fully implemented by every member of the team. If I am out of the kitchen in a meeting, going through finances with Nicola or writing recipes for this book for example, then my sous chef is controlling every aspect of the prep in the kitchen in readiness for lunch or dinner. So yes, in a way my sous chef has to be a dictator to make sure everything is 100% right 100% of the time. **Continued on page 143.**

Halibut | Cauliflower | Dill
Serves 4

Herb Crust

This will make more than you need but it freezes exceptionally well if stored between silicone paper in an airtight container.

125g butter
½ medium onion (finely diced)
250g panko breadcrumbs
25g chervil (roughly chopped)
25g chives (roughly chopped)
25g coriander (roughly chopped)
25g parsley (roughly chopped)
150g mature Cheddar (grated)
2 egg yolks

Melt the butter in a pan, add the onion and sweat gently for 2-3 minutes until soft but with no colour. Add half the breadcrumbs, half the herbs and cook for a further 2 minutes. Meanwhile, combine the rest of the breadcrumbs and herbs in a large bowl. Pour the onion mixture over this and stir well. Transfer to a blender. Add the cheddar and egg yolks and blend on a high speed until smooth and well incorporated.

Roll out the mixture between 2 sheets of silicone paper until ¼cm thick, then chill in the fridge. Using an 8cm round cutter, cut out 4 discs. The trimmings can be re-blended; simply repeat the process of rolling out and cutting. Store the discs in the fridge until required.

Potato Tuiles

200g potato (peeled)
sea salt
1 tsp fennel seeds
1 litre vegetable oil (for deep frying)

(Prepare ahead)

Boil the potatoes in salted water until tender. Drain and blend in a high speed blender. Spread out on a silicone mat or lined baking tray to a 3mm thickness and sprinkle over the fennel seeds. Transfer to a dehydrator on the highest setting for 4-5 hours.

Break into varied shards and deep fry until golden brown at 180°C.

Salt Dough

250g plain flour
2 egg whites
150g rock salt
75ml water

(Prepare ahead)

Combine the flour, egg whites and rock salt in a mixer for 4 minutes. Slowly add the water until it becomes a tight dough, keep mixing for a further 10 minutes.

Salt Baked Beetroot

1 golden beetroot
1 candy beetroot

(Prepare ahead)

Preheat the oven to 180°C.

Roll out the salt dough to a ½cm thickness, then wrap it around the beetroots. Place on an oven tray and cook for 1½ hours.

Break open the crust, discard, and allow the beetroot to cool naturally. Do not cool with the crust on as the beetroot will end up too salty. Peel and dice into 1cm cubes.

Cauliflower Purée

60g butter
1 cauliflower (diced including the stalk)
¼ large onion (diced)
sea salt
110ml milk
110ml double cream
¼ tsp xanthan gum

Melt the butter and add the cauliflower. Cook over a medium heat until the cauliflower has turned nut brown, be careful not to colour it too much otherwise it will go bitter. Add the diced onion and add a generous pinch of salt, continue to sweat the mixture for another 3-4 minutes before adding the milk and cream and bringing to a simmer.

Drain the liquid from the cauliflower and reserve.

Blend the cauliflower, slowly pouring the liquid back in as you blend, until a thick purée consistency is achieved. Add the xanthan gum and blend for another 2-3 minutes. Pass through a fine chinois and keep warm until needed.

Dill Jelly

570ml fish stock (cold) (see page 240)
4.7g gellan gum
½ tbsp watercress purée (see page 244)
3 tbsp dill (chopped)

Blend the fish stock, gellan gum and watercress purée together with a stick blender in a pan, then bring to a simmer. Add the dill and return to the boil.

Pour out onto an acetate sheet to a 2mm thickness. Using a 12cm round cutter, cut circles from the jelly. Use a 10cm diameter round cutter to cut out the centres to form rings of jelly.

Cauliflower

½ cauliflower
20g butter

Break the cauliflower into tiny florets, reserve 6 of these for each serving. Slice the remaining florets very thinly allowing 6 per plate and reserve the slices in ice water.

Melt the butter to a nut brown colour, add the whole cauliflower florets and cook for a minute until golden brown.

Kale

green and purple kale (handful of, picked, washed)
20g butter

Sweat down the kale in the butter for 30 seconds.

Pan Roasted Halibut

4 x 180g halibut fillet (skinned, deboned)
rapeseed oil (drizzle of)
sea salt
30g butter
½ lemon (juice of)

Heat up a non-stick pan until almost smoking hot. Add a drizzle of rapeseed oil, place the halibut in and turn down the heat. Cook the fish slowly until it is cooked halfway up the fish. Add a sprinkle of salt, the butter and lemon juice. Remove the pan from the heat, turn the fish over, and allow to finish cooking in the residual heat.

To Assemble

Place a jelly ring around each plate with a disc of herb crust in the centre. Decorate half of the ring with 6 cubes of beetroot. Arrange the roasted cauliflower between the beetroot cubes, then the raw cauliflower between the beetroot and roasted cauliflower. Interleave this with kale and potato tuiles.

Dot over the roasted cauliflower purée and finish by arranging the halibut in the centre of each plate.

Beef | Ash | Asparagus
Serves 4

Smoked Pomme Purée

4 large Rooster potatoes
sea salt
75ml milk
175g butter
1 portable smoker
applewood smoking chips

Preheat the oven to 185°C.

Prick the potatoes all over with a fork, place them on a layer of salt on a baking tray and bake for 2 hours.

Meanwhile, pour the milk into a stainless steel bowl and cover well with cling film.

Lift up one edge of the cling film and using the smoker, pipe in smoke for 2 minutes. Re-cover the bowl making sure none of the smoke is lost and allow to sit for 30 minutes.

Cut the potatoes in half, scoop out the flesh and weigh out 400g.

Mash the potato through a drum sieve and transfer to a heavy-based pot.

Melt the butter into the smoked milk and pour slowly into the potatoes while stirring. Season with salt and keep warm until required.

Black Onion Gel

3 onions
700ml vegetable stock (see page 244)
20g-30g Ultratex
smoked sea salt

Cut the onions in half and remove the skins.

Using a non-stick pan over a medium heat, blacken the onions all over, turning every 3 or 4 minutes. This step should take a good half hour.

Place the onions in a heavy-based pot, pour over the vegetable stock and simmer for 30 minutes until the stock has almost evaporated.

Transfer to a blender and blend on a medium speed for 10 minutes, scraping down the sides halfway through.

Add the Ultratex a spoonful at a time until a glossy, smooth purée is achieved. Season with smoked salt to taste. Pass through a fine chinois and decant into a squeezy bottle until required.

Wild Garlic Crisps

4 wild garlic leaves
rapeseed oil (drizzle of)
sea salt

Cut the garlic leaves in half and trim off the edges so the leaves become straight.

Cling film a plate that will fit inside the microwave and pull the cling film tight so there are no creases. Oil the cling film well with rapeseed oil and season with salt.

Place the garlic leaves on the oil and smooth them out. Season the leaves with a little more salt.

Cook in the microwave for 20 second bursts until the leaves become transparent and crisp. Please note the leaves will crisp up more on cooling.

Drain the leaves on absorbent paper and store in an airtight container until required.

Sirloin Of 40 Day Dry Aged Aberdeen Angus Beef

4 x 200g 40 day dry aged sirloin steaks (fully trimmed)
80g butter
4 sprigs thyme
4 cloves garlic (crushed)
rapeseed oil (drizzle of)
sea salt

Preheat a water bath to 55°C.

Vacuum pack each steak individually with 20g butter, a sprig of thyme and 1 clove of garlic. Cook in the water bath for 35 minutes.

Remove from the water bath, remove the steaks from the vacuum pack bags and pat dry.

Heat up a cast iron pan until it is almost smoking. Drizzle a little rapeseed oil and salt over each steak. Place the steaks in the pan and colour on each side for just a moment, making sure to get a great colour. Remove the steaks from the pan and allow to rest on a cooling rack for 5 minutes.

Thyme Jus

400ml veal jus (see page 244)
6 sprigs thyme

Simmer the thyme in the veal jus for 5 minutes, then pass through a muslin cloth.

Pour the jus into small serving jugs and allow guests to pour it over the beef themselves.

To Assemble

4 asparagus spears
300ml butter emulsion (see page 238)
1 tsp black onion ash (see page 238)
24 thin slices black truffle
4 button mushrooms (cut into a selection of cubes and thin slices, seasoned with a little sea salt)

Remove and discard the woody ends of the asparagus spears. Pare down the ends using a peeler, then poach in the butter emulsion for 2-3 minutes until just tender.

Sprinkle a line of black onion ash 1½cm wide across each plate. Place one quenelle of smoked pomme purée towards the top of each line of ash and 2 smaller quenelles to the right of each line. Add 8 dots of black onion gel to the left of the onion ash.

Carve all of the fat off the sirloin and cut each steak into 3 pieces. Arrange the pieces on each plate, placing one on the onion ash and 2 on the smaller quenelles of pomme purée.

Rest the slices of truffle and mushroom against the pomme purée and sirloin. Scatter a couple of the mushroom cubes on each plate. Place one spear of asparagus down the centre of the ash on each plate. Garnish each plate with 2 garlic crisps immediately before serving.

Monkfish & Chicken
Serves 4

Fennel & Dill Purée

75g butter
3 shallots (diced)
2 bulbs fennel (thinly sliced)
300ml milk
300ml double cream
75g dill (finely chopped)
sea salt

Melt the butter in a heavy-based saucepan and add the shallots and fennel. Sweat until the fennel is cooked and almost falling apart but with no colour; this should take approximately 30 minutes on a low heat. Add the milk and cream and simmer for 15 minutes. Transfer to a blender and blend on a medium speed for 8 minutes. Add the dill and blend for a further 4 minutes. Pass through a fine chinois. Season with salt, to taste. Keep warm until needed.

Confit Chicken Wings

8 chicken wings
500g duck fat
6 sprigs thyme (picked, finely chopped)
sea salt

Preheat the oven to 120ºC.

Cut a small incision in the end of each wing. Twist and pull out the thinner of the 2 bones. Trim off any loose bits of fat or sinew. Push the meat down to the end of the bone.

Melt the duck fat and season the chicken wings with salt and chopped thyme.

Place the chicken wings into a casserole dish and cover them with the duck fat. Place in the oven for 3 hours until the meat is meltingly soft. Drain the chicken wings.

Confit Carrots

150g butter
4 baby carrots
1 clove garlic (crushed)
3 sprigs thyme
1 orange (zest of)

Melt the butter in a pan. Add the rest of the ingredients and simmer very gently for 11 minutes, or until the carrots are tender. Remove the carrots.

Carrot Ribbons

1 carrot (peeled)

Using a peeler, cut 8 strips of carrot lengthways. Cut the strips into rectangles measuring 3cm x 12cm. Pour boiling water over the ribbons and allow to cool.

Roasted Monkfish

rapeseed oil (drizzle of)
1 monkfish tail (600g)
sea salt (pinch of)
30g butter
½ lemon (juice of)

Heat up a non-stick pan until almost smoking hot, then add a drizzle of
rapeseed oil. Place the monkfish in the pan, add a sprinkle of salt, cook for
2-3 minutes and turn the fish over.

Add the butter and lemon juice and baste the fish. Take the pan off the heat,
turn the fish over and allow it to finish cooking in the residual heat.

Cardamom Foam

1 shallot (peeled, diced)
25g butter
8 cardamom pods (toasted, crushed)
150ml white wine
300ml fish stock (see page 240)
400ml milk
8g sugar ester (see page 243)

Sweat the shallot in the butter. Add the cardamom pods, then the white
wine and reduce until the wine has almost evaporated. Pour in the fish
stock, stir well and reduce until the stock has almost evaporated.

Add the milk and the sugar ester and bring to a gentle simmer.

Remove from the heat and allow to cool for 15-20 minutes. Pass the liquid
through a fine chinois.

Gently reheat the liquid, ensuring it does not go above 70°C.

Foam the mixture with a stick blender, allow to settle for 1-2 minutes and
spoon off the foam from the top to garnish.

To Assemble

dill sprigs (to garnish)
vegetable oil (for deep frying)

Drain the carrot ribbons and season with a little sea salt. Wrap each ribbon
into a tube and arrange 2 tubes on each plate.

Drag a spoonful of the purée across each plate. Cross that with a drained
baby carrot.

Reheat the chicken wings by deep frying them in the vegetable oil at 185°C
for 2-3 minutes.

Place 2 chicken wings on each plate.

Divide the monkfish into 4 and place a piece in the middle of each plate.

Garnish with sprigs of dill and cardamom foam.

Duck

When searching for the best possible ducks available in Scotland, Gartmorn Farm was a name that came up over and again. Roger and Susan Lucey specialise in slow grown, mature poultry and their ducks really are second to none. The farm is situated in an idyllic location on the north shore of the Gartmorn Country Park, nestled just beneath the Ochil Hills - the ideal growing conditions for ducks. Roger and Susan take pride in the fact they have complete control over the whole process from day old ducklings, right up to the delivery of the final product. With a stockman and butcher on site, they ensure all aspects of the production are carefully monitored. Every ingredient I buy has to come from people equally as passionate as we are, and I find the job that Roger and Susan do is outstanding, leading to a fantastic end product we are proud to use.

The farm itself has been in the family since 1968 when it began as a seasonal turkey enterprise. It quickly expanded and grew to be a sizeable wholesale business. During the late 90s, the wholesale market became very competitive and intensive farming became the norm.

Roger and Susan made the decision to move away from this and focus on the careful rearing of their birds. They said goodbye to the commodity priced production in order to maintain a superior product. Their dedication means the ducks arriving in my kitchen are the best you can buy in Scotland. They are big enough to have the equipment and knowledge to produce a quality welfare friendly product but small enough to care and take the time and attention. I have been lucky enough to work with them over the past year and the duck dishes on my menu have grown in popularity as a result. A duck main course is always available at the restaurant, although the accompaniments change with the seasons. Knowing that the star of the dish is always of superior quality gives me the freedom to do whatever I like to help this amazing ingredient shine through.

Duck | Red Cabbage | Salsify
Serves 4

Gartmorn Farm Duck Breast

1 duck crown

Preheat a water bath to 55°C.

Trim the duck crown, remove any excess fat and vacuum pack (a butcher can do this for you).

Cook in the water bath for 2 hours, then plunge straight into ice water for half an hour.

Remove the breasts from the crown and trim away any excess fat or sinew.

Store in the fridge until ready to use.

Purple Carrots

2 purple carrots
100ml butter emulsion (see page 238)

(Prepare ahead)

Cut off the top and bottom of the carrots.

Quarter and remove the core from the carrots but leave the skin on.

Place the carrots in a vacuum pack bag with the butter emulsion and seal tightly in a vacuum pack machine to remove all the air.

Plunge into boiling water and simmer for 20 minutes until the carrots are just soft to the touch.

Cut the top off the bag and re-vacuum pack the carrots, sealing the bag tightly.

Allow to sit in the fridge for 24 hours so that the purple colour bleeds through the inside of the carrot.

Chips

2 Maris Piper potatoes (washed)
300ml duck fat

Using an apple corer, core the potatoes to get 16 cylindrical shapes.

Cut the cylinders to 4½cm lengths.

Lay silicone paper at the base of a heavy-based pot and fill the pot with the duck fat.

Gently simmer the potatoes in the duck fat so they are just tender but not broken up. This should take about 8-9 minutes.

Drain the potatoes on absorbent paper and allow to cool completely.

Red Cabbage & Red Onion Compôte

½ red cabbage
6 red onions

Chiffonade the red cabbage and red onion as thinly as possible and keep them separate.

Place the red onion on a low heat in a heavy-based pan.

In a separate heavy-based pan, place the red cabbage on a low heat.

Cook down the red onion and red cabbage slowly and once they have both broken down slightly, turn up the heat to a medium heat.

Stirring occasionally, allow all the natural sugars to come out of the red cabbage and red onion.

If it starts to catch slightly on the pan, add a few drops of water just to loosen the mixture and continue to cook down. The onions should take about 1 hour and the cabbage 1½ hours.

Once both mixtures are ready, mix them together and allow to cool. Refrigerate until required.

Bread Tubes

2 slices white bread (crusts removed)
50g clarified butter (see page 239)
vegetable oil (for deep frying)

Using a pasta machine, pass the bread through each size setting twice until the last setting is reached.

Cut each slice of bread into 3cm x 8cm rectangles - there should be 8 rectangles.

Brush a metal tube measuring approximately 2½cm in diameter, with a little oil and wrap it in silicone paper.

Lightly brush the bread rectangles with clarified butter.

Wrap the rectangles around the pipe, one at a time, pressing the edges together to form a tight seal.

Deep fry in the oil at 180°C until golden and crispy. Slide the bread off the pipe and allow to cool.

Repeat with the remaining bread.

Salsify

2 sticks salsify
125ml butter emulsion (see page 238)
1 clove garlic (crushed)
1 stalk tarragon

Peel and wash the salsify well.

Working quickly, place the salsify in a vacuum pack bag and pour in the butter emulsion, garlic and tarragon. Vacuum pack tightly to expel all the air.

Cook in simmering water for 20 minutes or until the salsify is just tender. Plunge the whole bag into ice water.

Fig Purée

200g caster sugar
300g ripe figs

Make a dry caramel with the sugar, taking it to a golden brown colour.

Top and tail the figs, then cut into quarters.

Drop the figs into the caramel and cook down until water has come out of the figs and evaporated.

Blend to a smooth purée, pass through a fine chinois and decant into a squeezy bottle. Store in the fridge.

Tarragon Jus

250ml red wine
500ml duck stock (see page 240)
2 stalks tarragon

Reduce the wine in a pot until it has almost evaporated. Add the stock and reduce to 150ml, then remove from the heat. Add the tarragon and allow to infuse for at least 1 hour.

To Assemble

80g honey
sea salt (pinch of)
vegetable oil (for deep frying)
16 nasturtium leaves

Remove the duck breasts from the fridge and allow to come up to room temperature for about 10 minutes.

Preheat the oven to 200°C.

Place the duck breasts skin-side down in a cold pan. Bring the duck up to a medium heat and render out all the excess fat (ensuring it doesn't cook too fast and colour the skin before the fat has a chance to render out all of the way).

Once an even golden colour is achieved, turn the duck over and turn up the heat to colour the underside of the breast. Turn the duck back onto its skin and place in the oven for 6 minutes. Remove the duck from the oven and drizzle honey and a pinch of salt over the skin. Allow the duck to rest for 10 minutes.

Cut the salsify and carrots into 10cm lengths. Using some of the emulsion from the salsify, warm the carrots and salsify through, then place in the oven for 5 minutes until piping hot.

Deep fry the chips at 185°C for 2-3 minutes until crisp and golden. Season these well with a little salt.

Carve each duck breast in half lengthways and trim off the rounded edges.

Place a piece of salsify and carrot on each plate. Lay one piece of duck at the head of each plate.

Fill each bread tube with a spoonful of the red onion and red cabbage compôte and place 2 on each plate.

Scatter around the chips, dots of the fig purée and nasturtium leaves.

Warm the tarragon jus through and serve separately so that guests can pour it themselves.

Salmon | Cucumber | Saffron

Serves 4

Cucumber

2 cucumbers

Peel both cucumbers.

Using a blow torch, burn one of the cucumbers all over. Vacuum pack the charred cucumber and refrigerate for 2 hours. Remove from the vacuum pack bag and cut the flesh of the cucumber into 4cm x 2cm rectangles.

Pass the other cucumber through a spiralizer and set aside.

Saffron Mayonnaise

1 whole egg
1 egg yolk
1 tsp Dijon mustard
2 tbsp sherry vinegar
saffron (large pinch of)
30ml water
500ml rapeseed oil
sea salt

Combine the egg, egg yolk, mustard and vinegar in the container of a food processor.

Bring the saffron to the boil in the water.

Set the food processor on a medium speed and gradually drizzle in the oil while blending. Add the saffron water. Once emulsified, taste and season with salt. Store in a small squeezy bottle or piping bag.

Salmon

4 x 140g wild salmon fillets
rapeseed oil (drizzle of)
sea salt (pinch of)
50g butter
½ lemon (juice of)

Cut each salmon portion into 4 equal size pieces.

Heat up a non-stick pan until almost smoking hot and add a drizzle of rapeseed oil.

Place the salmon skin-side down in the pan and turn down the heat. Cook the salmon slowly on its skin-side until it is cooked halfway up the fish. Add a sprinkle of salt, the butter and lemon juice.

Take the pan off the heat, turn the fish over and allow it to finish cooking in the residual heat of the pan, basting the butter mixture over the fish.

Remove the salmon from the pan and keep warm until plating up. The salmon should be rare in the middle but warmed all the way through.

To Assemble

dill (to garnish)
chives (to garnish)

Place 4 pieces of salmon down the centre of each plate. Spread 5 rectangles of cucumber around the fish, 3 at the back and 2 in front of the fish. Drape the cucumber laces over and under the salmon. Dot the saffron mayonnaise over and around the salmon. Garnish the plates with dill and chives.

SALMON | CUCUMBER | SAFFRON

Fish | Chips | Peas

Serves 4

'Ketchup' Leather

8 very ripe tomatoes
1 clove garlic (sliced)
3 sprigs thyme (picked)
50g Demerara sugar
70ml cider vinegar
sea salt (pinch of)
1 tsp xanthan gum
½ tsp crytex

(Prepare ahead)

Preheat the oven to 85°C.

Slice all the tomatoes in half, scatter over the garlic and thyme and cook in the oven for 5 hours.

Remove the garlic and thyme from the tomatoes and discard.

Make a light caramel with the sugar by melting in a dry non-stick pan until golden brown.

Add the vinegar, being careful as this is extremely hot. Stir in the tomatoes and cook down the mixture for 20 minutes on a gentle simmer. Season to taste with a pinch of salt.

Blend to a smooth purée and add the xanthan gum and crytex.

Spread onto a silicone mat to a ¼cm thickness. Dehydrate for 12 hours on the machine's highest setting. Cut into 9cm squares and return to the dehydrator until you are ready to serve.

Plaice

4 x 180g plaice fillets (skinned, deboned)
sea salt (pinch of)
¼ lemon (juice of)

Roll up each plaice fillet tightly in cling film to form a cylinder and tie off the ends. Place in the fridge to set for 1 hour.

Cook in a water bath set at 62°C for 40 minutes. Remove from the water bath and discard the cling film. Season each fillet with a little salt and lemon juice.

Potato Laces

2 Rooster potatoes (peeled)
vegetable oil (for deep frying)
sea salt (pinch of)

Put the potatoes through a spiralizer. Lightly oil and season with salt.

Pick out strands about 1m in length. One by one, place the strands in the fryer gathering up all the strands to make loose nests. Fry until golden brown for about 4-5 minutes. Drain on absorbent paper and season with a little more salt.

Pea Purée

60g butter
1 shallot (finely diced)
½ clove garlic (finely sliced)
100ml chicken stock (see page 239)
100ml milk
100ml double cream
150g peas (fresh or frozen)
sea salt

Gently melt the butter in a pan, add the shallot and garlic and sweat until softened but with no colour. Add the stock and reduce by half. Pour in the milk and cream and bring to a rapid boil. Add the peas and quickly bring back to the boil, then remove from the heat.

Pass the mixture through a fine sieve, reserving the liquid and the peas separately. Blend the peas, adding in the liquid until a smooth consistency is achieved. Season with salt to taste.

Peas

200g fresh peas (out of the pod)

Boil the peas in salted water, then refresh in ice water.

Purple Carrots

4 baby purple carrots (peeled)
200ml butter emulsion (see page 238)

Gently poach the carrots in the butter emulsion for 4 minutes. Cut each carrot into 4 pieces.

To Assemble

baby parsley (to garnish)

Scrunch up the 'ketchup' leather and allow to come to room temperature. This will crisp up as it cools.

Place one of the potato nests in the centre of each plate and top with a piece of 'ketchup' leather. Arrange the purple carrot pieces into the holes in the nest. Flake a plaice fillet over each plate. Scatter over the peas and dot the pea purée on and around the plaice and potato laces. Top with baby parsley.

Grouse | Heather Honey | Aubergine
Serves 4

Parsnip Bark

1 parsnip
vegetable oil (for deep frying)
sea salt

(Prepare ahead)

Peel the parsnip and cut into quarters. Using a mandoline, slice the parsnips as thinly as possible.

Lay the slices onto silicone mats and dehydrate for 24 hours at the machine's highest setting.

Deep fry at 180°C until golden brown, drain on absorbent paper and season with a little salt.

Hazelnut & Oatmeal Granola

45g pine nuts
45g puffed millet
60g hazelnuts (skins removed, halved)
135g rolled oats
110g pinhead oats
60g pumpkin seeds
2 garlic cloves (chopped)
110ml liquid glucose
85g duck fat
135g Parmesan (grated)
180g basil leaves
vegetable oil (for deep frying)
sea salt (pinch of)

Preheat the oven to 180°C.

Place the pine nuts, puffed millet, hazelnuts, oats, pumpkin seeds, garlic, liquid glucose and duck fat in a large baking tray and mix well. Place in the oven for 25 minutes, mixing every 7-8 minutes.

Spread the Parmesan on a silicone mat and bake for 7-8 minutes until melted together and golden. Allow to cool and break into crumbs.

Deep fry the basil leaves at 180°C until crispy and drain on kitchen paper.

Mix the Parmesan and basil with the other ingredients and season with a little sea salt, being careful as Parmesan can be salty.

Aubergine Crisps

½ aubergine
rapeseed oil (drizzle of)

Preheat the oven to 185°C.

Slice the aubergine lengthways as thinly as possible on a mandoline.

Place an oiled piece of silicone paper on a baking tray and lay the slices of aubergine on the tray.

Oil another sheet of silicone paper and lay on top of the aubergine slices. Top with a baking tray of equal size. Place in the oven 12 minutes.

Potato Fondant

1 large Rooster potato (peeled, cut into 2cm thick slices)
150ml chicken stock (see page 239)
150g butter
1 sprig thyme
1 clove garlic (skin on, crushed)

Preheat the oven to 185°C.

Using a 3cm cookie cutter, cut out 4 rounds of potato.

Add all the ingredients to an ovenproof dish and bake in the oven for 35 minutes or until the potato is tender.

Honey & Juniper Roast Root Vegetables

1 parsnip (peeled)
½ celeriac (peeled)
4 baby carrots (peeled)
3 Brussels sprouts
20g butter
80g heather honey
6 juniper berries (crushed)
100ml chicken stock (see page 239)
sea salt (pinch of)

Dice the parsnip and celeriac to 1cm cubes.

Pick the leaves off the sprouts and shred the heart of the sprouts.

Blanch the carrots, celeriac and parsnip separately in boiling water for approximately 2 minutes each until tender.

Melt the butter until it starts to foam. Place the celeriac and parsnip in the butter and add the honey and juniper. Cook the vegetables in the honey mix until they start to colour slightly. Add in the carrots and cook for a further 2 minutes. Pour in the chicken stock and add a pinch of salt. Add in the shredded Brussels sprout hearts and toss vigorously. Lastly, add the Brussels sprout leaves.

Grouse

4 grouse
rapeseed oil (drizzle of)
50g butter
1 clove garlic (crushed)
1 sprig thyme

Preheat the oven to 190°C.

Brown the grouse evenly on all sides with a drizzle of rapeseed oil in a large pan.

Transfer the pan to the oven and roast the grouse for 8 minutes. Remove the pan from the oven and add the butter, garlic and thyme. Baste the juices over the birds.

Allow the grouse to rest in the pan for 6 minutes. Remove the legs and breasts from the grouse and keep warm. Reserve the bones for the jus.

Grouse Trimming Jus

reserved bones from the grouse
400ml red wine
6 juniper berries (crushed)
1 litre chicken stock (see page 239)

Brown the grouse bones well in a heavy-based sauté pan.

Add the red wine and juniper berries and reduce the wine until it has almost evaporated. Pour in the chicken stock and reduce until there is 200ml left in the pan.

Pass through a fine chinois and serve separately so guests can pour the sauce at the table.

To Assemble

1 leaf radicchio (ripped into pieces)
12 nasturtium leaves

Place 2 grouse legs on each plate and lay over 2 breasts.

Set a potato fondant disc on top. Spoon a generous amount of the roasted root vegetables in front of the breasts and top with a generous spoon of the granola, enough to cover the vegetables.

Top with an aubergine crisp, some parsnip bark, ripped radicchio and nasturtiums.

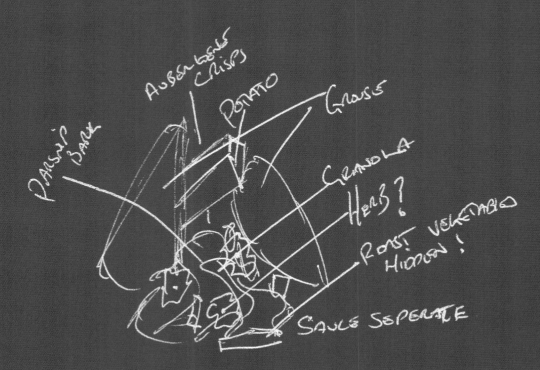

Hake | Cannelloni | Shellfish
Serves 4

Fennel Bisque

400g lobster shells (crushed)
200g prawn shells (crushed)
250g butter
3 bulbs fennel (thinly sliced)
1 shallot (peeled, finely diced)
2 stalks thyme
3 cloves garlic (crushed)
60ml Pernod
30ml brandy
100ml white wine
12 very ripe tomatoes (skinned, seeds removed)
2 litres fish stock (see page 240)
sea salt

Preheat the oven to 185°C.

Roast the lobster shells and prawn shells in the oven for 30 minutes, turning every 10 minutes.

Melt the butter in a heavy-based pan. Add the fennel, shallots, thyme and garlic and sweat well for 10-15 minutes without colour.

Add the shells to the pot with the fennel and cook down for 5 minutes. Pour in the Pernod and brandy and flame to burn off the alcohol.

Add the white wine and reduce until the wine has almost evaporated. Stir in the tomatoes and cook for a further 10 minutes. Add the fish stock and simmer for 1½ hours.

Transfer everything to a blender and blend on a medium speed for 10 minutes - this will need to be done in batches.

Pass through a fine chinois and then through a muslin cloth.

Bring the bisque back up to the boil and reduce by half. Check the seasoning and add salt to taste. Pass once more through a muslin cloth and keep warm until required.

Shellfish Mousse

250g plaice fillets (skinned, deboned)
160g scallops (roe removed)
1 egg
sea salt (pinch of)
175ml double cream
50g cockles (cooked, shells removed)
50g mussels (cooked, shells removed)
½ tbsp dill (chopped)

Blend the plaice, scallops and salt together. Pass through a drum sieve. Add back into a clean blender with the egg. While blending, drizzle in 125ml of the cream until combined. Chill the mixture for half an hour.

Fold the remaining cream through the mixture, then add the cockles, mussels and dill. Place the mixture into a piping bag and return to the fridge for half an hour.

Pipe onto rolled out cling film. Roll up into 4 cylinders; each should measure 11cm in length and 2cm in diameter. Refrigerate until required.

Pasta

200g pasta flour
5 egg yolks
5ml olive oil
1 whole egg

Place the flour on a board. Make a well in the centre and add the egg yolks and olive oil.

Using your fingertips, mix the ingredients together until it resembles breadcrumbs.

Add the whole egg and mix until it forms a dough. Wrap the dough well in cling film and refrigerate for 1 hour.

Roll the dough through a pasta machine until the fourth last setting.

Black Pasta

200g pasta flour
2 tsp carbon black
5 egg yolks
5ml olive oil
1 whole egg

Sieve the flour and carbon black together. Make a well in the centre and add the egg yolks and olive oil. Using your fingertips, mix the ingredients together until it resembles breadcrumbs.

Add the whole egg and mix until it forms a dough. Wrap the dough well in cling film and refrigerate for 1 hour.

Roll the dough through a pasta machine until you reach the fourth last setting.

Striped Pasta

Place the sheet of black pasta directly on top of the sheet of white and gently press together.

Using a sharp knife, slice the pasta widthways into ¾cm strips.

Layer the strips together using a little cold water if the pasta won't stick naturally.

Continued: Hake | Cannelloni | Shellfish

Continue doing this until the pasta has 21 layers of alternate black and white layers.

Vacuum pack the pasta on the machine's highest setting.

Re-set the pasta machine to its widest setting and feed through the striped pasta dough, feeding it through each setting twice until the second last setting.

Trim up the edges of the pasta sheet and cut into 14cm x 10cm rectangles.

Layer between silicone paper and store in an airtight container in the fridge.

Fennel & Dill Purée

75g butter
2 bulbs fennel (thinly sliced)
3 shallots (diced)
300ml milk
300ml double cream
½ pack dill (finely chopped)
sea salt

Melt the butter in a heavy-based saucepan and add the shallots and fennel. Sweat until the fennel is cooked and almost falling apart but with no colour; this should take approximately 1 hour.

Add the milk and cream and simmer for 15 minutes. Add the dill and blend in a high speed blender until smooth and glossy. Season to taste with salt, then pass through a fine sieve. Keep warm until required.

Leeks

rapeseed oil (drizzle of)
sea salt (pinch of)
1 leek (sliced into 1½cm slices)

Heat up a non-stick pan to a medium to hot heat.

Drizzle the rapeseed oil over the leeks and sprinkle with a pinch of sea salt. Place the leeks in the pan and cook until slightly scorched and tender, this will take 2-3 minutes.

Hake

rapeseed oil (drizzle of)
4 x 180g hake portions (pin boned)
sea salt (sprinkle of)
30g butter
½ lemon (juice of)

Heat up a non-stick pan until almost smoking hot. Add a drizzle of rapeseed oil then place the hake skin-side down in the pan and turn down the heat. Cook the hake slowly on its skin-side until it is cooked halfway up the fish. Add a sprinkle of salt, the butter and lemon juice.

Take the pan off the heat, turn the fish over and allow it to finish cooking in the residual heat.

Clams & Cockles

200g clams
200g cockles
1 clove garlic (crushed)
25g butter
100ml white wine

Rinse the clams and cockles under cold running water for half an hour.

Simmer all the ingredients in a pan with a lid on until the shellfish have opened. Pick the clams and cockles out of their shells. Pass the cooking liquor through fine muslin.

Reserve the liquor to reheat the clams and cockles when serving.

To Assemble

4 sprigs dill (leaves picked)
sea salt
¼ salt baked celeriac (see page 243)

Poach the mousse cylinders in simmering water for 6 minutes. Cut one end of the cling film and slide out the cylinders of mousse.

Heat the clams and cockles through in the reserved cooking liquor.

Cook the pasta sheets in salted boiling water for 1 minute only. Drain and season with a little salt.

Place each mousse cylinder onto a sheet of pasta and roll up completely.

Transfer to the plates and unroll the pasta, but leave enough rolled around mousse to create the cannelloni effect.

Arrange a piece of hake on the unrolled section of each pasta sheet and dot with the fennel and dill purée. Plate the remaining elements around and over the hake. Finally, top with picked dill leaves.

Lamb | Milk Skin | 'Shepherd's Pie'
Serves 4

Milk Skin Crisp

1 litre milk
50ml double cream
30g milk powder

Preheat the oven to 185°C.

Blend all the ingredients together using a stick blender.

Gently warm the milk mixture up to 65°C until the milk is not quite simmering. Pull the milk off the heat and put it in the oven for roughly 7-8 minutes, or until a full skin is formed over the milk.

Carefully remove from the oven and peel off the skin, placing it on silicone paper.

Place the pot back in the oven and repeat the process until you have 3 more fully formed milk skins.

Place these in a dehydrator set at the highest setting for 5 hours.

Once dehydrated, colour the milk skin with a blow torch or under a very hot grill, being extremely careful as this will burn very easily.

Mash Potato

2 large Rooster potatoes
90g butter
40ml milk
sea salt

Preheat the oven to 185°C.

Prick the potatoes all over with a fork, place them on a layer of salt on a baking tray and bake for 2 hours.

Cut the potatoes in half, scoop out the flesh and weigh out 400g.

Mash the potato through a drum sieve and transfer to a heavy-based pan.

Melt the butter and add the milk. Bring up to a simmer and remove from the heat.

Slowly pour the milk and butter mixture into the potatoes while stirring vigorously. Season with a little salt to taste. Keep warm until required.

Shepherd's Pie Filling

100g butter
½ carrot (peeled, cut into brunoise)
1 stick celery (peeled, cut into brunoise)
1 leek white only (peeled, cut into brunoise)
1 clove garlic (crushed)
500g minced lamb rump
200ml red wine
1 fresh bay leaf
1 litre lamb stock (see page 241)

Melt the butter in a heavy-based pan and add all of the vegetables. Sweat down for 4-5 minutes with no colour. Add the garlic and cook for a further 2 minutes.

Add the lamb mince and cook until it is well browned but not burnt. Stir in the red wine and bay leaf and reduce the red wine until it has almost evaporated. Add the lamb stock and lower the heat until it is just simmering. Simmer gently for 1 hour. The stock should almost be gone and the mince should be sticky and glossy.

Allow the mixture to cool at room temperature for half an hour.

Cabbage Wrap

4 leaves Savoy cabbage
sea salt (pinch of)

Blanch the cabbage in salted, boiling water for 2 minutes. Refresh in ice cold water.

Remove the stalks from the cabbage leaves and set aside. Season the leaves with a little salt.

To Assemble The Shepherd's Pie

Line a 6cm ring mould with cling film ensuring there is a decent overhang of film.

Lay in a cabbage leaf and press into the corners of the ring.

Add a generous spoon of the mash potato to the bottom of the cabbage in the ring.

Add some of the mince filling on top of the mash potato so it comes three quarters of the way up the mould.

Gather the cling film together and twist the cabbage so it forms a small parcel.

Peel down the cling film and trim off any excess cabbage, folding the cabbage in on itself to cover all of the mince.

Remove the ring and twist the cling film to achieve a tight ball shape. Tie off the cling film so it becomes watertight.

Repeat this process to create 4 parcels.

Roasted Shallot Purée

200g butter
1kg shallots (peeled, sliced)
250ml chicken stock (see page 239)
300ml milk
100ml double cream
sea salt

Place the butter and shallots in a heavy-based pan.

Slowly cook down the shallots, stirring frequently. Once the shallots start to colour, stir vigorously so that they caramelise but not burn.

Add the chicken stock and reduce by half. Pour in the milk and cream and cook out for 10 minutes.

Pass the liquid off the shallots and reserve.

Blend the shallots, adding the liquid back in until a thick, glossy purée is achieved.

Pass through a fine chinois and season with salt to taste.

Roasted Lamb Jus

rapeseed oil (drizzle of)
100g lamb shoulder (diced)
1 sprig rosemary
1 clove garlic (lightly crushed, skin on)
400ml red wine
100ml sherry
1½ litres lamb stock (see page 241)
sea salt

Heat up the oil until it almost smokes and add the diced lamb. Cook the lamb until well browned and reduce the heat.

Add the rosemary and garlic then pour in the red wine and sherry. Reduce until the red wine and sherry have almost evaporated, then add the lamb stock.

Reduce the sauce, skimming every 10-15 minutes, until it becomes a coating consistency but not too sticky.

Pass through fine muslin cloth and season with a little salt to taste.

Lamb Loin

rapeseed oil (drizzle of)
4 x 180g centre cut lamb loin
50g butter
2 cloves garlic (lightly crushed, skin on)
2 stalks rosemary

Preheat the oven to 185°C.

Drizzle a non-stick pan with the rapeseed oil.

Place the lamb loin in the cold pan skin-side down. Bring the pan up to a medium heat to render the fat out from the lamb.

Once rendered, turn the heat up slightly and brown the skin. Turn the lamb over and brown the meat for a couple of minutes.

Turn back onto the skin and cook in the oven for 6 minutes. Remove from the oven and turn the meat over. Add the butter, garlic and rosemary. Using a spoon, baste the foaming butter over the lamb.

Rest the lamb on a cooling rack for 10 minutes in a warm place.

Blackened Onions

2 pearl onions
sea salt (pinch of)

Blanch the pearl onions in salted, boiling water for 3 minutes, then refresh in ice cold water.

Peel the onions and cut in half. Using a blow torch, scorch the onions. Separate out the individual layers of onion. Keep warm until required.

Samphire

100g samphire (well washed)
40ml butter emulsion (see page 238)

Warm the samphire through in the butter emulsion just before serving.

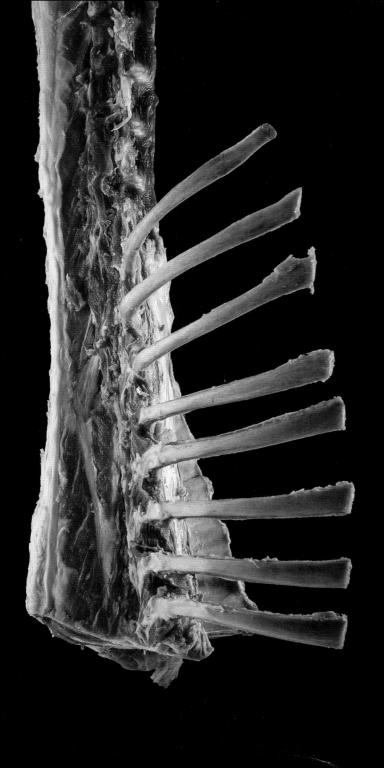

To Assemble

reserved cabbage stalks
100ml butter emulsion (see page 238)

Poach the shepherd's pie for 4 minutes in boiling water and remove the cling film.

Fill 4 of the blackened onion halves with some roasted shallot purée.

Simmer the cabbage stalks in the butter emulsion for 2 minutes.

Place a spoonful of the roasted shallot purée to the left of each plate and top with a shepherd's pie parcel.

Arrange a piece of lamb to the right of each plate and a filled onion half at the front of each plate.

Heat the jus and decant into jugs for guests to pour themselves.

Garnish each plate with a milk skin crisp and a cabbage stalk. Scatter over the samphire and dot around the roasted shallot purée.

LOBSTER & POTATO

Lobster & Potato
Serves 2

Lobster

1 whole lobster

Place the lobster in the freezer for 10 minutes; this will render it unconscious.

Push the tip of a sharp, heavy knife through the centre of the cross on its head.

Remove the claws from the body and cook them in salted, boiling water for 8½ minutes.

Cook the body in salted, boiling water for 6 minutes.

Allow to cool at room temperature. Once cool to the touch, remove the meat from the body and claws. Slice each piece of claw meat in half and the body meat into 6 pieces.

Confit Potatoes

2 large Dunbar Rover potatoes (washed)
400g duck fat
sea salt (pinch of)
1 lemon (zest of)

Add the potatoes to a pan and cover them in duck fat. Season well with a pinch of salt. Gently simmer the potatoes for 10-12 minutes until tender, then remove from the fat.

Dice the potatoes into 3cm cubes. Season again with a little salt and the lemon zest.

Marinated Courgette

1 courgette
1 tsp thyme leaves
½ lemon (juice of)
sea salt (pinch of)

Using a vegetable peeler, peel down the courgette to create courgette ribbons.

Lay the ribbons flat in a large vacuum pack bag. Season with the thyme leaves, lemon juice and salt.

Vacuum pack on the machine's highest setting. Refrigerate for 30 minutes.

Drain off the courgette ribbons and return to the fridge until required.

Potato Crisps

1 Dunbar Rover potato (washed)
vegetable oil (for deep frying)
sea salt (pinch of)

Using a mandoline, slice the potato as thinly as possible.

Cover the potato slices with boiling water and leave to cool. Once cool, drain and dry the potato slices well.

Deep fry at 185°C until they are golden brown and crisp. Drain on absorbent paper and season with a little sea salt.

Carrot Purée

200g carrots (peeled, sliced)
75g butter
1 large shallot (peeled, diced)
2 star anise
sea salt (pinch of)
½ tsp xanthan gum
double cream (splash of)

Add the carrots, butter, shallot, star anise and a pinch of sea salt to a vacuum pack bag and seal on the highest setting.

Simmer in a pan of boiling water for 40 minutes or until the carrots have softened.

Strain the liquid off the carrots and discard the star anise but keep all of the liquid.

Blend the carrots on a medium speed in a blender until smooth and glossy, adding the liquid back in as needed. Add the xanthan gum and continue to blend for a further 2-3 minutes. Add a splash of double cream if needed and blend until combined.

Season to taste with sea salt, pass through a fine sieve and keep warm until needed.

Parmesan Crisps

100g Parmesan (finely grated)
20g fresh white breadcrumbs

Preheat oven to 185°C.

Sprinkle the Parmesan and breadcrumbs evenly over an oven tray lined with silicone paper.

Cook in the oven for approximately 7 minutes or until the Parmesan has melted but not coloured.

Remove the tray from the oven and whilst the Parmesan is still hot, cut it into squares.

Return back to the oven and cook for a further 5 minutes until the Parmesan squares turn golden brown. Remove from the oven and rest the squares on absorbent paper. Reserve in an airtight container until needed.

Basil Mayonnaise

¼ bunch parsley (leaves of)
1 bunch basil (leaves of)
500ml rapeseed oil
1 whole egg
1 egg yolk
1 tsp Dijon mustard
2 tbsp cider vinegar
sea salt

Blanch half of the parsley in salted boiling water and refresh in iced water. Once chilled, squeeze out any excess water.

Place the basil, the blanched and fresh parsley and the rapeseed oil in a blender. Blend on a high speed for 6 minutes. Pass through a fine chinois and refrigerate.

Combine the egg, egg yolk, mustard and vinegar in a blender. Blend on a medium speed and gradually drizzle in the basil oil while blending.

When all of the oil has been added, taste and season the mayonnaise with salt. Place in a piping bag and store in the fridge until required.

To Assemble

frisée lettuce (to garnish)
chicory (to garnish)
6 hazelnuts (skins removed, toasted)
1 tsp salmon caviar

Using a palette knife, swipe some carrot purée across the centre of each plate.

Place 5 slices of lobster on the purée.

Arrange the rest of the ingredients between the lobster slices and top with basil mayonnaise, toasted hazelnuts and salmon caviar.

Weave a courgette ribbon through the centre of the elements.

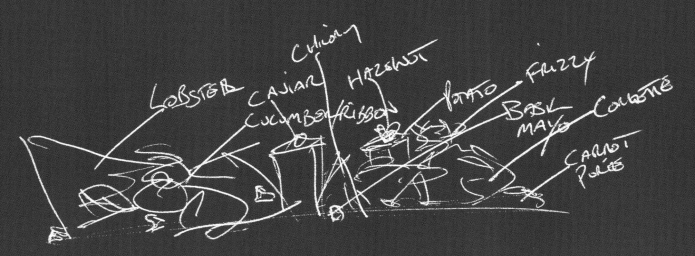

Mackerel | Peas | Orange

Serves 4

Sweetcorn

1 yellow sweetcorn
1 purple sweetcorn
sea salt
50ml butter (melted)

Simmer the yellow corn in salted water for 15 minutes. Remove the corn from the cob and season with butter and a little salt.

Simmer the purple corn in salted water for 1½ hours. Remove from the cob and season with a little salt and butter and mix with the yellow corn. Keep warm until needed.

Pea Purée

60g butter
1 shallot (finely diced)
½ clove garlic (finely sliced)
100ml chicken stock (see page 239)
100ml milk
100ml double cream
150g peas (fresh or frozen)
sea salt

Melt the butter in a pan, add the shallot and garlic and sweat until softened but with no colour.

Add the stock and reduce by half. Pour in the milk and cream and bring to a rapid boil. Add the peas and quickly bring back to the boil. Remove from the heat.

Pass the mixture through a fine sieve, reserving the liquid and the peas separately.

Blend the peas in a high speed blender adding in the liquid until the desired consistency is achieved. Season with salt to taste.

Roasted Fennel

rapeseed oil (drizzle of)
1 bulb fennel (quartered)
80g butter

Heat the drizzle of rapeseed oil in a pan over a medium heat.

Roast the fennel for 2-3 minutes then add the butter and baste the juices over the fennel. Keep turning the fennel until just tender.

Spring Onions

4 spring onions
sea salt (pinch of)

Blanch the spring onions in salted, boiling water, then refresh in ice cold water. Trim the spring onions so they are 10cm in length.

Mackerel

4 fillets mackerel (deboned)
sea salt (pinch of)
½ lemon (juice of)

Blow torch the skin-sides of the mackerel fillets until blackened. Season lightly with salt and a squeeze of lemon.

To Assemble

4 fresh peas in the pod
½ frisée lettuce (picked, washed)
100g fresh peas (blanched, refreshed)
4 orange segments
8 thin slices radish

Swipe the pea purée across each plate and top with a mackerel fillet.

Gently warm the spring onions through in a medium oven or under the grill.

Place a piece of fennel beside the mackerel and top with a spring onion. Pile the sweetcorn to one side and top with a fresh pea pod. Pipe some more of the pea purée into the pod.

Top the mackerel with fresh peas, frisée, an orange segment and slices of radish.

Partridge | Purple Sprouting Broccoli | Pear
Serves 4

Salt Dough

250g plain flour
3 egg whites
150g rock salt
75ml water

Mix the flour, egg whites and rock salt in a mixer for 4 minutes. Slowly add in the water until it becomes a tight dough. Keep mixing for a further 10 minutes.

Salt Baked Pear

3 pears
salt dough

Preheat the oven to 180°C.

Remove the stalks from the pears and discard.

Roll out the salt dough as thinly as possible, using a little flour if necessary.

Wrap each pear in dough, making sure there are no air bubbles or rips.

Bake the pears for 25 minutes. As soon they are ready, remove the pears from the oven and crack open the dough. Leave to cool.

Using a pastry knife, top and tail the pear and remove the skin. Cut each pear into 4 and dice into ½cm cubes. Store in an airtight container in the fridge.

Broccoli Purée

30g butter
2 shallots (finely diced)
100ml chicken stock (see page 239)
200ml milk
50ml double cream
2 heads broccoli (stalks removed)
100g baby spinach
sea salt

Melt the butter in a heavy-based pan and sweat the shallot over a medium heat with no colour.

Add the chicken stock and reduce by half. Pour in the milk and cream and cook for 6-7 minutes.

Add the broccoli and spinach and cook for 2 minutes only. Drain the liquid from the broccoli and spinach mixture and set aside.

Transfer the broccoli and spinach to a blender and blend on a high speed, adding a little of the liquid at a time, to achieve a thick, glossy purée.

Pass the purée through a fine chinois and season with a little salt to taste. Keep warm until needed.

Partridge

4 partridges
rapeseed oil (drizzle of)
50g butter
1 clove garlic (crushed)
1 sprig thyme

Preheat the oven to 190°C.

Brown the partridges evenly on all sides in a large pan with a drizzle of rapeseed oil.

Transfer the pan to the oven and roast the birds for 9 minutes.

Remove the pan from the oven and add the butter, garlic and thyme. Baste the juices over the birds and allow the partridges to rest in the pan for 6 minutes.

Remove the legs and breasts from the partridges and keep warm. Reserve the bones for the jus.

Partridge Trimming Jus

reserved bones from the partridges
400ml red wine
6 juniper berries (crushed)
1 litre chicken stock (see page 239)

Brown the bones well in a heavy-based sauté pan.

Add the red wine and juniper berries and reduce the wine until it has almost evaporated. Pour in the chicken stock and reduce until there are 200ml left in the pan. Pass through a fine chinois and serve separately so guests can pour the sauce at the table.

Continued:
Partridge | Purple Sprouting Broccoli | Pear

Purple Sprouting Broccoli

12 spears purple sprouting broccoli
30g butter (melted)
1 tbsp sesame seeds
vegetable oil (for deep frying)
sea salt

Remove the leaves from the broccoli and set aside.

Blanch the broccoli in boiling, salted water for 1½ minutes.
Drain and toss through the melted butter and some of the
sesame seeds.

Deep fry the leaves at 185°C. Drain on absorbent paper and
season with salt and a sprinkle of sesame seeds.

To Assemble

1 tbsp black onion ash (see page 238)

Sprinkle the onion ash all over each plate. Using the tip of a
clean tea towel, run a finger holding the tip around the plate to
form a perfect circle.

Place the partridge in the centre of the plate and the purple
sprouting broccoli below the partridge.

Lay the crispy leaf above the partridge.

Scatter the diced pear around the dish and finally, dot the purée
between the pears.

Continued From Page 101

We strive to ensure the business is consistent from a financial standpoint, but if we aren't putting out consistent food or providing consistent service how can it be? That is not to say we keep 100% of customers happy. I have learned over the last 24 years as a chef, that keeping every single customer happy all of the time is impossible. However, it doesn't stop us giving our all each and every minute of every day.

So would I say I was a dictator? No definitely not, I would rather use the carrot than the stick; I have had my fair share of dressing-downs over the years. I was once even attacked and left black and blue at only 16 in a kitchen. I was given a verbal warning for being insubordinate even though I ended up with a black eye, bloody nose and cracked rib - but that's a story for another day.

My leadership works like many chefs where there is a great deal of sarcasm balanced out with a huge amount of respect for the team and this in turn is given back to me. We spend about 14 hours a day together so, although we are very disciplined in what we do, we also have a great bit of banter and camaraderie. The team you employ needs to want to work with you and not for you. They need to want the same things as the business does and strive for the same goals otherwise they won't and don't last. The youngsters who come into the industry because they want to be famous or to be on TV never last. We call them glory hunters or star chasers and only glancing at their CV tells a whole story. One month here, two months there, never lasting in any one place once they realise it is a lot harder than it looks on the TV.

We get youngsters in who love the idea of working for me, rather than actually working for me. It is hard graft and yes, I do raise my voice when needed, and if I do, then you definitely know something is wrong. I have to instil discipline and demand standards otherwise the business will never grow or get better, but I would like to think the days of shouting TV style chefs are well and truly behind us. If carrots aren't peeled properly or the potatoes are undercooked for the mash then it upsets me, very minor details but just as important as properly cooked fillet steak or the more expensive ingredients. I always focus on the little things and on getting them right and this is something which I instil in every member of my team. After all, each good plate of food is made up of doing lots of little things right.

Building A Dream

Ever since my very first day (well, technically second day) of being a chef, I knew that I wanted to own my own restaurant or hotel one day.

So what was my dream? I have always been driven to succeed; I am not sure why, I just have. When I was a commis chef I always wanted to be better than the other commis chefs. I think it is human nature to be competitive, so I knew I wanted my own restaurant where I could be the boss and where I could cook what I wanted to cook, the way I wanted to cook it. That still is the dream, only now I am 'the boss' and it is a whole lot harder than I ever thought it would be.

When you are a young chef starting out you want to open your own place, but the idea of exactly what you want changes drastically over the years. It actually takes time to realise your dream and for it to come to fruition. I had no idea about the cost of things - pots, pans, cutlery, crockery, glassware never mind vacuum pack machines and fancier bits of kit!

Realising my dream has been a lot tougher than I ever imagined. Firstly, the standard of restaurant we have achieved is nothing short of a miracle, considering our budget. By constantly putting the money back into the business each week and not taking a proper salary we have developed the look and feel of the restaurant and can afford the very best ingredients. **Continued on page 161.**

Roast Chicken Dinner
Serves 4

Potato Fondant

2 large Rooster potatoes (peeled, cut into
3cm thick slices)
150ml chicken stock (see page 239)
150g butter
1 sprig thyme
1 clove garlic (skin on, crushed)

Preheat the oven to 185°C.

Add all the ingredients to an ovenproof dish and
place in the oven for 35 minutes, or until the
potato is tender.

Allow the potatoes to cool for 10 minutes. Remove
them from the tray and cut into 3cm cubes.

Keep in a warm place.

Chicken Jus

rapeseed oil (drizzle of)
1kg chicken wings
1 clove garlic (crushed)
200ml white wine
2 litres chicken stock (see page 239)

Heat up the rapeseed oil in a heavy-based pan.

Cook the chicken wings on the stove over a
medium heat until golden brown all over. Add
the garlic and cook for 2 minutes.

Drain off all the fat and add the white wine.
Reduce until the wine has almost evaporated,
then add the chicken stock and reduce down to
200ml. Pass through a fine muslin cloth and
reserve until needed.

Roast Chicken

rapeseed oil (drizzle of)
1 chicken crown
85g butter
2 leaves sage

Preheat the oven to 190°C.

Drizzle a non-stick pan with the rapeseed oil.
Place the chicken in the cold pan, skin-side down.

Bring the pan up to a medium heat to render the
fat from the chicken.

Turn the chicken onto the other breast, increase
the heat slightly and brown the skin. Turn the
chicken over and brown the base for a couple
of minutes.

Place in the oven, breast-side up, for 22 minutes.

Remove from the oven and turn the chicken onto
the breasts. Add the butter and sage and, using a
spoon, baste the foaming butter over the
chicken. Rest the chicken on a cooling rack for
10 minutes in a warm place.

Carve the breasts off the bird and cut each
breast into 2 rectangles.

Honey Roast Parsnips

500g parsnips (peeled)
100ml honey
100ml water
60g butter
sea salt (large pinch of)
100ml chicken stock (see page 239)

Cut the parsnips in half lengthways and remove
the core.

Place all the ingredients, except the chicken
stock, into a large, non-stick pan and bring to the
boil, then reduce the pan to a simmer. Cook the
parsnips until the honey starts to caramelise.
Once caramelisation starts, be very careful as the
honey can burn quickly.

Check the parsnips are cooked by piercing
them with a toothpick or small knife; they are
ready when it goes through the parsnip without
any resistance. If still a little firm, add a drizzle
of the chicken stock to loosen the honey so it
doesn't burn before the parsnips are fully
cooked. Cover and keep warm until needed.

Poached Baby Turnip

4 baby turnips
300ml chicken stock (see page 239)

Remove the stalks from the baby turnips and
set aside. Simmer the turnips in the chicken
stock for 8-10 minutes until just tender. Remove
from the heat and cool the turnips down by
removing from the chicken stock.

Just before serving, heat the turnips back up in
the chicken stock and, using a small knife, pierce
a hole in the top of each turnip. Place a stalk
back into the top of each turnip.

Toast Purée

4 slices sourdough bread
2 shallots (peeled, diced)
20g butter
200ml chicken stock (see page 239)
100ml milk
50ml double cream
½ nutmeg (grated)
sea salt

Toast the sourdough bread until dark brown but not burnt, take this as far as you dare.

Sweat the shallots in the butter on a medium heat for 2 minutes with no colour.

Break up the toast and add to the shallots. Add the chicken stock, milk, cream and nutmeg and bring to the boil. Simmer for 4-5 minutes.

Transfer to a blender and blend on a medium speed to a smooth purée. Pass through a fine chinois and season with salt to taste.

To Assemble

12 turnip stalks

Place the chicken back into the oven just before serving, covered with either foil or buttered silicone paper, to warm the chicken through.

Heat the jus through and pour into jugs for guests to pour themselves.

Place 2 cubes of potato and 1 rectangle of chicken on each plate.

Arrange 1 piece of parsnip and 1 baby turnip on each plate. Dot some of the toast purée around the dish. Garnish with 3 turnip stalks.

Turbot | Red Wine | Chocolate
Serves 4

Bread Crostini

½ loaf brioche (cut lengthways)
rapeseed oil (drizzle of)
sea salt (pinch of)

Freeze the brioche for 2 hours.

Preheat the oven to 185°C.

Using a meat slicer or an extremely sharp knife, slice the brioche lengthways as thinly as possible.

Place an oiled piece of silicone paper on a baking tray. Lay out the slices of brioche on the tray and sprinkle over the salt.

Oil another sheet of silicone paper and place on top of the bread slices. Top with a baking tray of equal size and place in the oven for 7-9 minutes until golden brown.

Caramelised Cauliflower Purée

60g butter
1 cauliflower (diced including the stalk)
¼ large onion (diced)
sea salt (pinch of)
110ml milk
110ml double cream
¼ tsp xanthan gum

Melt the butter and add the cauliflower.

Cook over a medium heat until the cauliflower has turned nut brown; be careful not to colour it too much otherwise it will go bitter. Stir in the diced onion and add a generous pinch of salt. Continue to sweat the mixture for another 3-4 minutes. Add the milk and cream and bring to a simmer. Continue to cook for 5-7 minutes.

Drain the liquid from the cauliflower, reserving the liquid.

Blend the cauliflower, adding the liquid back in as it is blending, until a thick purée consistency is achieved. Add the xanthan gum and continue to blend for another 2-3 minutes. Pass through a fine chinois and keep warm until required.

Golden Beetroot

2 golden beetroots
rapeseed oil (drizzle of)
sea salt (pinch of)
1 sprig thyme
1 sprig dill
1 clove garlic (crushed)

Preheat the oven to 185°C.

Lightly wash and dry the beetroot. Drizzle the rapeseed oil over the beetroot and season with salt.

Wrap the beetroot in foil along with the thyme, dill and garlic. Bake in the oven for 25 minutes.

Remove the beetroot from the foil and allow to cool slightly. Gently rub the beetroot with your fingertips to remove the skin. Discard the skin and cut each beetroot into 6 segments.

Tomatoes

2 large plum tomatoes (blanched, peeled, seeds removed)

Cut the tomato flesh into 12 5cm x 3cm rectangles.

Crab

3 large brown crab claws
½ lemon (zest and juice of)
sea salt

Boil the crab claws in salted, boiling water for 7 minutes. Remove from the water and allow to cool naturally. Crack open the claws and remove the meat, being careful to remove any small shards of shell. Break the claw meat into chunks and season with a little lemon juice, lemon zest and salt. Set aside until required.

Roasted Cauliflower

½ cauliflower
rapeseed oil (drizzle of)
40g butter
sea salt (pinch of)

Slice 4 slices of the cauliflower on a mandoline as thinly as possible through the root so it holds its shape.

Break the remainder of the cauliflower into small florets.

Heat up a non-stick pan with a drizzle of rapeseed oil on a high heat. Gently place in the slices of cauliflower and the butter, being careful that the slices don't break. Cook the cauliflower for 3 minutes until it starts taking on a little colour. Remove the slices of cauliflower carefully from the pan.

Place the cauliflower florets in the same pan back on the heat and cook for 1-2 minutes over a high heat so there is still a little crunch left in the florets but they are golden brown. Season the slices and florets with a pinch of salt.

Dark Chocolate & Red Wine Poached Turbot

750ml red wine
150ml chicken stock (see page 239)
125g 70% dark chocolate pistoles
4 x 120g turbot portions (fully trimmed)

Reduce the red wine and chicken stock to 450ml. Remove from the heat and add in the chocolate. Stir until the chocolate has melted.

Drop the turbot into the red wine and chocolate liquid, place back on the stove and simmer gently for 3 minutes. Pull the pan off the heat and leave to sit for 10 minutes to finish cooking the fish.

Remove the turbot and keep warm.

Pass the sauce through a fine muslin cloth and transfer to a clean pan. Reduce the sauce to a coating consistency and keep warm.

To Assemble

12 sprigs chervil

Using a pastry brush, brush a square measuring 11cm x 11cm of the red wine and chocolate sauce directly onto the middle of each plate.

Place a slice of the cauliflower directly on the sauce. Top with a piece of turbot.

Scatter around the roasted cauliflower florets. Rest a brioche crostini against the back of the turbot.

Place 3 of the tomato rectangles around the turbot, 2 at the back and 1 at the front. Scatter the crab claw meat around the turbot. Dot the roasted cauliflower purée at the front of the turbot, scatter the beetroot around the dish, and garnish with sprigs of chervil.

Rabbit | Chestnut | Leek
Serves 4

Celeriac & Chestnut Purée

75g butter
3 shallots (peeled, diced)
1 celeriac (peeled, diced into even pieces)
100g peeled chestnuts
150ml chicken stock (see page 239)
300ml milk
300ml double cream
sea salt

Melt the butter in a heavy-based saucepan and sweat the shallots for 3-4 minutes. Add the celeriac and chestnuts, then continue to sweat down for another 5-6 minutes until softened but with no colour. Pour in the chicken stock and bring to the boil. Add the milk and cream and simmer for 15-18 minutes.

Blend in a high speed blender until smooth and glossy. Season to taste with salt, then pass through a fine chinois. Keep warm until required.

Ballotine Of Rabbit Saddle

1 rabbit saddle (deboned, a butcher can do this although the bones are also required)
10 basil leaves
sea salt

Lay the rabbit saddle out flat on cling film. Place the basil leaves to create a flat layer running down the middle of the saddle. Season well with salt.

Roll up the rabbit into a cylinder shape and tie the ends of the cling film. It may need to be wrapped in a few further layers of cling film to create a tight cylinder.

Cook in a water bath at 64°C for 2 hours.

Remove from the water bath and discard the cling film. Re-wrap the rabbit in cling film to create a very tight boudin shape. Plunge into ice water and allow to cool for 30 minutes.

Rack Of Rabbit

rapeseed oil (drizzle of)
8 racks of rabbit (a butcher can provide these)
1 clove garlic (crushed)
40g butter
3 sprigs thyme
sea salt (pinch of)

Heat up the rapeseed oil in a non-stick pan on a medium to high heat. Place the racks of rabbit in the pan and gently brown one side. Add the garlic, butter, thyme and salt and turn the racks of rabbit over.

Baste the rabbit with the foaming butter for 2-3 minutes.

Remove the racks of rabbit from the pan and rest on a cooling rack for 10 minutes.

Rabbit Bone Jus

1kg rabbit bones
200ml white wine
1 cardamom pod
1 star anise
2 litres chicken stock (see page 239)

Preheat the oven to 180°C.

Roast the rabbit bones for 40 minutes turning the bones every 10 minutes so they colour evenly.

Remove the bones from the oven tray and pour in the white wine, cardamom and star anise. Scrape the tray well with a wooden spoon or spatula to release all of the caramelised bits from the tray.

Pour the wine mixture into a pot with the rabbit bones and add the chicken stock. Reduce the stock to 350ml, skimming every 10-15 minutes. Pass through a fine muslin cloth and transfer to a clean, small pan.

Confit Carrot

150ml chicken stock (see page 239)
20g butter
3 star anise
2 cardamom pods
6 coriander seeds
4 baby carrots (peeled)

Bring the chicken stock to a gentle simmer with the butter, star anise, cardamom pods and coriander seeds. Add the carrots and poach for 3 minutes. Once tender allow to cool in the stock.

Deep Fried Parsnip

1 parsnip (peeled)
vegetable oil (for deep frying)
sea salt (pinch of)

Using a vegetable peeler, shave the parsnip down to the core and discard the core. Pour boiling water over the parsnip shavings and allow to cool naturally. Drain the parsnip shavings and dry thoroughly.

Deep fry the parsnips at 150°C until golden and crisp. Drain on absorbent paper and season with a little salt.

Crispy Leeks

rapeseed oil (drizzle of)
sea salt
4 wild leeks (green part only)

Cling film a plate that will fit inside the microwave and pull the cling film tight so there are no creases. Oil the cling film well with rapeseed oil and season with salt.

Place the leeks on the oil and smooth them out. Season the leaves with a little more salt.

Cook in the microwave for 20 second bursts until the leaves become transparent and crisp. Please note the leaves will crisp up more on cooling.

Drain the leaves on absorbent paper and store in an airtight container until required.

Wild Leeks

4 wild leeks
100ml butter emulsion (see page 238)
sea salt (pinch of)

Trim the wild leeks so they are 11cm in length.

Poach the leeks in the butter emulsion with the salt for 30 seconds only. Serve immediately as they will overcook very quickly.

To Assemble

4 slices crispy pancetta (see page 239)

Preheat the oven to 200°C.

Cut the rabbit ballotine into 4cm thick slices and warm through in the oven for 6-7 minutes.

Place the rack of rabbit on a small skillet, cover with buttered silicone paper, and transfer to the oven for 3-4 minutes.

Place 2 slices of the rabbit ballotine on each plate.

Carve one rabbit rack and keep the other whole. Place next to the rabbit ballotine.

Spoon a generous amount of the purée to the left of each plate. Lay the crispy leek and poached leek on one of the rabbit slices, drape the cooked baby carrot over another. Also add the pancetta and parsnip crisp onto one of the slices.

Heat the jus and add to jugs so guests can pour it themselves.

Straight From The Farm
Serves 4

Carrot Powder

1kg carrots (sliced)
sea salt (pinch of)

(Prepare ahead)

Boil the carrots in salted, boiling water for 11 minutes. Drain the carrots; they should not be fully cooked at this stage. Blend in a high speed blender to a smooth purée and season with a little salt, to taste.

Spread out on a silicone mat to a ½cm thickness. Dehydrate at 55°C for 24 hours.

Blend in a spice blender to a fine powder.

Potato Crumble

1 Rooster potato (peeled, diced into equal sized pieces)
20g butter
20g crème fraîche
sea salt (pinch of)

(Prepare ahead)

Boil the potato in salted water until tender. Drain the potatoes and return to the pan. Dry the potatoes out over a medium heat, then transfer to a blender and blend on a medium speed. Add the butter and crème fraîche, season with a little salt to taste.

Pass the potato mixture through a drum sieve. Spread onto a silicone mat to a ½cm thickness. Dehydrate at 55°C in a dehydrator for 18 hours.

Blend to a coarse powder and store in an airtight container.

Potato Tubes

1 large potato (peeled)
rapeseed oil (drizzle of)
sea salt
1 litre vegetable oil (for deep frying)

Using a spiralizer, spiralize the potato.

Pick out 6 of the longest strands of potato; they will need to be approximately 2 metres long.

Douse each strand in a little rapeseed oil and sprinkle with salt.

Using a metal tube 9cm long, 5cm in diameter, wrap the tube with oil and silicone paper.

Wrap a strand of the potato around the tube from end to end ensuring there are no gaps. Secure the ends with steel paperclips.

Deep fry at 160°C until golden brown. Allow to cool slightly and remove from the tube.

Repeat with the remaining potato strands.

Salt Dough

250g plain flour
3 egg whites
150g rock salt
75ml water

Mix the flour, egg whites and rock salt in a mixer for 4 minutes. Slowly add in the water until it becomes a tight dough. Keep mixing for a further 10 minutes.

Salt Baked Vegetables

4 candy beetroot (washed)
1 baby red beetroot (washed)
1 baby golden beetroot (washed)
4 baby turnips (washed)

Preheat the oven to 200°C.

Roll out the salt dough and place all of the beetroots and turnips at one end. Fold the dough back on itself to encapsulate all the vegetables within it.

Place the vegetables on a baking tray and bake for 35 minutes.

Crack open the salt dough and discard it as soon as you take the vegetables out of the oven.

Using your fingertips, rub the skins off the beetroot and turnip. Cut into quarters. Keep the vegetables warm until plating up.

Carrot Purée

200g carrots (peeled, sliced)
75g butter
60g candied stem ginger
1 large shallot (peeled, diced)
sea salt
½ tsp xanthan gum
double cream (splash of)

Add the carrots, butter, ginger, shallot and a pinch of sea salt to a vacuum pack bag and seal on the highest setting.

Simmer in a pan of boiling water for 40 minutes or until the carrots have softened. Strain the carrots, reserving the liquid.

Blend the carrots in a blender on a medium speed until smooth and glossy, adding the liquid back in as needed. Add the xanthan gum and continue to blend for a further 2-3 minutes. Add a splash of double cream if needed and blend until combined. Season to taste with sea salt. Pass through a fine sieve and keep warm until required.

Corn On The Cob

1 corn on the cob (washed)
20g melted butter
sea salt (pinch of)

Cook the corn in gently simmering, lightly salted water for 25 minutes.

Whilst still hot, cut the kernels off the cob, but cut a little closer to the cob than normal so all the kernels stay in one piece and don't fall apart. Drizzle with a little butter and a pinch of salt.

Asparagus

10 spears asparagus (washed)
200ml vegetable stock (see page 244)
30g butter
1 sprig thyme
3 star anise

Take 8 spears of asparagus and cut the woody ends off. Pare down the bottom ends of these spears using a peeler.

Bring the stock, butter, thyme and star anise to a rolling boil.

Cook the asparagus for 1 minute 45 seconds, then drain on absorbent paper.

Using a vegetable peeler, shave the 2 uncooked spears and set aside.

Heritage Carrots

180g butter
8 baby orange carrots (peeled)
8 baby purple carrots (peeled)
sea salt

Gently melt the butter and add all the carrots to the butter. Cover the carrots with a cartouche made out of silicone paper and simmer for 11 minutes. Drain and season with a pinch of salt.

To Assemble

16 popcorn shoots
16 yellow viola flowers
16 purple viola flowers

Sprinkle a generous amount of the potato powder and carrot powder over each plate.

Using the tip of a clean tea towel run it around the plate but the powder shouldn't look too neat.

Arrange the vegetables in the centre of each plate. Break up the potato tubes and scatter over each plate. Spread the asparagus shavings equally between the plates. Stick the popcorn shoots out of the vegetables to add height and dot the carrot purée between the vegetables to fill any gaps. Lightly sprinkle a little more carrot powder over the vegetables.

Add the viola flowers just before serving.

Venison

Venison is such a diverse meat; it is not only rich in flavour but also low in fat, if that's your thing.

We have been buying our venison from Ardgay Game for longer than I even knew. It was through my supplier Ochil Foods (page 072) that I was first introduced to them.

I remember being a young apprentice and we would get the whole deer into the kitchen. We would break it down into its separate parts and then marinate it all in red wine, port, Madeira, juniper berries, black peppercorns, bay leaf, garlic and shallots for at least a week before chef would allow us to cook it. It was horrible stuff, far too gamey; so, so strong in flavour and it really put me off venison for a few years as I thought that's how you 'had' to cook it. Now we get the venison and keep it as natural as possible. We don't age it and we certainly don't marinate it for weeks at a time. I think this probably put a lot of people off venison in days gone by but thankfully it is not a practice that happens anymore, well not in my kitchen anyway.

Not only is venison delicious it is also extremely versatile. Here, I have done a very simple roasted loin of venison with some root vegetables. Loin is extremely easy to cook and the method I have used is a simple one. Currently on our menu we have a venison carpaccio, similar to the beef carpaccio on page 043, so why not give it a go? Just substitute the beef for venison haunch or loin. Equally, if you look at the lamb 'shepherd's pie' on page 130 this would work equally as well with venison; be creative and remember there are no real rules in cooking.

The history of eating game meat is integral to Scotland's food culture. In the past, game meat, such as venison, was as commonplace in the Scottish household as roast chicken is today. In recent years, venison and indeed all game has once again become a popular choice.

Ardgay Game is a second generation family business. Established in 1982 by Les Waugh, the company was originally based in the small village of Ardgay. The opportunity then arose to expand and Ardgay Game took over the Bonar Venison Group.

Over the years Les and his son Ruaridh have driven the company forward to reach today's position as a prominent wholesaler of premium venison and game, sourcing and supplying some of Scotland's finest products. Key to Ardgay Game's success has been building strong relationships based on family values, gaining them an excellent reputation. Over recent years, the British public has become more appreciative of this natural, healthy, 'home grown', seasonal product and domestic consumption has grown substantially.

Venison | Chocolate | Root Vegetables
Serves 4

Parsley Pomme Purée

4 large Rooster potatoes
sea salt
175g butter
75ml milk
1 tbsp parsley (chopped)

Preheat the oven to 185°C.

Prick the potatoes all over with a fork, place them on a layer of salt on a baking tray and bake for 2 hours.

Cut the potatoes in half, scoop out the flesh and weigh out 400g. Mash the potato or pass it through a drum sieve, then transfer to a pan.

Melt the butter into the milk and pour slowly into the potatoes while stirring. Season with salt. Fold through the parsley and keep warm until required.

Shallot Rings

2 banana shallots
100ml milk
60g plain flour
vegetable oil (for deep frying)
sea salt (pinch of)

Slice the shallots as thinly as possible. Separate all the rings and discard the core or central rings.

Soak the shallot rings in milk for 1 hour. Drain off the milk and pat the shallot rings dry. Douse in flour.

Deep fry at 155°C until golden brown and crisp. Drain on absorbent paper and season lightly with salt.

Carrot Purée

200g carrots (peeled, sliced)
75g butter
1 large shallot (peeled, diced)
2 star anise
sea salt (pinch of)
double cream (splash of)
½ tsp xanthan gum

Add the carrots, butter, shallot, star anise and a pinch of sea salt to a vacuum pack bag and seal on the highest setting.

Simmer in a pan of boiling water for 40 minutes or until the carrots have softened. Strain the carrots, discarding the star anise and reserving the liquid.

Blend the carrots in a blender on a medium speed until smooth and glossy, adding the liquid back in as needed. Add the xanthan gum and continue to blend for a further 2-3 minutes. Add a splash of double cream if needed and blend until combined. Season to taste with sea salt, pass through a fine sieve and keep warm until required.

Salsify

4 sticks salsify (each measuring approximately 12cm in length)
125ml butter emulsion (see page 238)
1 clove garlic
1 stalk tarragon

Peel and wash the salsify well.

Working quickly, place the salsify in a vacuum pack bag and pour in the butter emulsion, garlic and tarragon.

Vacuum pack tightly to expel all the air. Cook in simmering water for 20 minutes or until the salsify is just tender.

Venison

1 x 600g venison loin
rapeseed oil (drizzle of)
sea salt (pinch of)
60g butter

Preheat the oven to 200°C.

Heat up a non-stick pan on a high heat until almost smoking.

Oil the venison loin and season well with salt. Cook the venison in the pan until well coloured on each side. Place the pan in the oven and cook for 5 minutes, turning the venison halfway through.

Pull the pan out of the oven, add the butter and place back over the heat. Baste the venison with the foaming butter, then remove the venison from the pan. Allow the meat to rest for 10 minutes.

Cut the venison into 4 equal portions, removing the end pieces.

Continued: Venison | Chocolate | Root Vegetables

Dark Chocolate Jus

100ml red wine
1 litre chicken stock (see page 239)
2 litres venison stock (see page 244)
30ml double cream
40g 70% dark chocolate pistoles
20g butter

Reduce the red wine in a pan until it has almost evaporated. Add the chicken and venison stocks and reduce down to 400ml.

Remove from the heat and add the cream, chocolate and butter. Blend with a stick blender. Return to the heat and simmer gently for 5-7 minutes. Pass through a fine muslin cloth.

Baby Carrots

150ml chicken stock (see page 239)
sea salt (pinch of)
20g butter
4 baby carrots (peeled)

Bring the chicken stock to a gentle simmer, add a pinch of salt and the butter. Add the carrots and cook for 2 minutes. Pull the pan off the heat and allow the carrots to cool down naturally in the stock.

Celery

2 sticks of celery (peeled)
sea salt (pinch of)

Slice the celery as thinly as possible, sprinkle with a touch of salt and set aside until required.

To Assemble

24 70% dark chocolate pistoles

Using hot plates, place a spoonful of the parsley pomme purée in the centre of each plate.

Place the venison on top. Cut each carrot and salsify stick into 4 pieces and arrange around the rim of the plates.

Dot the carrot purée around the rim of the plate. Place on some chocolate pistoles which will melt naturally due to the heat of the plate.

Rest the shallots and celery against the carrots and salsify.

Serve the jus separately for the guests to pour themselves.

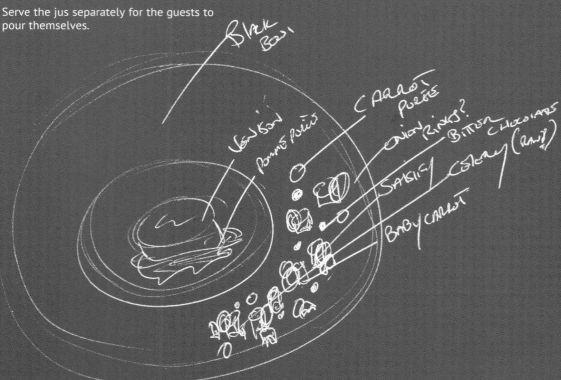

When we decided to open Restaurant Mark Greenaway on North Castle Street we were severely underfunded. However, this was our dream so after a lot of hard graft we welcomed our first customers on January 16th 2013. As I write this, the restaurant has only been open two and a half years and it has gone from strength to strength but not without hiccups.

Everyone has heard of the saying 'if you build it they will come'. Well, to get the restaurant open, we literally had to build it ourselves. We had Paul, our chef de partie of two years at the time, who was an ex-joiner. He and one of the part-time waiters, Andrew, also an ex-joiner, built the wine cellar for us. A regular customer of ours just so happened to own a timber yard so that was an easy swap, some wood for the wine cellar for some credit he could use in the restaurant whenever he liked. A painter friend of mine had his guys work all day and night just getting the place painted from top to bottom. The chefs and full-time waiting staff were all here in their scruffy clothes doing all the manual labour and clearing out. We had set ourselves such an unrealistic target of two weeks to get the place open, but it had to be done as I was about to appear on the BBC's Great British Menu for the second time, so we couldn't afford not to be open. The exposure that the show brings to a restaurant is huge, and we did it. On opening day, the paint barely dry, I was in full whites giving interviews to the press in the restaurant, very calm, as if we had been ready for ages. Meanwhile, the team in the back were frantically running about like headless chickens preparing the canapés for the opening night celebrations.

When we bought the restaurant the kitchen was old; we had to refurbish it all before we opened. It was stripped back to the bare minimum and cheap linoleum flooring installed by the chefs who collected it themselves from the local hardware shop for £80. The under counter fridges and hot passé were bought from my good friend Gary in Glasgow and paid for on a payment plan over four months, it was the only way we could afford it at the time. The only thing we couldn't change were the cookers. We had two six-burner stoves and an old smokehouse salamander grill. It pumped out so much heat my then sous chef on the garnish section, William, had to change his jacket mid shift as he would be soaked in sweat. We had to work like this for the first seven months as we simply couldn't afford new ones. As soon as we completed our first Edinburgh Fringe Festival, often the busiest month of the year in the city for restaurants, we stripped out the cookers and sent the salamander grill to scrap heaven. We now have an infrared grill that switches on and off at the touch of a button. New 'proper' kitchen flooring was laid and we fitted new air valves to keep it at a decent working temperature.

People often think restaurateurs are wealthy but trust me, after two and half years of being open, we are still making improvements to the building and interiors, so every spare penny not going to staff, the tax man or suppliers goes straight back into the restaurant. From the addition of new chairs to the opening of our private dining room in 2014, there is no end to the possibilities but also, it seems, no end to the investment needed.

I often tease the boys in the kitchen that the kitchen porter gets paid more than what I make from the restaurant and in its first two years this was certainly true, but it has always been about the long game for me, the ultimate goal, and never about short term gain.

Pride in having my own restaurant has only increased along the way. This is due to so many factors; to see customers becoming regulars, and even friends, returning again and again, is my biggest achievement so far. The team has also been recognised with numerous awards and accolades, from our 3 AA Rosettes for Culinary Excellence to having been named number 13 in the UK's Top 100 Restaurants in 2015 by Square Meal, and many more. These awards instil such a sense of pride in the team but it puts extra pressure on what we produce and present, as I still have the same feeling that I did back when I was a commis - just wanting to be better and better.

So in essence, I did build my dream but as things progress then so does the dream. I am extremely proud of all that Restaurant Mark Greenaway has achieved thus far but I am also excited for the future and what it has in store for myself, Nicola and the restaurant team.

CHEESE

Blue Murder | Pear | Walnut
Serves 4

Pear Crisps

50g caster sugar
70ml water
25ml lemon juice
2 pears

(Prepare ahead)

Bring the sugar, water and lemon juice to the boil, then allow to cool completely.

Slice the pears as thinly as possible lengthways using either an extremely sharp knife or a mandoline. Dip each slice into the sugar syrup and drain well. Lay each piece onto a silicone mat until you have at least 12 slices, place another mat on top and dehydrate in a dehydrator at 100°C for 18 hours.

Frozen Grapes

200g grapes

Using scissors, cut up the grapes leaving at least 3 grapes on each stalk. Freeze for 4 hours.

Toasted Walnuts

100g walnuts
sea salt (pinch of)

Lightly toast the walnuts under a hot grill or in a hot, non-stick pan on the stove.

Crush the walnuts and season lightly with sea salt.

To Assemble

300g Blue Murder cheese
3 pears (thinly sliced)
watercress (to garnish)
Dijon mustard (to garnish)

Cut the Blue Murder cheese into 4cm squares, 1cm in thickness. Sandwich 3 squares of cheese between 3 slices of fresh pear for each plate. Scatter around the frozen grapes, watercress, walnuts and pear crisps. To finish, dot Dijon mustard around the plate.

Brie | Kumquat | Rhubarb
Serves 4

Lavosh Crackers

6 egg yolks
500g plain flour
3 whole eggs
125ml water
20g poppy seeds

(Prepare ahead)

Mix the egg yolks with the flour until it resembles fine breadcrumbs.

Whisk together the 3 whole eggs and the water. Add the whole eggs and water to the egg yolk and flour mixture, knead until it forms a tight dough. Wrap tightly in plenty of cling film and refrigerate for 4 hours.

Preheat the oven to 165°C.

Using a pasta machine, roll the dough through each setting twice until the third last setting is reached. Sprinkle the poppy seeds down the centre of the dough, then fold it in half to seal the seeds inside.

Pass the dough back through the pasta machine. Put it through each setting twice, starting at the widest setting until the second last setting is reached. Cut the dough into 3 equal lengths and place onto silicone paper. Bake for 10-12 minutes until the dough is golden brown and slightly puffed.

Allow to cool, then break into various sized shards.

Store in an airtight container until needed.

Kumquat & Rhubarb Compôte

150g candied kumquats (see page 238)
6 sticks garden grown rhubarb
110g soft brown sugar
200ml red wine vinegar
100ml water
3 star anise
6 coriander seeds
2 cardamom pods (crushed)

Dice the kumquats. Dice the rhubarb into 1cm cubes.

Bring the sugar, vinegar and water to the boil, add the star anise, coriander and cardamom. Reduce by half before passing through a fine chinois into a clean pot. Add half of the rhubarb and all the kumquats and gently simmer until almost all the liquid has evaporated. Remove from the heat, add the rest of the rhubarb and mix thoroughly. The residual heat should just cook the rhubarb, giving a coarse texture.

Allow to cool completely, then store in a sterilised jar in the fridge.

Baked Brie

1 small Brie

Preheat the oven to 190°C.

Remove the Brie from its wooden case and discard the wrapper. Line the wooden case with silicone paper and place the cheese back in. Bake for 12-15 minutes.

To Assemble

Spoon a generous amount of compôte onto the centre of the Brie. Arrange the crackers in and around the cheese.

Serve as pictured for guests to help themselves.

Goat's Cheese | Macadamia Nut | Honey
Serves 4

Whipped Goat's Cheese

8 juniper berries (crushed)
150ml double cream
200g goat's cheese (rind removed)

Add the juniper berries to the cream and infuse gently on the stove for 20 minutes. Pass the cream through a fine chinois before placing in the fridge to cool.

Whip the goat's cheese in a mixer, adding the cream slowly until all is incorporated. Refrigerate until required.

Sourdough Toasts

12 slices wholemeal sourdough bread
rapeseed oil (drizzle of)
sea salt (pinch of)
9 juniper berries (crushed)

Preheat the oven to 185°C.

Lay the slices of sourdough on a non-stick tray. Drizzle over the rapeseed oil and sprinkle with the salt and crushed juniper berries. Bake for 7-9 minutes until the bread has toasted and warped.

Dill Tempura

50g cornflour
50g plain flour
6 ice cubes (crushed)
90ml sparkling water
6 sprigs dill
vegetable oil (to deep fry)
sea salt (pinch of)

Mix together the cornflour and plain flour.

Add the crushed ice to the sparkling water. Mix with the flour mixture and whisk to a batter. Be sure not to over mix, lumps should be left in the batter.

Dip each sprig of dill into the tempura batter and deep fry at 180°C for 3-4 minutes. Break the dill into pieces, drain on absorbent paper and season lightly with sea salt.

To Assemble

100g macadamia nuts (toasted)
heather honey (drizzle of)

Quenelle or rocher a generous spoon of goat's cheese onto each plate. Scatter around the dill tempura and macadamia nuts, drizzle over the honey and serve the toasts to the side.

DESSERTS

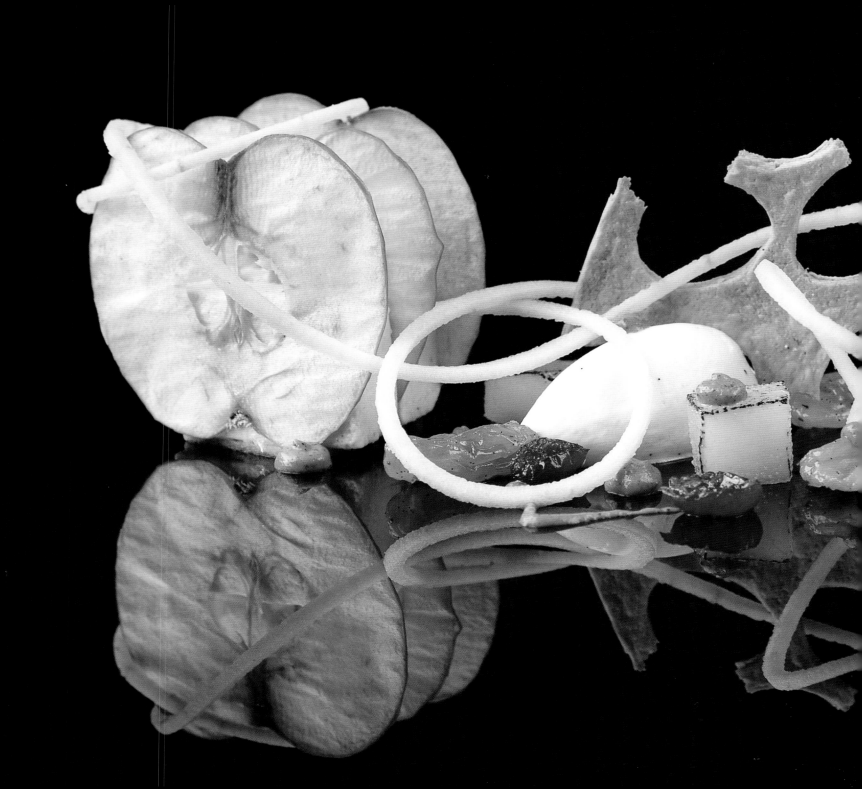

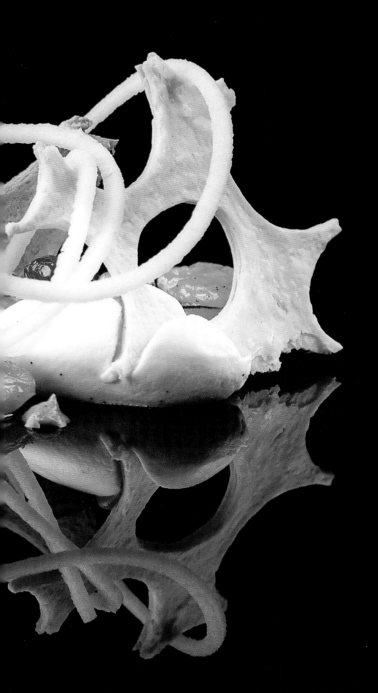

APPLE | CINNAMON | RAISIN

Apple | Cinnamon | Raisin
Serves 6

Puff Pastry

150g puff pastry (see page 242)

Preheat the oven to 165°C.

Roll the puff pastry out to a 0.3cm thickness and cut out random holes using a variety of round cutters 1cm, 2cm and 3½cm in diameter.

Place the puff pastry onto silicone paper and cover with another piece of silicone paper.

Bake between 2 trays, with a weight on top, for 15-20 minutes until golden brown.

Leave to cool completely and break into random shards.

Apple Crisps

150g caster sugar
150ml water
½ vanilla pod
2 Granny Smith apples

(Prepare ahead)

Make a stock syrup by adding the sugar, water and vanilla to a pot and bringing to the boil. Allow the syrup to cool.

Using a mandoline, slice the apples as thinly as possible. Dip each slice into the stock syrup and shake off the excess liquid. Place the slices, spaced apart, on a silicone mat. Place another silicone mat on top of the slices to ensure they stay flat.

Dehydrate at 57°C for 24 hours.

Store between layers of silicone paper in an airtight container.

Cinnamon Ice Cream

5 sticks cinnamon
80g ground cinnamon
1.8 litres double cream
14 egg yolks
650g caster sugar
40g liquid glucose
3 leaves gelatine (soaked in cold water)
6 egg whites

(Prepare ahead)

Place the cinnamon sticks and ground cinnamon into 900ml of the double cream and place over a low heat. Simmer for 25 minutes, then remove from the heat. Wrap the pot in cling film and leave to infuse for 30 minutes.

Whip the remaining double cream to soft peaks.

Place the egg yolks, 425g of the sugar and the glucose into a Thermomix at 80°C for 5 minutes on setting 6.

Add in the gelatine and continue to blend for a further 5 minutes.

Whisk the egg whites to soft peaks and gradually add in the remaining 225g of sugar until a stiff French meringue is achieved.

Slowly add the egg yolk mixture to the semi-whipped double cream and stir until fully incorporated. Fold the French meringue into this mixture. Finally, fold in the cinnamon infused double cream.

Set the ice cream in an airtight container in the freezer for 24 hours.

Burnt Apple Purée

6 Granny Smith apples (stalks removed)
150g caster sugar
25ml olive oil
75ml apple juice

Preheat the oven to 200°C.

Place the whole apples in a heavy-based tray and cover with the sugar.

Put the tray in the oven and bake for 1 hour until completely burnt.

Transfer the apples to a blender and blend on a low speed. Add in the olive oil and apple juice and blend until emulsified.

Pass the purée through a fine chinois and transfer to a piping bag.

Refrigerate until required.

Golden Raisins & Cranberries

100g caster sugar
100ml water
1 vanilla pod (seeds of)
50g golden raisins
15g dried cranberries

Make a stock syrup by placing the sugar, water and vanilla seeds into a pot and bring them to the boil.

Leave to cool slightly, then pour over the raisins and cranberries. Leave to steep.

Refrigerate until required.

Poached Apples

350g caster sugar
300ml apple juice
150ml apple cider
1 vanilla pod (seeds of)
1 stick cinnamon
½ lemon (juice of)
2 Granny Smith apples

Combine all the ingredients, except the apples, in a pot and bring to the boil.

Peel the apples and place them in the stock syrup. Poach gently on a low heat for 35 minutes until soft and tender. Drain the apples and allow to cool.

Dice into 1cm cubes and refrigerate until required.

Apple Laces

1 Granny Smith apple (peeled)
acidulated water

Top and tail the apple with a sharp knife to create a flat surface.

Place the apple into a spiralizer. Spiralize 1 long strand of apple. Keep in the acidulated water until required.

Brown Sugar & Vanilla Whipped Cream

150ml double cream
22g brown sugar
½ vanilla pod (seeds of)

Whip all of the ingredients together to soft peaks. Refrigerate until required.

To Assemble

Cut the cinnamon ice cream into squares big enough to sandwich between the apple crisps.

Place 4 cubes of poached apple around each plate. Dot some of the burnt apple purée on the plates and on the apple cubes. Scatter over several of the golden raisins and cranberries.

Rocher 3 spoonfuls of the brown sugar whipped cream on each plate, stick 2 shards of the puff pastry coming out of the cream. Sandwich together 2 squares of ice cream between 3 apple crisps, then gently drape some of the apple laces over each dish.

Cherries | Cherries | Cherries
Serves 6

Set Cherry Mousse

400g cherry purée (see page 239)
5 egg whites
160g caster sugar
400ml double cream
2 vanilla pods (seeds of)
4 leaves gelatine (soaked in cold water)

Place the cherry purée into a heavy-based pot and reduce down to 200g. Remove from the heat and allow to cool completely.

Place the egg whites into a bowl and whisk to soft peaks. Slowly add in the sugar while whisking to a sturdy French meringue.

Whip the double cream with the vanilla seeds to soft peaks. Stir the meringue into the cream.

Place 100g of the cherry purée in a pot over a low heat and add the bloomed gelatine, stirring to dissolve. Remove from the heat and add in the remaining purée.

Slowly add the purée to the cream and meringue mixture while stirring.

Place the mousse into a 3cm deep tray and leave to set for at least 4 hours in the fridge. Portion the mousse into 5cm squares and store in the fridge.

Cherry Granola Clusters

300g fresh cherries (pitted, soaked in 250ml kirsch for 1 week)
400g cherry purée (see page 239)
480g rolled oats
220g pinhead oats
300g blanched flaked almonds
80g blanched hazelnuts (skins removed, chopped)
240g brown sugar
240ml maple syrup
180ml olive oil
20g vanilla salt (see page 243)

(Prepare ahead)

Drain the cherries. Dehydrate at 57°C for 24 hours on a tray lined with silicone paper.

Place the cherry purée in a pan and reduce on a high heat to 100g.

Preheat the oven to 180°C.

Toast the oats, almonds and hazelnuts together for 10 minutes, then place them in a large bowl.

Reduce the oven temperature to 150°C.

Place the sugar, maple syrup, olive oil and salt into a pan and dissolve the sugar on a low heat. Pour this mixture onto the oats and nuts and mix thoroughly. Spread onto a tray lined with silicone paper. Bake in the oven for 30-40 minutes, mixing every 5-10 minutes. In the last 5 minutes of cooking, add the cherry reduction and work it through the granola. Remove from the oven.

Add the dehydrated cherries and scrunch together with the granola into small 'clusters'. Dehydrate the clusters at 43°C for 12 hours on a tray lined with silicone paper. Store in an airtight container.

Cherry 'Meringues'

300ml cherry juice
6g Hy-Foamer
4g xanthan gum
3g Crisp Film
10g caster sugar

(Prepare ahead)

Place the cherry juice in a mixer bowl.

In a separate bowl add the Hy-Foamer, xanthan gum, Crisp Film and sugar and rub together until incorporated.

Add the sugar mixture to the cherry juice. Whisk on full speed for approximately 12 minutes until the mixture starts to climb up the whisk and is very thick and glossy.

Transfer the meringue to a piping bag fitted with a 1½cm nozzle. Pipe small mounds onto a tray lined with silicone paper.

Dehydrate at 64°C for 24 hours. Keep the meringues in the dehydrator until ready to use.

Cherry Paint

200g cherry purée (see page 239)
10g caster sugar

Place the cherry purée and sugar in a heavy-based pot over a high heat. Reduce the purée, whilst continually stirring, down to 50ml; it will be very thick.

Continued: Cherries | Cherries | Cherries

Cherry Laces

150g cherry purée (see page 239)
150ml stock syrup (see page 243)
4g gellan gum type F
4 leaves gelatine (soaked in cold water)

Add the cherry purée and stock syrup to a pot. Add the gellan gum and blend together using a stick blender.

Place the cherry mixture over a high heat and bring the mixture to the boil. Add in the drained gelatine and blend the mixture again. Pour the liquid into a piping bag and leave to cool for about 5-6 minutes.

Set up 2 sheets of silicone paper on top of 2 baking trays.

Cut a very fine pinhole in the piping bag, about 0.1mm. Carefully pipe long strands of the lace onto the sheets; if it is still too liquid, let it stand for a further 3-4 minutes and start again.

Place the baking trays in the fridge to fully set.

Cherry Sorbet

333g caster sugar
600ml water
66ml kirsch
45g liquid glucose
1kg cherry purée (see page 239)

(Prepare ahead)

Bring the sugar, water, kirsch and glucose to the boil. Pour this mixture over the cherry purée and whisk together well. Allow to cool and pour into a container. Freeze for 24 hours.

Cut the mixture into rough cubes. Transfer to a blender and blend on a low speed until smooth and lighter in colour. Pour back into a container and store in the freezer.

Cherry Gel

6g gellan gum type F
150g caster sugar
600g cherry purée (see page 239)

Rub the gellan gum through the sugar. Add the cherry purée and blend with a stick blender. Place on the heat and slowly bring up to the boil, stirring constantly. Once boiled, remove from the heat and blend once more with a stick blender.

Pass through a fine chinois and pour into a tray. Refrigerate for 1 hour.

Once fully cooled, add the set gel to a blender and blend on full power to a smooth, silky gel. Transfer the gel to a squeezy bottle.

To Assemble

18 fresh cherries
picked thyme leaves (to garnish)

Paint the base of each plate with the cherry paint. Using a palette knife, place one square of cherry mousse on each plate on top of the paint. Rocher a spoonful of sorbet onto each square of cherry mousse and rocher 2 further spoonfuls of sorbet onto each plate. Scatter all the elements around it, finally draping the cherry laces on top.

Treacle Tart | Honeycomb | Vanilla
Serves 8

Treacle Tart

180g brown bread (crusts removed, roughly torn)
85g butter
3 medium eggs
75ml double cream
9g sea salt
750g golden syrup

Preheat the oven to 180°C.

Place the bread in a food processor and pulse to fine breadcrumbs.

Heat the butter in a pan until browned, then strain through a fine sieve into a bowl, leaving the sediment behind.

Mix the eggs, cream and salt in a bowl until well combined.

Gently heat the golden syrup in a pan and stir in the strained butter.

Pour the golden syrup mixture into the egg mixture and stir in the breadcrumbs.

Pour the mixture into a tin approximately 15cm x 20cm, lined with silicone paper.

Bake in the oven for 25 minutes.

Turn the oven temperature down to 140°C and bake for a further 20 minutes, or until the tart is golden brown and bubbling.

Remove from the oven and allow to cool for 1½ hours at room temperature before turning out and cutting into slices 4cm x 11cm.

Honeycomb

butter (for greasing)
315g caster sugar
125g liquid glucose
50g honey
60ml water
15g bicarbonate of soda

Grease a 20cm square tin with the butter.

Mix the sugar, liquid glucose, honey and water in a pan and stir over a gentle heat until the sugar has melted.

Once completely melted, turn up the heat a little and simmer until you have an amber coloured caramel or until it reaches 147°C on a sugar thermometer. Turn off the heat, tip in the bicarbonate and beat in with a wooden spoon until it has all disappeared and the mixture is foaming. Scrape into the tin immediately but be careful as the mixture will be hot.

The mixture will continue bubbling. Leave it to set for about 1 hour and the honeycomb will be ready to snap into chunks.

Vanilla Cream

200ml double cream
2 tbsp icing sugar
½ vanilla pod (seeds of)

Whip all of the ingredients together until the cream forms soft peaks.

Vanilla Lollipop

900ml double cream
2 vanilla pods (seeds of)
7 egg yolks
325g caster sugar
420g liquid glucose
3 leaves gelatine (soaked in cold water)
3 egg whites

(Prepare ahead)

Whip the double cream with the vanilla seeds to soft peaks.

Place the egg yolks, 200g of the sugar and the glucose into a Thermomix at 80°C for 5 minutes on setting 6. Add in the gelatine and continue to blend for a further 5 minutes.

Whisk the egg whites to soft peaks and gradually add in the remaining sugar until a stiff French meringue is achieved.

Slowly add the egg yolk mixture to the semi-whipped double cream and stir until fully incorporated. Fold the French meringue into this mixture.

Pour the mixture into 2 piping bags and tie off the ends.

Pipe the mixture evenly into 60mm x 20mm easy moulds. This amount will make 20 lollipops, leftover lollipops can be stored in the freezer. Place the moulds in the freezer for 3 hours. Before they freeze completely, place in the lollipop sticks.

Treacle Syrup

3g gellan gum type F
25g caster sugar
200ml cold water
120g treacle

Rub the gellan gum through the caster sugar. Blend the sugar mixture through the cold water with a stick blender. Bring the water mixture to a gentle boil.

Once boiling, add the treacle and blend again with a stick blender. Return to the boil.

Once the boil is reached, pour onto a non-stick 20cm square tray and allow to cool completely.

Scrape the mixture into a blender and blend on a medium speed for 10 minutes until smooth and glossy. Decant into a squeezy bottle.

Almond Salted Praline

120g caster sugar
90g liquid glucose
50ml water
135g whole almonds
4g vanilla salt (see page 243)
½ vanilla pod (seeds of)
9g butter
4g bicarbonate of soda

Place the sugar, glucose and water in a heavy-based pot and bring to the boil over a high heat.

Bring the syrup to 115°C and add the almonds. Stirring continuously, bring the mixture to 150°C then remove from the heat and add the salt, vanilla seeds and butter and stir vigorously.

Finally, add the bicarbonate of soda and turn out onto a tray lined with silicone paper. Leave to cool and smash into pieces. Store in an airtight container.

Pecan Tuiles

160g caster sugar
10g pecans

Make a dry caramel from the sugar and pour over the pecans on a silicone paper lined tray.

Preheat the oven to 180°C.

Once cold, blend the mixture to a fine powder.

Sift the powder onto a silicone mat so a thin, even layer is achieved. Bake for 9-10 minutes until evenly melted together. Allow to cool and break into random shards.

To Assemble

Place a slice of the treacle tart just off-centre on each plate and place a vanilla lollipop behind it.

Place 2 rochers of the vanilla cream on each dessert, one on top of the tart and one on the plate.

Scatter over some honeycomb and dot some treacle syrup on the plate and tart. Scatter some of the almond praline on the plates.

Stick 2 pecan tuiles coming out of the cream on each dessert.

Rhubarb | Hibiscus | Candy Floss
Serves 12

Hibiscus Syrup

98g dried hibiscus flowers
2 litres water
675g caster sugar
½ vanilla pod
½ lemon

Place all the ingredients into a large pot and bring to the boil. Reduce the heat and simmer for 1 hour. Remove from the heat, cover the top in cling film and allow to infuse for another hour.

Pass the syrup through a fine chinois into a large container. Store in the fridge until required.

Rhubarb Purée

3kg rhubarb (roughly chopped)
650ml hibiscus syrup

Place the rhubarb in a vacuum pack bag with the syrup. Vacuum pack on the machine's highest setting. Simmer the bag in a pot of boiling water for 30 minutes. Remove from the bag and place in a blender. Blend until smooth, then pass through a fine chinois.

Ginger Custard

5 egg yolks
100g caster sugar
250ml milk
250ml double cream
1 tbsp ground ginger

Whisk the egg yolks and sugar over a bain-marie until light and foamy.

Place the milk, cream and ginger in a pot and bring up to the boil.

Pour some of the milk mixture into the egg and sugar mixture and stir, then add the egg and sugar mixture into the rest of the milk mixture. Cook over a low heat whilst stirring until thickened, then pass the mixture through a fine chinois. Store in the fridge until ready to use.

Rhubarb Curd

170g rhubarb purée
170ml hibiscus syrup
270g whole eggs
270g caster sugar
350g butter
4g gellan gum type F
3 leaves gelatine (soaked in cold water)

Place all the ingredients, excluding the gelatine, into a Thermomix on setting 5 for 10 minutes at 90ºC.

Add the gelatine and blend for a further 5 minutes.

Pass the mixture through a fine chinois into a large bowl.

Press cling film onto the surface and refrigerate until ready to use.

Frozen Rhubarb Espuma

2 leaves gelatine (soaked in cold water)
200ml double cream
800g rhubarb purée
220g caster sugar
2 egg whites

(Prepare ahead)

Place 12 large rubber hemispherical moulds in the freezer.

Dissolve the gelatine in the double cream over a medium heat, then add the rhubarb purée and sugar. Pour the mixture into an espuma gun with the egg whites and charge twice, shaking well between charges.

Refrigerate the mixture for 2 hours, then empty into the frozen moulds. Freeze for 24 hours.

Amaretti Biscuits

4 egg whites
340g ground almonds
340g caster sugar
30g Amaretto liqueur
20g butter (melted)

Preheat the oven to 170ºC.

Whisk the egg whites to stiff peaks in a large bowl.

Mix the sugar and the almonds gently into the egg whites. Add the Amaretto liqueur and fold in gently to a smooth paste.

Place some silicone paper on a baking sheet lightly brushed with butter.

Using a teaspoon, place small heaps of the mixture approximately 2cm apart as they will expand whilst cooking.

Bake in the oven for approximately 15 minutes until golden brown.

Turn off the oven and wedge the door open, allowing the biscuits to cool so they become crisp and brittle.

Amaretti Meringue

100g egg whites
200g caster sugar
150g Amaretti biscuits (crushed to a fine crumb with a rolling pin)

(Prepare ahead)

Whisk the egg whites to stiff peaks. Add in the sugar, a bit at a time, whisking well between each addition. Once all of the sugar has been added, whisk until the mixture is thick, firm and shiny. Fold through the biscuit crumbs.

Pipe onto a tray lined with silicone paper about ½cm round and 1cm high. Dehydrate for 24 hours at 60°C.

Rhubarb & Ginger Jelly

227ml rhubarb purée
56ml ginger syrup
1 litre hibiscus syrup
420ml cold water
25 leaves gelatine (soaked in cold water)

(Prepare ahead)

Place the rhubarb purée, ginger syrup, hibiscus syrup and water into a pot and bring to the boil. Add in the drained gelatine. Pour into a cling film lined tray 20cm x 40cm so the mixture is 2cm thick. Refrigerate for 6 hours.

Once set, cut into ½cm strips and refrigerate until required.

Poached Rhubarb

500g rhubarb
100ml hibiscus syrup

Slice the rhubarb into 4cm lengths and place into a vacuum pack bag with the syrup. Vacuum pack the bag on full power.

Remove the rhubarb and syrup from the bag and place in a new vacuum pack bag. Re-vacuum pack on full power, then repeat this step.

Poach the rhubarb in a water bath at 65°C for 25-30 minutes depending on the thickness of the rhubarb. When tender but not soft, take it out. Refresh in ice water.

Open the bag and place the contents in a new vacuum pack bag. Re-vacuum pack on full power.

Candy Floss Paper

150g caster sugar
1 candy floss machine

Make candy floss following the machine's instructions.

Divide the candy floss into 12. Place each portion between silicone paper and gently flatten with a rolling pin so it resembles paper. Each piece should measure approximately 20cm x 15cm so it can cover the full dessert. This will depend on the bowls being used.

Repeat until you have 12 pieces of candy floss paper.

Rhubarb Strips

2 stalks rhubarb
25ml hibiscus syrup

Using a vegetable peeler, peel the rhubarb into strips 15cm long. Soak the strips in the hibiscus syrup for no more than 5 minutes. Drain any excess syrup off the rhubarb.

To Assemble

lemon balm (to garnish)
candied fennel seeds (see page 238, to garnish)
15ml hibiscus syrup per dessert

Remove the frozen espuma from the freezer and remove from the moulds. Scoop out the centre of each hemisphere with a Parisienne scoop and allow to temper for 5 minutes before the next step. Fill the holes with some of the ginger custard.

Place the frozen espuma at one end of each bowl.

Wrap a strip of the jelly around the espuma and tail the end off as shown in the image.

Wind up 2 of the marinated rhubarb strips, place on the plate and fill the strips with ginger custard.

Dot the rhubarb curd around the frozen espuma.

Slice the poached rhubarb into 2cm lengths and place 3 on each plate. Scatter 6 Amaretti meringues on each plate.

Scatter a sprinkle of candied fennel seeds and a few sprigs of lemon balm over the whole dessert.

Place one candy floss paper over each dessert to totally cover it. Allow guests to pour the syrup over the candy floss paper and watch it disappear to reveal the dessert below.

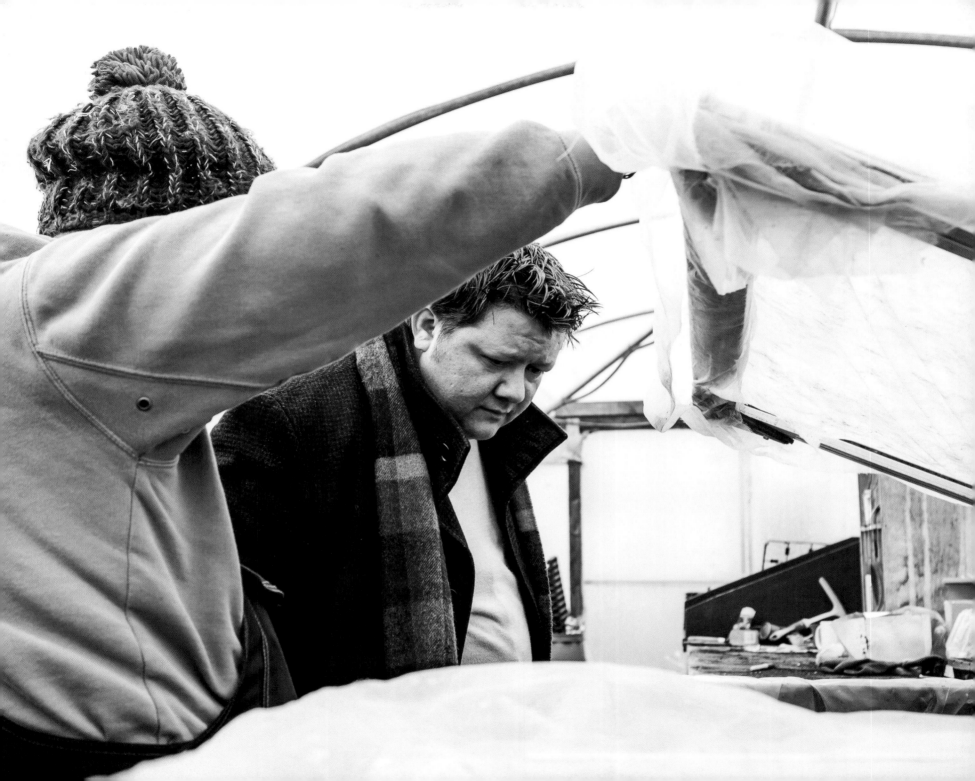

Peanut Caramel Cheesecake
Serves 10

Shortbread

1kg butter
500g caster sugar
1½kg plain flour

Cream together the butter and sugar, then mix in the flour. Divide the mixture into 3, shape into logs and wrap in cling film. Refrigerate for at least 1 hour.

Preheat the oven to 180°C.

Slice the shortbread to 2cm thick. Place the slices on non-stick baking mats and bake for 25 minutes or until just over-cooked. Leave the shortbread to rest for 20 minutes.

Transfer to a blender and blend on a medium speed until a liquid consistency is achieved.

Pour small amounts of the liquid shortbread onto silicone paper, cover with another sheet of silicone paper and roll until ½cm thick. Repeat until all the mixture is used up.

Place the sheets on a flat tray in the freezer for at least 1 hour.

When frozen, portion the shortbread using a pastry knife and ruler into 2½cm x 17½cm rectangles.

Store between silicone paper in the fridge.

Peanut Caramel

145g condensed milk
75g smooth peanut butter
65g golden syrup
60g butter

Place all the ingredients into a heavy-based pot. Stirring constantly, bring the mix slowly up to the boil. Boil for 2 minutes whilst whisking.

Pass through a fine chinois into a container and store in the fridge until required.

Cheesecake

220ml double cream
200g cream cheese
200g peanut caramel

Whip the double cream to soft peaks and set aside.

Place the cream cheese and peanut caramel into a large bowl and beat together until fully incorporated. Fold through the whipped cream and place into 2 piping bags. Store in the fridge until required.

Frozen Peanut Cheesecake

100g dark chocolate
250g peanut caramel cheesecake

Cut 10 thin strips of acetate into 8cm x 17½cm rectangles and lay out side by side.

Melt the dark chocolate and transfer to a piping bag. Cut a small hole in the bag and pipe the melted chocolate lengthways over the middle section of acetate in a criss-cross formation.

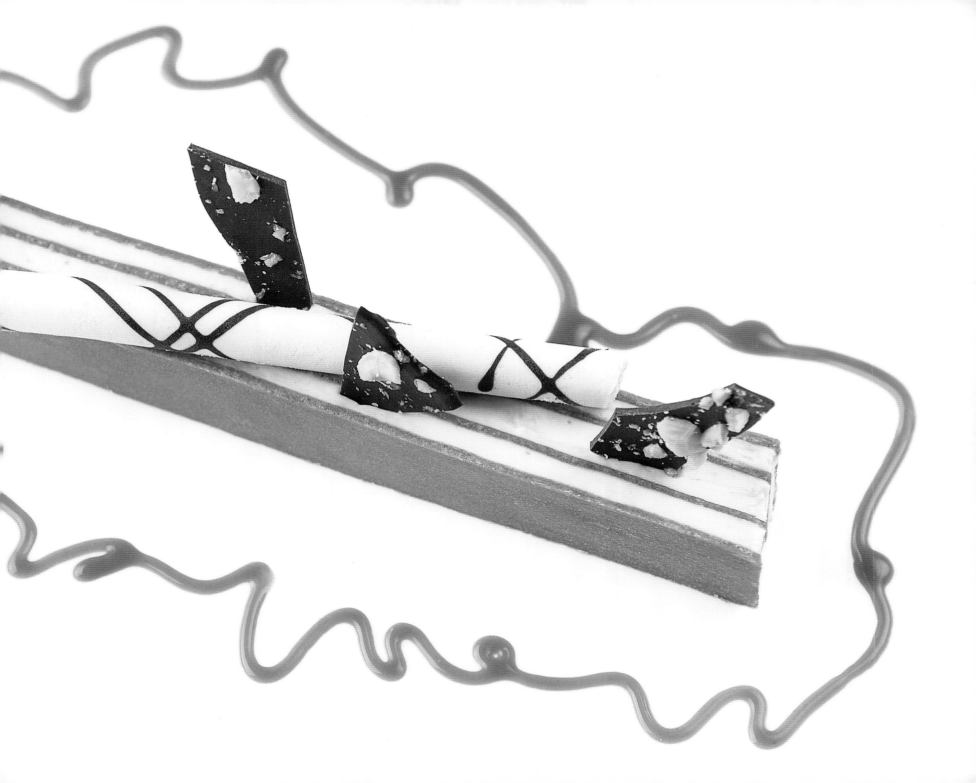

Continued: Peanut Caramel Cheesecake

Very gently roll the acetate rectangles into tubes being careful not to smudge the chocolate. Secure with Sellotape (the tubes should be roughly 1cm in diameter). Place the tubes in the freezer.

Take one of the piping bags of cheesecake and gently fill the tubes from one end until they are full.

Repeat until all of the tubes are full. Store them in the freezer.

Salted Caramel

300g caster sugar
20g sea salt
100g butter
200ml double cream

Place the sugar in a heavy-based pot and melt to a golden brown caramel. Add the salt and stir thoroughly. Stir in the butter until incorporated, then the cream. Strain though a fine chinois.

Store in the fridge until required.

Toffee Sauce

250g caster sugar
250g butter (diced)
500ml double cream

Place the sugar in a large, heavy-based pot and melt to a dark golden brown caramel. Stir in the diced butter. When all the butter is incorporated, add the cream and whisk. Bring the sauce up to the boil and reduce slightly. Pass through a fine chinois.

Store in the fridge until ready to use.

Peanut Tuile

100g unsalted peanuts
200g dark chocolate

Preheat the oven to 175°C.

Roast the peanuts for 14 minutes and allow to cool. Once cooled, roughly chop the nuts.

Melt the dark chocolate over a bain-marie, then spread it over a sheet of acetate to a ½cm thickness. Drop the chopped peanuts over the chocolate.

Store on a flat tray in the fridge until set. Once set, break into random shards.

To Assemble

Lay out 4 rectangles of frozen shortbread. Pipe the cheesecake mixture down both edges of frozen shortbread. Fill the middle space with the salted caramel.

Stack up the shortbread, making 4 layers of shortbread sandwiching 3 layers of cheesecake and salted caramel.

Repeat for each plate.

Place a 'sandwich' on its side in the centre of each plate.

Cut both ends off the frozen peanut cheesecake tubes to neaten up. Snip the Sellotape, gently unroll the acetate and place a tube on each dessert.

Stick shards of the peanut tuile out the top of each dessert.

Drizzle a generous amount of the toffee sauce around the dessert or serve on the side.

Baked Alaska
Serves 8

Salt Dough

500g plain flour
5 egg whites
300g rock salt
150ml water

Mix the flour, egg whites and rock salt in a mixer for 4 minutes. Slowly add in the water until it becomes a tight dough. Keep mixing for a further 10 minutes.

Salt Baked Pineapple

1 pineapple
salt dough

Preheat the oven to 185°C.

Twist off the top of the pineapple and discard.

Roll out the salt dough as thin as you can, using a little flour if it makes it easier. Wrap the pineapple in dough, making sure there are no air bubbles or rips in the dough.

Bake the pineapple for 80 minutes. As soon as it is ready, remove the pineapple from the oven and crack open the dough. Leave to cool.

Using a pastry knife, top and tail the pineapple and remove the skin. Cut the pineapple into 3 wedges. Trim up the sides of each wedge to form rectangles 1½cm thick. Portion each rectangle into 1½cm cubes.

Store in an airtight container in the fridge.

Vanilla Ice Cream

7 egg yolks
320g caster sugar
22g liquid glucose
3 leaves gelatine (soaked in cold water)
3 egg whites
2 vanilla pods
450ml double cream (semi-whipped)

(Prepare ahead)

Place the egg yolks, 210g of the sugar and the glucose into a food processor and blend on medium speed for 10 minutes, adding the gelatine in after 5 minutes.

Whisk the egg whites to soft peaks, then gradually add the remaining sugar until you get a stiff French meringue.

Split the vanilla pods and scrape the seeds into the double cream. Mix well.

Slowly add the egg yolk mixture into the semi-whipped double cream and incorporate fully. Finally, fold in the French meringue.

Freeze for 24 hours before use.

Swiss Meringue

4 egg whites
300g caster sugar
1½ tbsp ground coconut

Preheat the oven to 130°C.

Place the egg whites and sugar into a medium sized metal bowl and place the bowl over a bain-marie. Stir the egg whites and sugar until the sugar has completely dissolved. Remove from the heat.

Place the egg white mixture into a mixer and whisk on full for 8 minutes or until slightly cooled. Fold in the ground coconut.

Spoon into a piping bag and pipe the meringues onto a lined baking tray.

Bake in the oven for 15 minutes.

When the meringues are cooled, use a pair of tweezers or a turning knife to poke a small hole in the base of the meringue to create enough space to fill with ice cream.

Pipe the ice cream into the holes in the meringue and store in the freezer.

Green Tea Sponge

3 egg yolks
150g caster sugar
4g matcha green tea powder
2½g sea salt
35g toasted desiccated coconut
1½ limes (zest of)
110ml vanilla oil (infuse 1½ vanilla pods in 110ml rapeseed oil)
100ml coconut milk
140g plain flour
1½ tsp bicarbonate of soda

Add the egg yolks and sugar to a food processor and blend on a medium speed to make a sabayon.

Meanwhile, mix the green tea, salt, coconut and lime zest together in a large metal bowl.

Strain the vanilla oil and blend together with the coconut milk using a stick blender, then slowly pour into the sabayon mixture, continually blending.

Continued: Baked Alaska

When fully emulsified together, pour the mix in to the metal bowl and fold together until incorporated.

Sift in the flour and bicarbonate of soda, then fold together gently.

Place the mix into a lined tray and bake for 45 minutes.

Cool on a wire rack. When completely cold, portion into 5½cm batons.

Kaffir Lime Espuma

50ml milk
100ml double cream
100ml lime juice
4 kaffir lime leaves
4 egg yolks
70g caster sugar
¼ tsp xanthan gum

Place the milk, cream, lime juice and lime leaves in a heavy-based pot and slowly bring to the boil. Once at the boil, take off the heat, cover the pot in cling film and leave to infuse for 30 minutes.

Place the egg yolks and sugar in a food processor and blend on a medium speed to make a sabayon.

Strain the liquid in the pot through a fine sieve and very slowly add to the sabayon. Once fully incorporated, add the xanthan gum.

Blend on full speed for 10 seconds, then pour into an espuma gun. Charge the gun with 2 charges (shaking well after each charge) and refrigerate for 2 hours.

Green Tea Panna Cotta

6g matcha green tea powder
200ml double cream
70g caster sugar
1 leaf gelatine (soaked in cold water)

Place the green tea, cream and sugar into a pot and blitz with a stick blender. Slowly bring to a simmer, add the soaked gelatine and blitz again. Strain through a fine sieve into a small bowl. Cover with cling film and refrigerate for 3 hours.

Transfer the set mixture to a mixer with a whisk attachment. Whisk on full power for 2 minutes.

Divide between 2 piping bags and store in the fridge.

Alaska Cloches

400g egg whites
3 tsp cream of tartar
800g caster sugar

(Prepare ahead)

Preheat the oven to 110ºC.

Whisk the egg whites to soft peaks and add in the cream of tartar. Turn the mixer on to full speed and take the mixture to stiff peaks. Gradually add in the sugar.

When the meringue is fully whipped, using a large spoon, spoon the mixture onto trays lined with silicone paper.

The domes should be approximately 15½cm in diameter and 9cm in height.

Glaze the cloches with a blow torch, then bake in the oven for 15 minutes.

Place in the dehydrator set at its highest setting for 15 hours.

After the 15 hours, working one at a time, take a turning knife and score a circle around the flat base of the meringue approximately 12-13 cm in diameter, then make 4 scores in the diameter.

Using a large spoon, carefully scoop out the interior of the meringue so that you are left with a hollow and empty shell.

Glaze the inside of the shell with a blow torch and place back in the dehydrator for another 5 hours.

To Assemble

10g toasted coconut

Scatter the coconut over each plate, then square off the coconut to give an even shape to work on.

Arrange 3 pieces of the tea sponge in the middle of each plate. Place 3 Swiss meringues onto each plate, if any are broken just scatter these around as little extras.

Place 5 pineapple cubes onto each plate, some resting on the sponge and some directly on the plate. Dot 7 dots of the green tea panna cotta randomly over the pineapple and sponge.

Express 3 mounds of the espuma onto each plate.

At the last minute, rocher the ice cream onto each plate.

Place the meringue cloche over each plate to give the impression it is one extremely large Baked Alaska. Before guests dig into it, remove the cloche to very surprised guests.

Brown Bread | Orange | Fig
Serves 6

Burnt Orange Jelly

140g caster sugar
1 lime (zest of)
1 lemon (zest of)
1 orange (zest of)
2 vanilla pods (seeds of)
500ml fresh orange juice
7 leaves gelatine (soaked in cold water)

Place the sugar into a heavy-based pot and set
over a high heat. Stir with a wooden spoon
until the sugar is equally melted to a golden
caramel. Take off the heat and add the zests and
vanilla seeds.

Very slowly add the orange juice, stirring frequently
until all the liquid has been incorporated. Return
to the heat and bring to the boil. Add in the soaked
gelatine, stirring until dissolved. Pour the liquid
through a fine sieve and leave to cool.

Pour into a cling film lined, 20cm square tray to
a 2cm thickness and set in the fridge.

Once set, cut out circles from the jelly using a
9cm cookie cutter and set back in the fridge.

Brown Bread Parfait

450g brown sourdough (sliced)
120g light brown muscovado sugar
1 tsp cinnamon
½ tsp ground ginger
7 egg yolks
325g caster sugar
1½ tbsp liquid glucose
3 egg whites
3 leaves gelatine (soaked in cold water)
750ml double cream

(Prepare ahead)

Preheat the oven to 175ºC.

Break the bread into random shaped chunks and mix well with the brown sugar, cinnamon and ginger. Place on a non-stick baking sheet and toast in the oven for 20 minutes, turning the bread every 3 minutes. The bread should be well toasted.

Using a rolling pin, break up the toasted bread into rough breadcrumbs. Place the crumbs back in the oven for 6 minutes. Allow to cool at room temperature until cold.

Whisk the egg yolks until pale and light.

Boil 210g of the caster sugar with the liquid glucose until the soft ball stage is achieved (118ºC) and pour over the egg yolks. Stir in the softened gelatine and whisk until cold.

Whisk the egg whites and the remaining caster sugar to make a meringue.

Whip the double cream to soft peaks.

Fold all of the ingredients together, finally folding through the toasted breadcrumbs.

Pour into 4cm hemispherical moulds and freeze until firm.

When the parfait is frozen, turn out the moulds and stick the hemispheres together to make spheres. Place back into the freezer until ready to serve.

Chocolate Glass

80ml water
55g butter
45g liquid glucose
160g caster sugar
3g pectin
55g dark chocolate
12g cocoa powder

Preheat the oven to 180ºC.

Place the water, butter, glucose, sugar and pectin into a heavy-based pot and bring to the boil.

Mix the cocoa powder and chocolate together in a bowl and melt over a bain-marie. Pour the liquid mixture over the chocolate and blend with a stick blender. Pass the mixture through a fine chinois into a container and leave to cool.

Once fully cooled, pour onto a tray lined with silicone paper. Take another piece of silicone paper and place directly on top. Using a rolling pin, roll the mixture until flat. Place in the oven for 13 minutes, turning halfway through, and roll again with a rolling pin.

Remove from the oven and roll again so the mixture is really thin. Bake for another 5 minutes, remove from the oven and roll again. While the mixture is still hot, remove the top sheet of silicone paper. Use a sharp knife and portion strips measuring 11cm x 1cm. If it begins to cool down, return to the oven for a couple of minutes.

Working quickly, wrap each strip around a wooden dowel 2cm in diameter, 20cm in length to create a spiral. Slide the spiral off the dowel and store between layers of silicone paper. Repeat until all the mixture is used up.

Fig Purée

200g caster sugar
300g ripe figs

Make a dry caramel with the sugar taking it to a golden brown colour.

Top and tail the figs and cut into quarters.

Drop the figs into the caramel and cook down until water has come out of the figs and has evaporated.

Blend to a smooth purée and pass through a fine chinois. Decant into a squeezy bottle and store in the fridge.

Pistachio Powder

60g pistachios (shelled, peeled)
10g caster sugar
5ml pistachio oil

Preheat the oven to 180ºC.

Blend the pistachios with the sugar to a fine powder.

Spread out on a non-stick baking mat and drizzle with the oil. Bake for 5-6 minutes.

Cool and store in an airtight container.

To Assemble

Place a jelly circle in the centre of each plate and top with a sphere of parfait. Crumble a line of the pistachio powder up the side of the bowl. Dot the fig purée up the side of the bowl. Arrange a spiral of chocolate glass on top of each parfait.

Christmas Pudding | Brandy | Orange
Serves 12

Christmas Pudding

140g self-raising flour
40g ground ginger
½ tsp cinnamon
½ tsp mixed spice
½ tsp sea salt
55g butter
225g suet (chopped)
1 lemon (juice and zest of)
225g sultanas
225g currants
225g raisins
225g brown sugar
200g fresh breadcrumbs
115g cherries (chopped)
115g almonds (chopped)
170g apple (grated)
115g carrot (grated)
4 eggs
2 tbsp treacle
1 tbsp golden syrup
330ml stout

Preheat the oven to 120°C.

Mix the flour and spices together. Rub in the butter and add the suet followed by the lemon zest and all the remaining dry ingredients. Add the grated apple and carrot.

Beat the eggs and add to the mixture. Stir in the treacle, syrup and lemon juice. Add the stout, then pour the mixture into a terrine mould.

Place the terrine in a deep oven tray and fill the tray with water until it comes halfway up the terrine mould. Steam in the oven for 4 hours, then allow to cool.

Portion into rectangles 2cm x 4½cm x 14cm.

Caramelised Orange Jelly

160g caster sugar
3 oranges (zest of)
400ml fresh orange juice
7 leaves gelatine (soaked in cold water)

Place the sugar in to a heavy-based pan and set over a high heat. Stir with a wooden spoon until the sugar is equally melted to a golden caramel, take off the heat and add the zest.

Very slowly add the orange juice, stirring frequently until all the liquid has been incorporated. Return to the heat and bring to the boil. Add in the soaked gelatine, stirring until dissolved. Pour the liquid through a fine chinois and leave to cool.

Pour into a tray 2cm thick and set in the fridge. Once set, cut into 2cm cubes.

Cinnamon Parfait

2 sticks cinnamon
60g ground cinnamon
900ml double cream
6 egg yolks
320g caster sugar
20g liquid glucose
2 leaves gelatine (soaked in cold water)
3 egg whites

(Prepare ahead)

Place the cinnamon sticks and ground cinnamon into 450ml of the double cream and place over a low heat. Simmer for 25 minutes then remove from the heat. Wrap the pot in cling film and leave to infuse for 30 minutes.

Whip the remaining double cream to soft peaks.

Place the egg yolks, 125g of the sugar and the glucose into a Thermomix at 80°C for 5 minutes on setting 6. Add in the gelatine and continue to blend for a further 5 minutes.

Whisk the egg whites to soft peaks and gradually add in the remaining caster sugar until a stiff French meringue is achieved.

Slowly add the egg yolk mixture to the semi-whipped double cream and stir until fully incorporated. Fold the French meringue into this mixture. Finally fold in the cinnamon infused double cream.

Set the ice cream in an airtight container in the freezer for 24 hours. Cut into 3cm cubes.

Cinnamon Meringue

150g egg whites (room temperature)
280g caster sugar
cinnamon (to sprinkle over)

Whisk the egg whites on medium speed to soft peaks. Slowly add the sugar in a steady stream, while whisking, until incorporated and stiff peaks are achieved.

Spread the mixture thinly on silicone paper. Sprinkle the surface lightly with cinnamon and dry out in a dehydrator at the highest setting for 3 hours.

Once dry, break into shards and store in an airtight container.

Brandy Butter

250g butter (softened)
100ml brandy
85g icing sugar

Whip the butter in a mixer. Add in the brandy and icing sugar and whip until light and fluffy.

With a teaspoon, rocher onto a silicone paper lined tray, allowing 2 per person. Store in the fridge until ready to use.

Brandy Custard

5 egg yolks
100g caster sugar
250ml milk
250ml double cream
50ml brandy

Whisk the eggs yolks and sugar over a bain-marie until light and foamy.

Place the milk, cream and brandy in a pot and bring up to the boil. Pour some of the milk mixture into the egg and sugar mixture, then add the egg and sugar mixture into the rest of the milk mixture.

Cook the mixture over a low heat whilst stirring until thickened. Pass through a fine chinois.

Store in the fridge until ready to use.

To Assemble

lemon balm (to garnish)

Drizzle some of the brandy custard around each plate.

Place a rectangle of the Christmas pudding on each plate. Scatter 4 cubes of the caramelised orange jelly over the pudding and plate.

Place one rocher of the brandy butter on the pudding and one on a cube of the jelly.

Arrange 3 shards of meringue around each plate. Place one cube of cinnamon parfait on each slice of pudding. Scatter lemon balm over each plate.

Dairy

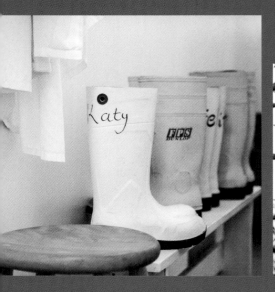

The milk and dairy products in Scotland are of outstanding quality and we once again have our climate to thank for this. The rainfall here means the grass grows better resulting in lush, green pastures on which the cows graze. It is not just the weather though that we have to thank. Scotland has a long history of dairy farming and a wealth of dedicated, knowledgeable dairy farmers who commit fully to their product with 3.30am starts 365 days a year - their dedication means us chefs are lucky enough to work with some of the best dairy products in the world.

The Rodger family has owned Knockraich Farm since the 1950s. The 80-acre farm, nestled between Stirling and the beautiful Trossachs, is home to 60 Friesians. The dairy cows and young stock are managed by Robert Rodger, but the wider diversified business - which includes a milk processing dairy - is very much a family affair. Keeping the cows in the fields and maintaining the farm for future generations is the biggest inspiration for the Rodger family as dairy farmers. Falling milk prices meant that their small dairy herd was under threat, so in 2011, Robert's wife Katy began to diversify and create a range of dairy products. She began with ice cream but this was a difficult market to break into so they reassessed their strategy and soon expanded the range. It was the yoghurt which really took off first. I first encountered Katy's amazing yoghurt in 2012 as a judge for the Scotland Food and Drink awards. To me this product was the obvious winner of the day in their category, and I petitioned hard. It got my vote and clearly impressed all the judges, not only winning their category but also the overall Product of the Year award.

Following on from this, I looked into the full Katy Rodger's Artisan Dairy range and began using her crème fraîche in some of the restaurant dishes. The range also includes natural yoghurt and Knockraich Crowdie. All products are made in a traditional manner with whole milk to retain the full flavour. The ingredients are simple and natural. They all have a fabulous consistency which makes them stable raw or in cooking. Last year I was on the hunt for some amazing Scottish butter to use on the tables in the restaurant. Given the amazing dairy in Scotland, it baffled me that I could not get quality table butter locally. I, like so many British chefs, was looking to France for quality but thankfully Katy stepped up. She is now providing me with fantastic cultured and lightly salted butter. I have been using her butter since day one and in the early days it arrived simply wrapped in greaseproof paper - I loved this as it showed how fresh from the farm it was. Along with bread, butter is the first thing guests receive when they come to the restaurant so it has to be perfect. The crunchy crystals of salt dispersed through this butter give not only flavour but also a little bit of texture which is not found in commercially produced butter.

'Knot' Chocolate Tart
Serves 8

Chocolate Jelly

6 eggs
320g caster sugar
800g chocolate
300ml milk
8 leaves gelatine (soaked in cold water)

(Prepare ahead)

Blend the eggs and sugar at 80°C in a Thermomix.

Melt the chocolate.

Bring the milk to the boil, then add the gelatine to the milk. Mix the chocolate into the milk mixture, then add this mixture to the sugar and eggs. Blend for a further 30 seconds.

Pour into a cling film lined tray to a thickness of 2cm. Set in the fridge for 10 hours.

Cut into strips the length of the tray and ½cm wide. Refrigerate until ready to assemble.

Kumquat Purée

1kg kumquats (halved, seeds removed)
1kg caster sugar
400ml water

Simmer the kumquats in the water and sugar for 3 hours. Blitz in a blender, then pass through a chinois. Decant into a squeezy bottle and reserve.

Coco Pops

120g caster sugar
80g Coco Pops

Make a dry caramel with the sugar. Carefully stir in the Coco Pops and allow to cool on a silicone mat. Smash into little pieces and reserve.

Crème Fraîche Parfait

7 egg yolks
375g caster sugar
1½ tbsp liquid glucose
450g crème fraîche
3 leaves gelatine (soaked in cold water)
3 egg whites
450ml double cream

Whisk the egg yolks until pale and light.

Boil 265g of the sugar with the glucose and just enough water to cover until it reaches 118°C. Pour over the egg yolks and whisk until cold.

Warm the crème fraîche and add in the gelatine.

Whisk the egg whites and remaining caster sugar to make meringue.

Whip the cream to soft peaks. Fold all of the ingredients together. Pipe the mixture into acetate tubes, secured with Sellotape, and freeze until required.

Salted Caramel

300g caster sugar
9g sea salt
100g butter
200ml double cream

Make a dry caramel with the sugar until it is deep brown in colour. Add the salt and butter, then stir in the cream. Bring back to the boil and pass through a fine chinois.

Decant into a squeezy bottle until required.

Frozen Chocolate Shortbread

300g flour
200g butter
100g caster sugar
75g 70% dark chocolate pistoles
60g white chocolate (for piping)

Preheat the oven to 165°C.

Rub the flour, butter and sugar together to form a dough. Rest the dough in the fridge for 10 minutes.

Roll out 20 shortbread biscuits and bake for 15 minutes or until dark brown.

Whilst still hot, blend the biscuits on a medium speed in a food processor, adding in the dark chocolate which will melt in.

Roll the paste between 2 sheets of silicone paper. Freeze for 30 minutes. Once frozen, cut into 5cm squares.

Melt the white chocolate and pipe it over the frozen squares. Return the shortbread to the freezer until required.

To Assemble

15g chocolate popping candy
16 candied kumquat halves (see page 238)

Tie each strip of chocolate jelly into a knot.

Remove the acetate from the parfait tubes and place a tube of parfait through the centre of each knot. Place in the centre of each plate and garnish with the remaining elements.

Brown Sugar | Bramble | Tomato
Serves 8

Brown Sugar Cheesecake

200g dark brown sugar
900g cream cheese
200ml double cream
3 tbsp plain flour
3 eggs
1 egg yolk
1 vanilla pod (seeds of)

Preheat the oven to 195°C.

Blend the brown sugar in a food processor to break it down. Add all the remaining ingredients to the sugar and blend until fully incorporated.

Pour into a silicone paper lined tray 20cm x 30cm. Bake for 10 minutes. Reduce the oven temperature to 110°C and bake for a further 25 minutes until it still has a slight wobble.

Turn off the oven and open the oven door for a cheesecake that's creamy in the centre, or leave it closed if you prefer a drier texture.

Allow to cool in the oven for 1½ hours.

Feuilletine Base

50g pistachios
50g hazelnuts (skins removed)
50g flaked almonds
125g caster sugar
15ml hazelnut oil
20g nibbed almonds
100g feuilletine
250g milk chocolate

Blend the pistachios, hazelnuts, flaked almonds, sugar and hazelnut oil on a low speed in a food processor to a coarse consistency.

Add the nut mixture to the nibbed almonds and feuilletine and mix.

Melt the milk chocolate and add it to the rest of the dry ingredients.

Spread the mixture between 2 pieces of silicone paper to a ½cm thickness. Store in the fridge for 1 hour or until fully set. Remove the top sheet of silicone paper.

Cut the feuilletine base to the size of the cheesecake tray. Turn the cheesecake out onto the base and return to the fridge.

Bramble Sorbet

665ml water
333g caster sugar
45g liquid glucose
1kg bramble purée (see page 238)

(Prepare ahead)

Bring the water, sugar and glucose to the boil. Pour this syrup over the bramble purée and whisk together well.

Allow the mixture to cool, pour into a container and freeze for 24 hours.

Cut the mixture into rough cubes and blend in a food processor on a medium speed until smooth and lighter in colour. Place back in a container and re-freeze until set.

Milk Biscuit

500ml milk
45g liquid glucose
sea salt (small pinch of)

(Prepare ahead)

Gently heat the milk, glucose and salt together to 75°C. Blend with a stick blender until foam starts to form. Scoop off the foam and place it onto a 30cm x 20cm tray lined with silicone paper. Dehydrate at 60°C for 24 hours.

Tomato Caramel

10 ripe plum tomatoes
500g caster sugar
1 lime (juice and zest of)

Blow torch the tomatoes and peel off the skin. Quarter them and discard the seeds. Weigh out 400g of tomato petals and leave to one side.

Place the sugar in a heavy-based pot and make a dry caramel until it reaches a walnut brown.

Add the tomato petals and stir into the caramel. Simmer for 10 minutes until the tomatoes have broken down into the sugar. Add the lime zest and juice. Remove from the heat and leave to cool completely. Transfer to a squeezy bottle and refrigerate.

To Assemble

16 fresh brambles

Cut the cheesecake into 5cm x 11cm rectangles and place in the centre of each plate.

Put 2 brambles on each dish. Break up the milk biscuit and scatter on the plates, sticking 2 out of each slice of cheesecake to give height. Rocher the bramble sorbet, either onto a spare piece of feuilletine or straight onto each plate.

Drizzle the cold tomato caramel to finish.

Orange | Chocolate | Honeycomb
Serves 6

Salted Marmalade Caramel

300g caster sugar
20g sea salt
100g butter
80g thick cut marmalade
200ml double cream

Place the sugar in a heavy-based pot and stir over a medium heat until golden brown. Add the salt and stir thoroughly. Mix in the butter and marmalade and stir until incorporated. Pour in the cream and bring back to the boil. Pass through a fine chinois.

Decant into a squeezy bottle.

Honeycomb

315g caster sugar
125g liquid glucose
50g honey
60ml water
15g bicarbonate of soda
butter (for greasing)

Grease a 20cm square tin with the butter.

Mix the sugar, liquid glucose, honey and water in a pan and stir over a gentle heat until the sugar has melted.

Once completely melted, turn up the heat a little and simmer until you have an amber coloured caramel or until it reaches 147°C on a sugar thermometer. Turn off the heat, tip in the bicarbonate and beat in with a wooden spoon until it has all disappeared and the mixture is foaming.

Scrape into the tin immediately but be careful as the mixture will be hot.

The mixture will continue bubbling. Leave it to set for about 1 hour and the honeycomb will be ready to snap into chunks.

Orange Curd

200ml freshly squeezed orange juice
185g caster sugar
4 eggs
3 egg yolks
155g butter

Place the juice, sugar, eggs and yolks in a bain-marie and stir until the sugar has dissolved and the mixture reaches 82°C. Leave to cool down completely.

Pour the mixture into a blender with the butter and blend until smooth and shiny.

Store in the fridge.

Candied Ginger Ice Cream

8 egg yolks
375g caster sugar
1½ tbsp liquid glucose
150g crème fraîche
3 leaves gelatine (soaked in cold water)
3 egg whites
750ml double cream
100g candied ginger (diced)
80g ginger syrup

(Prepare ahead)

Whisk the egg yolks until pale and light.

Boil 265g of the sugar with the glucose until soft boil (118°C). Pour over the egg yolks and whisk until cold.

Warm the crème fraîche and add in the gelatine.

Whisk the egg whites and remaining caster sugar to make meringue.

Whip the cream to soft peaks, then fold through the diced ginger, followed by the ginger syrup.

Fold all of the ingredients together.

Gently spoon the mixture into a 2 litre container and freeze without a lid for 8 hours. Cover with a lid and store in the freezer until required.

Chocolate & Marmalade Fondant

50g white chocolate
50g dark chocolate
70g thick cut marmalade
125g caster sugar
125g butter
4 eggs
155g plain flour

Preheat the oven to 190°C.

Melt the chocolates, marmalade, sugar and butter together over a bain-marie and remove from the heat. Add the eggs and mix thoroughly with a whisk. Gently fold in the flour.

Divide the mixture evenly between 6 dariole moulds greased with butter and sugar or 6 ring moulds lined with silicone paper. Bake for 9 minutes and serve immediately.

To Assemble

200g burnt white chocolate (see page 238)
6 macarons (see page 241, filled with orange curd)

Place some burnt white chocolate at one side of each plate and place a fondant at the top of each plate.

Using a dessertspoon, make a rocher out of the candied ginger ice cream and place on the burnt white chocolate.

Dot some of the curd at the edge of the white chocolate and dot some of the salted caramel around each plate. Break up the honeycomb and scatter on the dessert. Finish by placing a macaron at the bottom of each plate.

Raspberry Bonfire
Serves 6

Raspberry Tubes

400ml fresh raspberry purée (see page 242)
150g icing sugar
2 tsp crytex

(Prepare ahead)

Blend the raspberry purée, icing sugar and crytex together. Spread the mixture on a silicone mat to a 3mm thickness. Dehydrate for 24 hours at 57°C.

Portion the mixture into rectangles measuring 11cm x 6cm. Wrap the rectangles around a small wooden dowel with a 1½cm diameter. Slide the tubes off the dowels and place in an airtight container between silicone paper, making sure they are not touching. Store in the freezer until ready to fill.

Raspberry Curd

270ml fresh raspberry purée (see page 242)
270g caster sugar
270g whole eggs
4g gellan gum type F
250g butter (diced)

Place the raspberry purée, sugar, eggs and gellan gum into a Thermomix and blend on setting 6 for 7 minutes at 80°C. Add the butter and continue to blend for a further 3 minutes.

Pass the mixture through a fine chinois into a container. Press cling film onto the surface of the mixture. Store in the fridge until required.

Raspberry Gel

6g gellan gum type F
100g caster sugar
600ml fresh raspberry purée (see page 242)

Rub the gellan gum through the sugar. Blend this sugar mixture through the purée with a stick blender in a pot. Place the pot on the heat and slowly bring up to the boil, stirring constantly. Once boiled, remove from the heat.

Blend the mixture once again with a stick blender. Pass through a fine chinois and pour into a non-stick tray. Set in the fridge.

Once fully cooled, place the gel in a blender and blend on full power to a smooth, silky gel. Transfer the gel to a squeezy bottle. Refrigerate until required.

Raspberry Rocks & Powder

300ml fresh raspberry purée (see page 242)
80g white chocolate
120g tapioca maltodextrin

(Prepare ahead)

Place the raspberry purée in a heavy-based pot. Place on a high heat and reduce down to 100ml. Stir in the white chocolate and remove from the heat.

Place the tapioca maltodextrin into a large bowl and pour over the raspberry and white chocolate mixture. Stir until everything is fully incorporated.

Using your hand, form 2 balls from about a third of the mixture. Break the balls into rough chunks and place onto a silicone mat. Dehydrate at 57°C for 24 hours.

Place the remaining mixture into a blender and blend on full to a fine powder. Dehydrate the powder for 24 hours at 54°C.

Store both the rocks and powder separately in the fridge.

Vanilla Crème Brûlée

15 egg yolks
2 vanilla pods (seeds of)
360g caster sugar
820ml double cream

Place the egg yolks, vanilla seeds and sugar into a mixer and whisk with a whisk attachment until doubled in size, thickened and fluffy.

Bring the cream up to the boil and pour over the egg yolk, vanilla seeds and sugar mixture.

Transfer to a large, wide-based pot and cook out the eggs over a gentle heat while stirring.

The mixture should coat a spoon and be extremely thick.

Pass the mixture though a fine chinois onto a large deep tray. Press cling film onto the surface of the mixture and refrigerate.

Once chilled and set, transfer the mixture to a piping bag and store in the fridge.

Continued: Raspberry Bonfire

Raspberry Mousse

400ml fresh raspberry purée (see page 242)
5 egg whites
160g caster sugar
400ml double cream
2 vanilla pods (seeds of)

Place the raspberry purée into a heavy-based pot and reduce down to 200ml. Remove from the heat and allow to cool completely.

Add the egg whites to a bowl and whisk to soft peaks. Slowly add the sugar while whisking to a sturdy French meringue.

Semi-whip the double cream with the vanilla seeds.

Fold the meringue mixture into the whipped cream. Slowly add the purée to the cream and meringue while stirring. Place the mousse into a piping bag and refrigerate until ready to use.

Lemon Sherbet

250g caster sugar
1 lemon (zest and juice of)
1 tsp ascorbic acid
1 tsp bicarbonate of soda

(Prepare ahead)

Mix all of the ingredients together. Dehydrate the mixture on a silicone mat for 48 hours at 60°C. Store in an airtight container.

Vanilla Sorbet

2 vanilla pods (seeds of)
1 litre milk
280g caster sugar
300ml double cream
40g liquid glucose

(Prepare ahead)

Place all of the ingredients into a large, metal bowl and whisk together.

Pour into a container and freeze for 24 hours. Portion the block into cubes and blend on a medium speed in a food processor until smooth. Spoon the mixture into a piping bag. Pipe into 12 of the raspberry tubes and return them immediately back into the freezer until required. Any leftover mix can be stored in the freezer for future use.

Raspberry Sorbet

666ml water
333g caster sugar
45g liquid glucose
1 litre fresh raspberry purée (see page 242)

(Prepare ahead)

Bring the water, sugar and glucose to the boil. Pour over the raspberry purée and whisk together well. Allow to cool. Pour into a container and freeze for 24 hours.

Cut the mixture into cubes and blend on a medium speed in a blender until smooth and lighter in colour. Place in a piping bag. Pipe into 12 of the raspberry tubes and return straight back into the freezer until required. Any leftover mix can be stored in the freezer for future use.

To Assemble

18 fresh raspberries

Scatter the raspberry rocks and powder around each plate.

Place the curd into a piping bag. Pipe the curd, mousse and brûlée into 12 tubes each.

Place the lemon sherbet into a piping bag and cut off just the tip; this is to guide it into the tubes. Pipe the sherbet into 12 tubes.

Stack 12 tubes rustically on each plate (2 of each flavour). Dot the gel around each plate and randomly on top of the tubes.

Scatter 3 fresh raspberries around each plate.

Pumpkin & Gingerbread
Serves 6-8

Ginger & Stout Cake

225g butter
225g brown sugar
225g treacle
2 eggs
340g plain flour
2 tsp ground ginger
2 tsp ground cinnamon
200ml milk
330ml stout (reduced to 85ml)

Preheat the oven to 180°C.

Melt the butter, sugar and treacle together in a large pot.

Pour the mixture into a mixer fitted with a paddle. Slowly add in the eggs while mixing. Sift in the flour and spices, then slowly pour in the milk and stout.

Pour into a tray lined with silicone paper. Bake for 30 minutes.

Leave to cool on a rack, then freeze for 2 hours to 'tighten up' the sponge and make it easier to slice. Portion into rectangles measuring 9½cm x 2cm x 2cm.

Pumpkin Purée & Syrup

2 large pumpkins

(Prepare ahead)

Preheat the oven to 180°C.

Remove the seeds from the pumpkins and portion each pumpkin into 20 similar sized pieces.

Place the pumpkin pieces in a large roasting tray and roast for 25-30 minutes until the pumpkin has started to caramelise. Remove from the oven and allow to cool for 15 minutes.

Using a large spoon, scoop out the flesh of the pumpkin and discard the skin.

Add the pumpkin flesh into a blender. Blend on a medium setting for 5 minutes. Transfer the purée to a muslin cloth and hang over a container for 24 hours.

Reduce the liquid that has fallen through the muslin to a thick syrup.

Pumpkin Jelly

1kg pumpkin purée
10 egg yolks
100g caster sugar
10 leaves gelatine (soaked in cold water)
60ml pumpkin syrup

(Prepare ahead)

Place the pumpkin purée into a Thermomix with the egg yolks and sugar and blend at 80°C on setting 5 for 5 minutes.

Add the gelatine and the pumpkin syrup reduction and blend for a further 5 minutes.

Set in a tray 20cm x 40cm lined with cling film. Refrigerate for a minimum of 5 hours.

Once set, portion into rectangles measuring 9½cm x 2cm x 4cm in height.

Pumpkin Curd

280g pumpkin purée
30ml pumpkin syrup
270g whole eggs
350g butter
180g caster sugar
5g gellan gum type F
4 leaves gelatine (soaked in cold water)

Place the pumpkin purée, syrup, eggs, butter, sugar and gellan gum into a Thermomix. Blend at 90°C on setting 5 for 5 minutes.

Add the gelatine and blend for a further 5 minutes. Pour into a 2 litre container and press cling film onto the surface to prevent a skin forming. Leave to cool for approximately 2 hours in the fridge or until cold.

When the mixture is completely cold, place into a mixer with a whisk attachment and whisk on full for 5 minutes. Transfer into piping bags and store in the fridge until needed.

Maple Stout Gel

660ml stout
200ml maple syrup
7g gellan gum type F

Reduce the stout down to 400ml, then add the maple syrup and gellan gum. Blend with a stick blender.

Bring the liquid to the boil, then blend again with a stick blender. Set in a container until solidified.

Blend the mixture in a blender on a medium speed for 6-7 minutes.

Spiced Caramel

480g caster sugar
10g cumin seeds
1 stick cinnamon
45g ground ginger
160g butter
400ml double cream

Place the sugar in a heavy-based pot and melt to a golden brown caramel. Add the cumin seeds, cinnamon and ginger and stir for 5 minutes. Add in the butter and stir until completely incorporated.

Slowly stir in the cream and bring to the boil. Pass the caramel through a fine sieve and leave to cool.

Microwave Pistachio Sponge

160g ground pistachios
150g caster sugar
50g plain flour
sea salt (pinch of)
300g egg whites

(Prepare ahead)

Place the ground pistachios, sugar, flour and salt in a blender. Blend on a medium speed for 10 seconds. Add in the egg whites and blend on full for 20 seconds.

Pass the mixture through a fine chinois straight into an espuma gun and add 2 charges. Refrigerate for 2 hours.

Pierce 6 holes in the bottom of 6 plastic cups. Empty 35g of mixture into each cup.

Place one cup at a time into a microwave for 40 seconds. Remove the cup from the microwave and immediately place the cup upside down on a cooling rack. Leave until completely cold.

Repeat until all of the mixture is used up.

Remove the microwaved sponge from the cups and place in the dehydrator at 60°C for 8 hours, turning the sponge over after 4 hours.

Milk & Yoghurt Sorbet

800ml milk
250g caster sugar
200ml double cream
300ml natural yoghurt

(Prepare ahead)

Place the milk, sugar and cream into a heavy-based pot and bring to the boil.

Remove from the heat and whisk in the yoghurt using a stick blender, blending the mixture thoroughly.

Pour into an airtight container and freeze for 24 hours.

After 24 hours, blend the sorbet in a food processor on a medium speed until smooth. Place back in the freezer and store until required.

Praline Tuile

300g caster sugar
water
30g sliced almonds

Place the caster sugar in a heavy-based pot and add just enough water to cover it. Bring to a rapid boil and cook until a golden caramel is achieved. Pour onto a non-stick baking mat, sprinkle over the sliced almonds and leave to cool completely.

Break the praline into shards. Blitz to a fine powder using a food processor.

Preheat the oven to 175°C.

Line a flat baking sheet with silicone paper. Sieve the sugar and almond powder straight onto the silicone paper until an even coating is achieved. Bake for 8-9 minutes until it all melts back together and is a shiny caramel colour. Allow to cool for 5 minutes. Cut strips 1½cm x 15cm in length. Allow to cool completely and store in an airtight container.

To Assemble

pecan nuts (toasted), 1 per plate

Arrange a rectangle of the sponge onto each plate and top with a rectangle of the pumpkin jelly.

Place 2 pieces of the pistachio sponge opposite the cake. Pipe some of the pumpkin curd between the sponges. Dot the spiced caramel and maple stout gel around and over the cake.

Rocher 2 scoops of the yoghurt sorbet, 1 on the plate and 1 on the cake. Top the sorbet on the cake with the praline tuile.

Pear Jam Jar
Makes 10 jam jars

Vanilla Parfait

7 egg yolks
325g caster sugar
24g liquid glucose
3 leaves gelatine (soaked in cold water)
4 egg whites
2 vanilla pods (seeds of)
900ml double cream

Place the egg yolks, 212g of the sugar and the glucose into a Thermomix at 80°C for 5 minutes on setting 6.

Add in the gelatine and continue to blend for a further 5 minutes.

Whisk the egg whites to soft peaks and gradually add in the remaining caster sugar until a stiff French meringue is achieved.

Add the vanilla seeds to the cream, then whip the cream to soft peaks.

Slowly add the egg yolk mixture to the semi-whipped double cream and stir until fully incorporated.

Fold the meringue into this mixture.

Pour the mixture into piping bags and pipe into jam jars to a 3cm depth. Set the jars in the freezer for 3 hours or until frozen, depending on the freezer.

Pear Jelly

5g gellan gum type F
50g caster sugar
300ml pear cider
300g pear purée (see page 242)

With your fingers, rub together the gellan gum and sugar.

Add the sugar mixture to the cider and blend with a stick blender. Add the pear purée, bring the mixture to the boil and blend again with a stick blender.

Pour into a cling film lined, flat tray, 2cm deep and allow to cool in the refrigerator for 1 hour.

Using a ring cutter, cut out discs of the jelly (the diameter will depend on the size of your jam jars).

Store the discs between layers of silicone paper in the fridge.

Pear Compôte

300g caster sugar
1kg pears (peeled, diced)

Make a dry caramel with the sugar, until golden brown, in a heavy-based pot.

Add in the pears and cook out over a low heat for 10 minutes until the pears start breaking down but before they turn into mush.

Pear Espuma

200g pear purée (see page 242)
100ml pear cider
100ml milk
100ml double cream
8 egg yolks
105g caster sugar
½ tsp xanthan gum

Place the pear purée, cider, milk and cream in a heavy-based pot. Slowly bring the mixture to the boil, then remove from the heat. Place the egg yolks and sugar in a Thermomix, blend on speed 5 for 5 minutes. Pour over the milk and pear mixture and blend on speed 5 at 80°C for a further 5 minutes. Add the xanthan gum and blend for a further 2 minutes. Pass through a fine chinois. Pour the mixture into an espuma gun, charge the gun with 2 charges, shaking well after each charge. Refrigerate for 2 hours.

Pear Tuile

200g pear purée (see page 242)
25g caster sugar
¼ tsp crytex

(Prepare ahead)

Blend all of the ingredients together. Spread thinly on a silicone mat and dehydrate for 24 hours at 60°C.

Portion the crisps into rectangles 2cm x 4cm. Store between layers of silicone paper in the freezer.

Pear Sorbet

665ml water
333g caster sugar
45g liquid glucose
1 litre pear purée (see page 242)

(Prepare ahead)

Bring the water, sugar and glucose to the boil. Once it reaches the boil, pour the syrup over the pear purée and whisk together well. Allow the mixture to cool and then freeze in an airtight container for 24 hours.

Cut the sorbet into rough cubes and blend in a food processor until smooth and lighter in colour. Re-freeze until set.

Rice Pudding

20g butter
300g pudding rice
150g caster sugar
3 vanilla pods (scraped)
1.2 litres milk

Melt the butter in a large pot. Add the pudding rice, sugar and vanilla pods and seeds and stir for 3-5 minutes over a medium heat.

Add half the milk and bring to the boil, then reduce the heat and slowly cook until al dente. Slowly add in the remaining milk, stirring until it is absorbed.

Discard the vanilla pods and store in the fridge until ready to serve.

To Assemble

milk (to loosen)

Heat up the rice pudding, loosening it with a little extra milk so it is glossy and creamy.

Add a spoonful of the compôte on top of the parfait at the bottom of the jar.

Add a circle of jelly and press down lightly to even out the compôte. Place a generous spoon of rice pudding on top of the jelly.

Express the espuma on top of the rice pudding.

Using an upturned jar lid, scoop a generous amount of sorbet onto each lid, top with pear tuile and serve immediately.

'Roks' & Moss
Serves 15

Liquid Chocolate

65g dark chocolate
45g milk chocolate
80ml milk
175ml double cream
30g honey
½ vanilla pod (seeds of)

(Prepare ahead)

Melt the dark and milk chocolates together in a metal bowl over a bain-marie.

Heat the milk, cream, honey and vanilla in a heavy-based pot. Remove from the heat as soon as it reaches the boil.

Pour the milk mixture over the melted chocolate and leave to stand for 5 minutes. Using a stick blender, blend everything together and pass through a fine chinois. Leave to stand for 5 minutes, then skim off the foam.

Set in a tray lined with silicone paper to a thickness of 1cm and freeze until required.

Cut the frozen chocolate using an oval cutter 8cm in length, then place the ovals back into the freezer. Defrost the trimmings, transfer to a mixing bowl and whisk on full power until stiff. Store in a container in the fridge until ready to serve.

Carbon Black Cocoa Butter

200g white chocolate
450g cocoa butter
6g carbon black

Melt the white chocolate and cocoa butter in a metal bowl over a bain-marie.

Add in the carbon black and blend with a stick blender until fully emulsified, then allow the mixture to cool to 20-30ºC.

Remove the oval-cut 'liquid chocolate' from the freezer and dip into the carbon black cocoa butter. Rest on a cooling rack for 10 seconds, then transfer to a tray lined with silicone paper. Store in the fridge in an airtight container until required.

Chocolate Ganache

400g dark chocolate
30g butter
80g icing sugar
300ml milk
300ml double cream
6 spearmint leaves (finely shredded)

(Prepare ahead)

Melt the dark chocolate, butter and icing sugar in a metal bowl over a bain-marie.

Heat the milk and cream in a heavy-based pot. Remove from the heat as soon as it reaches the boil. Pour the heated milk and cream over the melted chocolate and whisk together until emulsified and thick.

Fold in the spearmint leaves, then pour the mixture into 2 piping bags and leave to chill in the fridge. Once chilled, pipe the ganache into discs (3cm in diameter) onto flat trays lined with silicone paper. Freeze for 5 hours or until completely frozen.

Carbon Grey Cocoa Butter

200g white chocolate
450g cocoa butter
2g carbon black

Melt the white chocolate and cocoa butter in a metal bowl over a bain-marie.

Add in the carbon black and blend with a stick blender until everything is emulsified together, then let the mixture cool to 20-30ºC. Dip the frozen chocolate ganache into the carbon grey cocoa butter and rest on a cooling rack for 10 seconds. Transfer to a tray lined with silicone paper and store in an airtight container in the freezer until required.

Continued: 'Roks' & Moss

Honey Tuile

150ml double cream
60g butter
120g honey
450g caster sugar
120g plain flour
70g sesame seeds

Add the cream, butter, honey and sugar into a heavy-based pot and bring to the boil. Remove from the heat and add the dry ingredients to the mixture. Whisk together until fully incorporated. Allow to cool.

Preheat the oven to 175°C.

Scrape small amounts of the mixture onto trays lined with silicone paper, bake for 13 minutes until golden brown. Remove from the oven and place another sheet of silicone paper on top of the mixture, roll with a rolling pin until flat and glassy. Discard the top layer of silicone and portion the tuile into 1½cm x 30cm strips. Wrap each strip around a 9½cm diameter metal ring.

Remove from the metal ring and allow to cool. Store in an airtight container.

Pistachio Sponge

160g pistachios (peeled, blanched)
150g caster sugar
300g egg whites
50g ground almonds

Blend the pistachios to a fine powder on a medium speed in a food processor. Pour in the sugar, then blend again, scraping the sides of the mixer to ensure all the mixture is fully incorporated.

Add the egg whites and blend again for 20 seconds. Finally, add the almonds and blend on full power for 25 seconds. Pass the mixture though a fine chinois, then transfer into an espuma gun and charge 3 times.

Pierce 6 holes in the bottom of 6 plastic cups, fill each cup one third of the way up with the pistachio mixture. Microwave each cup on full power (850W) for 45 seconds. Remove from the microwave and turn upside down, leave to completely cool down inside the cup. Repeat until all of the mixture is used up. Once all are cooled, gently run a knife around the edge of the cups to release the sponge and rest on a tray lined with silicone paper. Dehydrate on the dehydrator's highest setting for 12 hours.

Break each 'sponge' into about 5 equal pieces, store in an airtight container in a cool dry place.

Crystallised Pistachios

200g pistachios (peeled, blanched)
200g caster sugar
150ml water

Preheat the oven to 175°C.

Roast the pistachios for 15 minutes.

Bring the sugar and water to the boil in a large, heavy-based pot. Stir well, bring the sugar syrup to 135°C, then pour in the pistachios. Keep stirring vigorously with a wooden spoon until crystallised. Allow the crystallised pistachios to cool on a tray lined with silicone paper, then store in an airtight container until required.

Coffee Macarons

125g caster sugar
120g egg whites
125g icing sugar
125g ground almonds
8g ground coffee

Preheat the oven to 150°C.

Combine the caster sugar and 60g of the egg whites in a metal bowl over a bain-marie, stir continuously until the sugar has dissolved. Transfer the mixture to a mixer and whisk on full power until cold.

Add the remaining egg whites, icing sugar, ground almonds and coffee to a food processor and blend at a medium speed until completely incorporated. Fold this paste into the meringue one third at a time, until completely combined. Pipe the macaron mixture into 3cm rounds onto flat trays lined with silicone paper, then leave to dry out at room temperature for 25 minutes. Once dry, bake the macarons for 15 minutes.

Remove the macarons from the oven, slide the silicone paper off the tray and allow to cool on a cold work surface. Once cooled, store in an airtight container in the freezer.

Candied Kumquats

1kg kumquats (halved, deseeded)
2kg caster sugar
500ml water

Add the kumquats, sugar and water into a large pot and simmer for 3 hours, or until soft and tender. Drain the kumquats, keeping just enough sugar syrup to cover. Reserve the excess syrup for the purée.

Kumquat Purée

Place half of the candied kumquats with the reserved kumquat syrup into a Thermomix at setting 4 and 80°C, blend until smooth.

Pass through a fine chinois, store in the fridge.

Honeycomb & Kumquat Cream

400ml double cream
100g caster sugar
50g kumquat purée
150g honeycomb (crushed, see page 240)

Whip the double cream and sugar to soft peaks. Fold through the kumquat purée and crushed honeycomb, then continue to whip until stiff peaks are formed. Store in the fridge in an airtight container.

To Assemble

Place a honey tuile in the bottom of each bowl with a dipped liquid chocolate in the centre. Arrange the dipped chocolate ganache, pistachio sponge, crystallised pistachios, candied kumquats and coffee macarons inside the tuile, dot with kumquat purée. Using a hot teaspoon, rocher the set 'liquid chocolate', honeycomb and kumquat cream, then place on the top of each dessert.

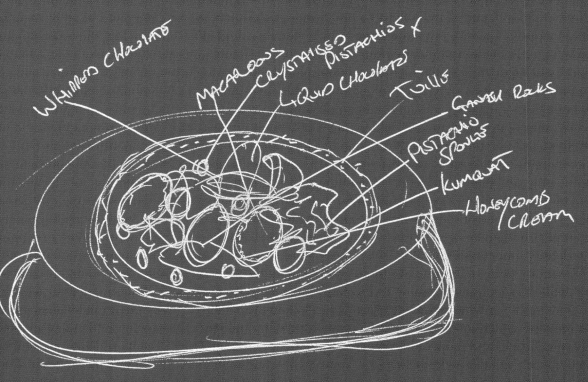

Berries

The summer months in Scotland bring an abundance of outstanding soft fruits. Soft fruit farming here has seen a steady growth in recent years and it is not difficult to see why the demand is so high. There is nothing more exciting for a Scottish chef than seeing the first strawberries of the season arrive in the kitchen. For me, they are second to none. During my five years in Australia, I never once put a strawberry dish on any of my menus. Once you have tasted Scottish strawberries then it is very difficult to settle for anything else. We have our wonderful climate to thank for our renowned berries. They thrive in the cooler summers where long daylight hours help them to ripen with plenty of flavour.

I choose Leadketty Fruit for berries during the summer months. They are set in the picturesque village of Dunning at the foot of the Ochil Hills. Their berries are handpicked, packed and delivered to the restaurant on the same day to ensure maximum freshness. Leadketty has been farming for the past 80 years under the capable stewardship of the Corrigall family. Harold Corrigall and son Stephen manage 16 hectares of strawberries, employing over 100 people every year for the picking season during the long, summer months.

For me, Scottish berries and in particular strawberries, are a source of pride. In my opinion, they are the best in the world. During my first appearance on Great British Menu back in 2012, I chose strawberries as the star ingredient in my version of Eton Mess, page 222. This much requested dish is one which appears on my menu each year just as soon as the Scottish berries begin to arrive in my kitchen.

I am often asked in interviews what my favourite ingredient is, and my normal answer is that it depends on the day or season. I would say though that during the summer it would have to be strawberries or raspberries and, to be honest, they would need to fight it out as I couldn't possibly decide between them.

Eton Mess
Serves 6

Strawberry Custard Jelly

500ml strawberry purée (see page 243)
6 egg yolks
120g caster sugar
6 leaves gelatine (soaked in cold water)

Place the purée, egg yolks and sugar in a Thermomix. Blend on setting 6 until the mixture reaches 80°C. Add the drained gelatine and continue to blend for a further 3 minutes.

Pass the mixture through a fine chinois onto a tray covered with cling film to a 1cm thickness. Set in the fridge for 4 hours, then cut into 1cm cubes. Place back in the fridge until ready to use.

Meringue

150g egg whites (room temperature)
280g caster sugar

Whisk the egg whites on medium speed until soft peaks are achieved.

Slowly add the sugar in a steady stream while whisking until fully incorporated and stiff peaks are created. Spread the mixture thinly on silicone paper and dry out in a dehydrator at the highest setting for 3 hours. Once dry, break into shards and store in an airtight container.

Strawberry Fluid Gel

6g gellan gum type F
150g caster sugar
600ml fresh strawberry juice

Rub the gellan gum through the sugar. Mix the strawberry juice with the sugar and gellan gum and place in a pot. Slowly bring the mixture to the boil.

Pass through a fine chinois, then refrigerate in a container for 30 minutes. Once set, blend on a medium speed for 10 minutes until smooth. Pass again through a chinois and store in a squeezy bottle.

Strawberry Leather

100ml strawberry purée (see page 243)
80g icing sugar
½ tsp Crisp Film

(Prepare ahead)

Blend all the ingredients together, then pass through a fine chinois onto a silicone mat to ¼cm thickness. Dry in a dehydrator at its highest setting for 12 hours. Cut into triangles whilst still warm and store between sheets of silicone paper in an airtight container.

Marshmallows

11 leaves gelatine
450g caster sugar
3 vanilla pods (seeds of)
375g liquid glucose
½ tsp sea salt
caster sugar (for dredging)

Soak the gelatine in 245ml of cold water and gently melt it in the same water. Pour this melted gelatine into a mixing bowl and start whisking.

Combine the sugar, vanilla and liquid glucose with 125ml of water and boil hard for 1½ minutes. Pour the boiling syrup onto the gelatine, add the salt and whisk for exactly 12 minutes, then scrape into a tray lined with cling film until 1½cm thick. Leave to set in the fridge for 1 hour. Cut into 1cm x 3cm rectangles and dredge in sugar.

Crème Chantilly

400ml double cream
1 vanilla pod (seeds of)
60g icing sugar

Whip all ingredients together until soft peaks are achieved. Store in the fridge until required.

Dipped Strawberries

200g caster sugar
6 strawberries

Place the sugar in a dry pan over a medium heat and melt to a light caramel. Allow the caramel to cool slightly. Dip the tip of each strawberry in the caramel and allow a thread to form.

To Assemble

10 strawberries (quartered)
1 punnet frozen raspberry cells (freeze the raspberries, then break up, store in freezer)
frozen strawberry espuma (see page 240)
1 packet baby basil (20g)

Plate the dish on 6 cold plates.

Scatter the strawberry quarters evenly between the plates. Place 4 cubes of the custard jelly onto each plate and dot the fluid gel around the jelly and strawberries.

Using a blow torch, lightly toast the top of each marshmallow and place one on each plate. Quenelle 3 teaspoons of crème Chantilly onto each dish. Scatter the meringue, frozen raspberry cells and frozen espuma. Place a dipped strawberry on each plate. Top with baby basil and strawberry leather.

Clootie Dumpling
Serves 6-8

Clootie Dumpling

230g butter
275ml water
180g caster sugar
15g treacle
230g plain flour
15g ground cinnamon
15g ground ginger
25g mixed spice
5g bicarbonate of soda
455g mixed dried fruit
2 eggs

Melt the butter, water, 115g of the sugar and the treacle together in a large, heavy-based pot.

Place the flour, ground spices, bicarbonate of soda and remaining sugar in a large metal bowl and combine well. Add these dry ingredients to the melted ingredients and mix well.

Stir in the dried fruit and beat in the eggs.

Divide the mixture in half. Roll each half of the mixture in cling film to make a log, about 30cm x 10cm, making sure you use plenty of cling film. Tie all the ends off securely either with string or extra cling film. Steam for 2 hours.

Burnt Orange Jelly

275g caster sugar
1 lime (zest of)
1 lemon (zest of)
1 orange (zest of)
4 vanilla pods (seeds of)
1 litre fresh orange juice
14 leaves gelatine (soaked in cold water)

Place the sugar into a heavy-based pot and set over a high heat. Stir with a wooden spoon until the sugar is equally melted to a golden caramel. Remove from the heat and add the zests and vanilla seeds. Very slowly, add the orange juice, stirring frequently until all the liquid has been incorporated.

Return to the heat and bring to the boil. Add in the soaked gelatine and stir until dissolved. Pass the liquid through a fine chinois and leave to cool. Pour into a tray 2½cm thick. Set in the fridge. Once set, cut into 2½cm cubes.

Treacle Meringues

100g treacle
50g caster sugar
50ml water
100g egg whites

(Prepare ahead)

Add the treacle, sugar and water to a pot and place over a high heat.

Meanwhile whisk the egg whites to soft peaks.

Bring the treacle mixture up to 113°C. Slowly pour the treacle mixture onto the egg whites while whisking. Continue to whisk until cool.

Place the mixture into a piping bag fitted with a 2cm nozzle. Pipe small meringues onto a tray lined with silicone paper. Dehydrate the meringues for 24 hours at 60°C.

Store in the freezer until required; this will keep them crisp on the outside and slightly chewy in the middle.

Treacle Gel

100g treacle
100ml stock syrup (see page 243)
2g gellan gum type F

Place all of the ingredients into a pot, blend with a stick blender, bring to the boil and blend again.

Pour into a bowl and allow to cool at room temperature. Once cooled, place in a blender and blend on a medium speed until smooth. Transfer the mixture to a piping bag and store in the fridge.

Crème Fraîche & Vanilla Sorbet

750ml crème fraîche
240g caster sugar
15g liquid glucose
2 vanilla pods (seeds of)
750ml water

(Prepare ahead)

Place all the ingredients into a large, metal bowl and whisk together vigorously. Pour the mixture into a container and freeze for 24 hours.

Portion the sorbet into cubes and blend on a medium speed in a food processor until smooth and silky. Pour the mixture back into a container and store in the freezer until ready to use.

Continued: Clootie Dumpling

Puffed Wheat Caramel

150g caster sugar
340g puffed wheat

In a non-stick pan, make a dry caramel with the sugar until completely melted and golden brown. Remove from the heat and add the puffed wheat. Mix through until well incorporated, then turn the mixture out onto silicone paper. Allow to cool.

Puffed Wheat Tuile

100g puffed wheat caramel

Preheat the oven to 200°C.

Blend the caramel to a fine powder and pass through a fine chinois onto a baking tray lined with silicone paper. Bake for 8 minutes until golden brown. Remove from the oven and allow to cool.

Break into random shards and store in an airtight container.

Treacle Cream

150ml double cream
½ vanilla pod (seeds of)
25g caster sugar
50g treacle

Place the cream, vanilla seeds and sugar into a bowl and whip to soft peaks. Fold through the treacle. Store in the fridge until ready to use.

To Assemble

Make sure the clootie dumpling is still warm and break it into random shaped chunks. If it has cooled down, reheat it in boiling water for 20 minutes. Scatter 5 pieces onto each plate.

Rocher 3 teaspoons of the treacle cream onto each plate.

Scoop or rocher a tablespoon of the ice cream onto the middle of each dish.

Sit 3 cubes of the jelly on each plate, making sure it is not touching the clootie as this will cause it to melt.

Scatter over 7 meringues and some broken puffed wheat caramel. Stick some of the puffed wheat tuile into the treacle cream.

Finally, randomly dot 11 dots of the treacle gel onto each plate.

Cranachan
Serves 6

Duck Egg & Whisky Set Custard

10 duck egg yolks
260g caster sugar
600ml double cream
350ml milk
50ml whisky
10 leaves gelatine (soaked in cold water)

(Prepare ahead)

Place the egg yolks and sugar into a mixing bowl and whisk until doubled in volume, thick and fluffy.

Place the cream, milk and whisky into a heavy-based pan and bring to the boil. Pour the hot liquid over the egg yolk mixture, place the mixture back into the pan and cook out to 85°C. The mixture should be thick and coat the back of a spoon.

Add the soaked gelatine, then pass the mixture through a fine chinois into a blender. Blend on full power for 25 seconds to get rid of any air and pour into ring moulds, 5cm in diameter and 6cm in height, but filling only three quarters of the way up the mould. Leave to set in the fridge for 24 hours.

Raspberry & Whisky Leather

300g raspberry purée (see page 242)
25ml whisky
45g caster sugar
¼ tsp crytex

(Prepare ahead)

Blend all the ingredients together and pass through a fine chinois. Spread the raspberry mixture out thinly on silicone mats and dehydrate for 24 hours at 60°C.

Once the leather has dehydrated, cut into 12cm squares, then scrunch each square up randomly to achieve height. Once these cool to room temperature they will become crisp and very fragile.

Raspberry & Whisky Granita

100ml whisky
150g caster sugar
500ml hot water
300g raspberry purée (see page 242)

(Prepare ahead)

Pour the whisky, sugar and water into a pot. Over a low heat, dissolve the sugar.

Once dissolved, mix in the raspberry purée.

Pour into a 30cm x 30cm tray and store in the freezer. Scrape the mixture every 30 minutes with a fork and leave in the freezer until completely frozen. This should take anywhere between 2-6 hours depending on the freezer.

Frozen Raspberry Cells

100g fresh raspberries

Place the raspberries on a tray lined with silicone paper and transfer to a freezer. After 2 hours, crumble the raspberries into cells and store in an airtight container in the freezer until required.

Praline Tuile

500g caster sugar
50g flaked almonds

Add just enough water to the sugar to make a paste and place over a high heat. Take this to a deep caramel, then add in the almonds. Pour onto a tray lined with silicone paper and allow to cool.

Break the caramel into rough pieces and blend in a food processor to a fine powder.

Preheat the oven to 180°C.

Line a flat baking tray with silicone paper. Pass the praline powder through a sieve onto the silicone paper to create a fine layer. Any leftover powder can be stored in the freezer and used for other dishes.

Bake for 5 minutes until the praline melts back down and creates a fine sheet of caramel that resembles glass. If a few holes form, dust on more praline powder and re-bake in the oven until melted back together.

Honey Granola

200g rolled oats (toasted)
126g flaked almonds (toasted)
80g brown sugar
80g honey
60ml rapeseed oil
6g vanilla salt (see page 243)

Preheat the oven to 150°C.

Place the oats and almonds in a large bowl.

Combine the sugar, honey, oil and vanilla salt in a pan and dissolve the sugar over a low heat.

Continued: Cranachan

Pour the mixture onto the oats and almonds and mix thoroughly.

Spread onto a tray lined with silicone paper and bake in the oven for 30-40 minutes until golden brown, mixing occasionally. Allow to cool and store in an airtight container.

Crystallised Almonds & White Chocolate

150ml water
200g caster sugar
200g almonds (toasted)
150g white chocolate

Pour the water over the sugar in a large heavy-based pan and bring to the boil whilst stirring. Take the sugar syrup up to 135°C. Pour the nuts into the pan and stir with a wooden spoon until crystallised. Leave to cool on a tray lined with silicone paper.

Melt the white chocolate.

Using a small fork, pick up each almond and dip into white chocolate. Allow any excess chocolate to drip off before transferring onto a silicone mat.

Burnt Honey Clotted Cream

400g honey
500g clotted cream

Place 300g of the honey in a large, heavy-based pot over a high heat and whisk constantly. Caramelise the honey to a deep golden brown. Remove from the heat, add the remaining honey and whisk until incorporated. Skim the excess fat off the clotted cream and discard.

Put the cream into a bowl and slowly add the caramelised honey to the cream, whisking constantly.

Keep whisking to a set cream. Refrigerate until required.

To Assemble

30 fresh raspberries

Scatter some of the granola over the base of each plate. Top with one of the set custards standing on its side. Sit the crumpled up raspberry leather next to the custard.

Scatter 5 raspberries and some of the frozen raspberry cells over the dish.

Using a teaspoon, rocher 2 spoons of the honey clotted cream onto each plate.

Lightly crush the almonds and scatter over the dessert.

Break up the praline tuile and stick into the set custard and honey clotted cream.

Finally, scrape the granita once more with a fork and scatter over the whole dessert.

Salt

Natalie Crayton of Hebridean Sea Salt has only been producing sea salt for the last five years but I have become a devoted fan of hers. My attitude is, and has always been, that if you don't support new local businesses producing something fantastic, literally on your doorstep, how are they meant to grow and hopefully sit on the shelves next to the market leaders? Now there isn't a shortage of sea salt producers in the UK. In fact, the global leader when it comes to sea salt is based in England. However, there was a shortage of Scottish sea salt producers when Natalie first set up her now growing empire, which consists not only of the purest, tastiest sea salt in my mind, but also peat smoked salt which is smoked with a mixture of oak and peat, cut from the surrounding moor and seaweed infused salt, which uses dried seaweed harvested locally and is a great addition to any fish dish or goes particularly well with lamb.

When planning for my first appearance on BBC's Great British Menu in 2012, I wanted to source a very Scottish larder of produce from suppliers who I knew and trusted. For the most part, I was convinced of my success in this until I arrived on set for the first day of filming and noticed that Alan Murchison had some unusual salt with him. This was my first look at Hebridean Sea Salt and I knew immediately that I wanted to use it at the restaurant. I contacted Natalie in the following weeks and asked if she could send me some samples. The salt arrived in the original test packaging and looked very different from the polished packages which arrive today. However, what hasn't changed is the amazing almost gem-like contents.

Hebridean Sea Salt is Scotland's first artisan salt producer. Nestled on the banks of Loch Erisort, on the Isle of Lewis in the Outer Hebrides, they harvest salt water from some of the most unspoilt coastline in the world. It is pumped into an open pan, heated and condensed and the sea salt flakes that are created are harvested and dried before packing.

It all began for Natalie in 2011 having identified a gap in the market. She couldn't believe no one in Scotland was producing sea salt when Scotland's west coast water is so pure - the waters around the Hebrides are crystal clear and have been given a grade A certification for purity. As a result, Natalie's salt is pure, white, crunchy sea salt that tastes fantastic. She spent more than a year in research and development, before putting some salt into friends' hands to test and get feedback. Natalie then went on to secure sales in 400 independent delis and shops and to expand into two more units in remote South Lochs. She now employs three people within the business. Keeping the team small means Natalie can control every part of the process from start to finish.

Salt is such a vital ingredient in any kitchen. And in my opinion, Hebridean Sea Salt packs a massive flavour and can transform even the most humble of dishes. There is a common misconception that salt is a flavour enhancer when in reality it actually dulls bitter and sour notes, allowing other flavours to shine through. This is why salt is so important in so many of my dishes and even gets used in desserts as well as savoury dishes.

Blueberry | White Chocolate | Lemon
Serves 8

Dehydrated White Chocolate & Poppy Seed Mousse

500g white chocolate
280ml double cream
3 egg whites
160g caster sugar
40g poppy seeds

(Prepare ahead)

Add the white chocolate to a bowl and set over a bain-marie to melt completely.

Whip the double cream to soft peaks and set aside.

Place the egg whites in a mixer with a whisk attachment and whisk on full speed to soft peaks. Slowly add the sugar to the egg whites while whisking to a French meringue.

Pour the melted chocolate into the double cream whilst stirring.

Fold the French meringue and poppy seeds into the cream mixture until fully incorporated.

Set the mousse in a 15cm x 30cm tray and refrigerate for 2 hours.

Once fully set, place the mousse in a dehydrator at 58°C for 24 hours in the same tray.

Once dehydrated, break into random pieces.

Lemon Curd

9 lemons (zest and juice of)
600g caster sugar
9 eggs
10 egg yolks
350g butter (cold, diced)

Place all the ingredients, except the butter, into a Thermomix on setting 4 at 80°C for 8 minutes. Add the butter and continue to blend on the same setting for a further 2 minutes. Pass the mixture through a fine chinois. Refrigerate until required.

Lemon Curd Ice Cream

450ml double cream
7 egg yolks
325g caster sugar
22g liquid glucose
3 leaves gelatine (soaked in cold water)
3 egg whites
450g lemon curd

Whip the double cream to soft peaks.

Place the egg yolks, 212g of the sugar and the glucose into a Thermomix on setting 6 at 80°C for 5 minutes. Add the gelatine and continue to blend on the same setting for a further 5 minutes.

Whisk the egg whites to soft peaks, then gradually add the remaining 113g of sugar and whisk to a stiff French meringue.

Slowly add the egg yolk mixture into the double cream and stir until incorporated. Fold in the French meringue to this mixture.

Finally, fold in the lemon curd. Pour the mixture into an airtight container and freeze.

Dehydrated Lemon Curd Crisps

200g lemon curd

(Prepare ahead)

Spread the lemon curd mixture thinly on to silicone paper and dehydrate for 24 hours at 56°C. Break into random shards and store in an airtight container.

Blueberry Gel

250g blueberries
500ml sparkling water
½ lemon (juice of)
175g caster sugar
1% gellan gum type F
25g caster sugar

Place the blueberries, sparkling water, lemon juice and 150g of the caster sugar into a bowl and cling film tightly.

Place the bowl over a pan of boiling water and cook for 1½ hours. Drain the liquid, discarding the blueberries.

Weigh the liquid and then weigh out 1% of gellan gum type F. Rub the gellan gum through the remaining 25g of sugar and blend through the liquid with a stick blender.

Place in a pot over a medium heat and slowly bring to the boil, stirring constantly. Once boiled, remove from the heat and blend again with a stick blender.

Pass the mixture through a fine chinois and set in a tray. Once fully cooled, transfer the set gel to a blender and blend on a high speed to a smooth, silky gel. Decant into a squeezy bottle.

Blueberry Jelly

1kg blueberry purée (see page 238)
100g caster sugar
4g gellan gum type F

(Prepare ahead)

Place the blueberry purée into a muslin cloth and hang in the fridge overnight.

Weigh out 400ml of the liquid, add in the sugar and gellan gum. Blend with a stick blender.

Place the mixture in a pot over a medium heat.

Place a sheet of acetate 60cm x 30cm on a flat surface ensuring there are no air bubbles.

Once the blueberry mixture has come up to the boil, remove it from the heat and blend once again with a stick blender.

Pour the liquid onto the acetate sheet evenly so it is flat. It should be about 2mm thick.

Cut lengths 2cm wide by 30cm long. Store in the fridge until required.

White Chocolate Microwave Sponge

110g white chocolate
208g whole eggs
82g caster sugar
2g vanilla salt (see page 243)
22g plain flour

Place the white chocolate into a bowl and set over a bain-marie to melt completely.

Place the eggs, sugar and salt into a blender and blend on a medium speed for 20 seconds. Add in the flour and blend again for 20 seconds.

Finally, add in the melted white chocolate and blend for 1 minute. Transfer the mixture to a 1 litre espuma gun and charge 3 times.

Pierce 5 holes in the bottom of 8 plastic cups.

Fill each cup a third of the way up with the white chocolate mixture. Microwave each cup on full power (850W) for 40 seconds. Remove from the microwave and turn upside down. Leave to completely cool down in the cup. Repeat until all the mixture is used up.

Once cool, gently run a knife around the edge of the cups, releasing the sponge.

Break into random chunks and store in an airtight container.

Poppy Seed Tuile

50ml double cream
20g butter
40g honey
150g caster sugar
40g plain flour
10g poppy seeds
3g Hebridean sea salt

Preheat the oven to 185°C.

Place the cream, butter and honey into a heavy-based pot and bring to the boil. Remove from the heat and add to the dry ingredients. Whisk together until fully incorporated. Allow the mixture to cool.

Scrape small amounts of the cooled mixture onto silicone paper lined trays. Bake in the oven for 13 minutes until golden brown.

Remove from the oven, place another sheet of silicone paper on top and roll until flat and glassy.

Remove the top layer of silicone paper and break the tuile into random shards.

Macerated Blueberries

150g caster sugar
1 vanilla pod (seeds of)
150ml water
1 lemon (zest of)
100g blueberries

Place the sugar, vanilla seeds, water and lemon zest into a pot and bring to the boil. Take off the heat and cool slightly. Pour the stock syrup over the blueberries and cover with cling film. Allow to cool.

To Assemble

120g lemon curd (in a piping bag)
gorse flowers (to garnish)

Place 4 chunks of the white chocolate sponge down the centre of each plate and add 4 pieces of the white chocolate mousse between the sponges.

Scatter some of the macerated blueberries on each plate on and over the sponge and mousse.

Interleave the blueberry jelly between the sponge and mousse. Dot 12 dots of the blueberry gel all over the ingredients.

Rocher 3 teaspoons of the lemon curd ice cream between the mousse and sponge.

Stick some of the lemon curd shards and poppy seed tuile in the ice cream and sponge.

Pipe some lemon curd over the ingredients and scatter some of the gorse flowers over the whole dish.

BLUEBERRY | WHITE CHOCOLATE | LEMON

Macarons | Passion Fruit Curd

Makes 50

Passion Fruit Curd

200ml passion fruit juice
200g caster sugar
3 eggs
3 egg yolks
115g butter

Place the juice, sugar, eggs and yolks in a bain-marie and stir until the sugar has dissolved and the mixture has reached 82°C. Leave to cool down completely.

Transfer the mixture into a blender with the butter and blend until smooth and shiny. Store in the fridge.

Macarons

150g egg whites
155g caster sugar
155g ground almonds
155g icing sugar

Place 75g of the egg whites and all the caster sugar in a bain-marie. Stir until the sugar has dissolved.

Meanwhile, place the remaining egg whites, the ground almonds and icing sugar into a blender and blend to a paste.

Whip up the egg whites and caster sugar to a meringue.

Fold the meringue into the paste then spoon the mixture into a piping bag. Pipe onto a baking tray lined with a silicone mat. Leave to dry out at room temperature for 20 minutes.

Preheat the oven to 150°C.

Bake for 15 minutes then lower the oven to 140°C and bake for a further 4 minutes.

Leave to cool.

To Assemble

Spoon a generous amount of passion fruit curd onto the flat side of half of the macarons and sandwich them together with the other half.

Chocolate Bars
Makes 12 bars

Salted Caramel

150g caster sugar
10g Hebridean sea salt
50g butter
100ml double cream

Place the sugar in a heavy-based pot over a medium heat. Melt to a golden brown caramel, add the salt and mix well. Stir in the butter until fully incorporated, followed by the cream. Allow to cool.

Chocolate

400g dark chocolate (70% callebaut)

Roughly chop 300g of the chocolate.

Finely chop the remaining 100g or process it in a food processor.

Place the roughly chopped chocolate in a bowl. Half fill a saucepan with hot water and place the bowl over it, making sure that the base of the bowl does not touch the water. Gently heat the water, ensuring it does not boil.

Stir using a spatula so that the chocolate melts smoothly and evenly. Check the temperature with a thermometer, when it reaches 55-58°C remove the chocolate from the bain-marie.

Set aside a third of the melted chocolate in a bowl in a warm place.

Add the 100g of finely chopped chocolate into the remaining two thirds of the melted chocolate, stirring constantly until it reaches 28-29°C.

Add the reserved melted chocolate to increase the temperature, it should reach 31-32°C. Stir until the correct temperature is reached. The chocolate is now 'tempered'.

Please check with your chocolate manufacturer as tempering guidelines may change depending on the brand of chocolate.

To Assemble

150g passion fruit curd (see page 242)

Pour the tempered chocolate into chocolate bar moulds. Tip out any excess and allow to set.

Fill the squares with the salted caramel and passion fruit curd and place in the fridge to set. Once set, top with a layer of tempered chocolate.

Allow to set before tipping the bars out of the moulds. Wrap each bar in tin foil, then a label or alternatively just serve them as they are.

Basic Recipes

Black Onion Ash

5 onions
smoked sea salt

(Prepare ahead)

Cut each onion into 5 thick slices and remove the skins. Season well with the salt.

Blacken the onions all over in a non-stick pan over a medium heat, turning every 3 or 4 minutes; this step should take a good half hour as the onions really do need to be black. Separate all of the onion layers and dehydrate on full power for 24 hours. Blend in a food processor, then pass through a fine chinois. Store in a clean, dry container.

Blueberry Purée

120g caster sugar
3 star anise
1kg fresh blueberries

Melt the sugar in a non-stick pan to create a light caramel. Add the star anise and blueberries. Cook for 5-6 minutes to break down the blueberries then remove the star anise. Blend to a smooth purée and pass through a fine chinois.

Bramble Purée

120g caster sugar
1½ sticks cinnamon
1kg fresh brambles

Melt the sugar in a non-stick pan to create a light caramel. Add the cinnamon sticks and brambles. Cook for 5-6 minutes to break down the brambles then remove the cinnamon sticks. Blend to a smooth purée and pass through a fine chinois.

Bread Tubes

6 slices white bread (crusts removed)
50g clarified butter
vegetable oil (for deep frying)

In a pasta machine, pass the bread through each size setting twice until the last setting is reached.

Cut each slice of bread into 2 rectangles.

Brush a metal tube, measuring approximately 2cm in diameter and 20cm in length, with a little oil and wrap it in silicone paper.

Lightly brush the bread rectangles with clarified butter. Wrap 2 of the rectangles around the pipe at a time pressing the edges together to form a tight seal.

Deep fry in the oil at 180°C until golden and crispy. Slide the bread off the pipe and allow to cool. Repeat with the remaining bread.

Burnt White Chocolate

300g white chocolate

Preheat the oven to 185°C.

Scatter the white chocolate evenly on a silicone mat and cook in the oven for 8 minutes.

Remove from the oven and mix through the chocolate well. Place back in the oven and cook for a further 5 minutes.

Remove from the oven and mix well again on the tray. Return to the oven and cook for 4 minutes.

Remove from the oven and mix well. Continue doing this until you have an even, walnut brown coloured, white chocolate. Allow to cool, then smash up into a crumble.

Butter Emulsion

1 litre water
250g butter
4g sea salt

Bring all the ingredients to the boil, then blend well with a stick blender. Keep warm and use as required.

Candied Fennel Seeds

100g caster sugar
70ml water
140g fennel seeds

Bring the sugar and water to 137°C. Pour in the fennel seeds and stir well to create crystallisation.

Cool on a flat tray. Store in airtight container until required.

Candied Kumquats

250g kumquats (halved, de-seeded)
900g caster sugar
1.8 litres water

Place the kumquats, sugar and water into a large pot and simmer for 2 hours until softened. Drain the kumquats and dice into 1cm cubes.

Candied Sea Buckthorn Berries

100g sea buckthorn berries
100g caster sugar
50ml water

Very gently mix together the sea buckthorn berries, sugar and water. Vacuum pack the ingredients and cook at 48°C for 3 hours in a water bath.

Cep Powder

200g ceps
100g button mushrooms
1½g sea salt

(Prepare ahead)

Clean all of the mushrooms well with a dry pastry brush.

Slice the mushrooms thinly and season with the salt. Place on a silicone mat and dehydrate for 24 hours on the dehydrator's highest setting. Blend in a food processor to a fine powder.

Cherry Purée

120g caster sugar
1 star anise
800g fresh cherries (stones removed)

Melt the sugar in a non-stick pan to create a light caramel. Add the star anise and the cherries. Cook for 10 minutes to break down the fruit. Remove the star anise and blend to a smooth purée. Pass through a fine chinois.

Chicken Stock

5kg chicken wings
5kg chicken carcases
1 bottle red wine

(Prepare ahead)

Preheat the oven to 185°C.

Roast the chicken wings for 35 minutes, turning every 10 minutes, until an even, golden brown colour is achieved.

Place the roasted chicken wings and uncooked chicken carcases in a large stockpot.

Cover with enough cold water to come 10cm above the bones. Bring to the boil and add the bottle of wine.

Skim any impurities from the top of the stock and simmer gently for 7 hours, skimming every 20 minutes or so.

Pass the chicken stock through fine muslin cloth. Refrigerate overnight, or for 8 hours.

Skim off any set fat from the stock.

Use as required.

Clarified Butter

250g unsalted butter

Gently melt the butter over a low heat in a saucepan until the butter starts to melt.

3 layers will form; the top layer, a white foam is the whey protein, and should be skimmed off with a spoon.

The milk solids will drop to the bottom of the saucepan and form a milky layer of sediment.

Pour off and keep the middle layer and discard the milky, bottom layer.

Crispy Pancetta

12 slices pancetta

Preheat the oven to 170°C.

Place the slices of pancetta between 2 sheets of silicone paper, then place between 2 baking trays.

Cook in the oven for 10-12 minutes until the pancetta is golden brown and crispy.

Double Chicken Stock

Step 1
5kg chicken wings
5kg chicken carcases
1 bottle red wine

(Prepare ahead)

Preheat the oven to 185°C.

Roast the chicken wings for 35 minutes, turning every 10 minutes, until an even, golden brown colour is achieved.

Place the roasted chicken wings and uncooked chicken carcases in a large stockpot. Cover with enough cold water to come 10cm above the bones. Bring to the boil and add the bottle of wine. Skim any impurities from the top of the stock and simmer gently for 7 hours, skimming every 20 minutes or so.

Pass the chicken stock through fine muslin cloth. Refrigerate overnight or for 8 hours.

Skim off any set fat from the stock and use in the next step.

Continued: Basic Recipes

Double Chicken Stock

Step 2
5kg chicken wings
5kg chicken carcases
1 bottle red wine

Preheat the oven to 185°C.

Roast the chicken wings for 35 minutes, turning every 10 minutes, until an even, golden brown colour is achieved.

Place the roasted chicken wings and uncooked chicken carcases in a large stockpot.

Cover with the stock from step 1. Bring to the boil and add the bottle of wine.

Skim any impurities from the top of the stock and simmer gently for 7 hours, skimming every 20 minutes or so.

Pass the chicken stock through fine muslin cloth. Refrigerate overnight or for 8 hours.

Skim off any set fat from the stock and use as required.

Duck Stock

2 duck carcases
2 bottles red wine (Malbec)

(Prepare ahead)

Preheat the oven to 185°C.

Roast the duck bones for 35 minutes, turning every 10 minutes, until an even, golden brown colour is achieved.

Remove the duck bones and place in a large stockpot. Cover with enough cold water to come 10cm above the bones.

Bring to the boil and add 1 bottle of wine.

Skim any impurities from the top of the stock and simmer gently for 7 hours, skimming every 20 minutes or so.

Pass the duck stock through fine muslin cloth. Refrigerate overnight or for 8 hours.

Skim off any set fat from the duck stock. Reduce the remaining bottle of wine in a heavy-based pot until it's a thick syrup consistency. Add the duck stock and bring to a rapid boil.

Skim the duck stock.

Elderflower Cordial

1 litre cold water
660g caster sugar
330g fresh elderflower flowers (picked)
2 lemons (zested, thinly sliced)
25g citric acid

(Prepare ahead)

Melt together the water and sugar in a deep saucepan. Allow to cool. When cold, add the elderflower flowers, lemons and citric acid.

Allow to infuse for 2 days. Pass through a double muslin cloth and store in sterile bottles.

Fish Stock

2kg white fish bones
2 coriander seeds
1 star anise
fennel pollen (pinch of)

(Prepare ahead)

Cover the fish bones with enough cold water to come 10cm above the bones. Bring to the boil and add the aromats.

Skim any impurities from the top of the stock and simmer gently for 20 minutes, skimming every 5 minutes or so.

Reduce the heat so it's not simmering and cook very, very gently for a further 20 minutes.

Refrigerate overnight or for 8 hours. Skim off any set fat that has formed on top of the stock.

Frozen Strawberry Espuma

65g caster sugar
200ml double cream
1 leaf gelatine (soaked in cold water)
800g strawberry purée

Freeze a cling film lined tray for 1 hour.

Add the sugar, double cream and gelatine to a pot and bring up to a simmer. Add the purée and pass through a fine chinois. Pour into an espuma gun, charge twice and refrigerate for 2 hours.

Express the mixture into the frozen tray and refreeze for a minimum of 4 hours. Break into random chunks and use as required.

Honeycomb

320g caster sugar
40g honey
120g liquid glucose
50ml water
12g bicarbonate of soda

Combine the sugar, honey, glucose and water in a wide heavy-based pot. Bring to the boil and cook out to 147°C, stirring constantly.

Whisk in the bicarbonate of soda and pour immediately onto a silicone paper lined tray.

Allow to cool for at least 60 minutes before using.

Lamb Stock

4kg lamb ribs (chopped)
2kg lamb leg bones and knuckles (chopped)
1 bottle red wine

Ask your butcher to chop up the bones for you so they fit in your largest stockpot.

(Prepare ahead)

Preheat the oven to 185°C.

Roast the lamb ribs for 35 minutes, turning every 10 minutes, until an even golden brown colour is achieved.

Place the roasted ribs, the uncooked lamb leg and knuckle bones into a large stockpot. Cover with enough cold water to come 10cm above the bones. Bring to the boil and add the bottle of wine.

Skim any impurities from the top of the stock. Simmer gently for 11 hours, skimming every 20 minutes or so.

Pass the lamb stock through fine muslin cloth. Refrigerate overnight or for 8 hours.

Skim off any set fat from the stock and use as required.

Macarons

135g egg whites
130g caster sugar
130g ground almonds
130g icing sugar

(Makes about 100)

Preheat the oven to 150°C.

Place 75g of the egg whites and all the caster sugar in a bain-marie and stir until the sugar has dissolved.

Meanwhile, place the remaining egg whites, the ground almonds and icing sugar into a blender and blend to a paste.

Whip up the egg whites and caster sugar to a meringue, then fold the meringue into the paste.

Spoon the mixture into a piping bag and pipe onto a baking tray lined with a silicone mat. Leave to dry out at room temperature for 20 minutes.

Bake for 15 minutes, then lower the oven to 140°C and bake for a further 4 minutes. Remove from the oven and run cold water between the baking mat and tray. Remove the baking mat from the tray immediately and place on a cold surface.

Once the macarons are cold, layer them between silicone paper and store in the freezer.

Mayonnaise

1 whole egg
1 egg yolk
1 tsp Dijon mustard
50ml sherry vinegar
500ml rapeseed oil
sea salt (to taste)

Combine the egg, egg yolk, mustard and vinegar in a bowl or the container of a food processor.

Set the food processor on medium speed, or whisk by hand, and gradually drizzle in the oil while whisking or blending. When all the oil has been added, taste and season with salt. If too thick, add a tablespoon of cold water to thin down.

Mushroom Powder

50g ceps
80g autumn chanterelles
300g button mushrooms
1½g sea salt

(Prepare ahead)

Clean all of the mushrooms well with a dry pastry brush, then slice thinly. Season with the salt.

Place on a silicone mat and dehydrate for 24 hours on the dehydrator's highest setting. Blend in a food processor to a fine powder.

Parsley Oil

300g flat leaf parsley (picked, stalks removed)
250ml rapeseed oil
sea salt (pinch of)

Blanch half of the parsley leaves in salted, boiling water for 30 seconds. Refresh in ice water until completely cold. Squeeze out all the excess water.

Add the blanched parsley, raw parsley and rapeseed oil to a blender and blend until smooth. Season with a pinch of salt. Pass through a fine sieve and reserve until required.

Passion Fruit Curd

180ml passion fruit juice
180g caster sugar
2 eggs
2 egg yolks
105g butter

Place the juice, sugar, eggs and yolks in a bain-marie and stir until the sugar has dissolved and the mixture has reached 82°C. Remove from the heat and leave to cool down completely.

Transfer the mixture to a blender with the butter and blend until smooth and shiny.

Store in the fridge.

Pear Purée

95g caster sugar
3 star anise
1kg fresh pears (peeled, deseeded)
60ml water

Melt the sugar in a non-stick pan to create a light caramel. Add the star anise and the pears.

Pour in the water, being careful as it will spit.

Cook for 5-6 minutes to break down the pears and introduce a light colour.

Remove the star anise, then blend to a smooth purée. Pass through a fine chinois.

Pork Crumb Crackling

20g pork rind crumble
vegetable oil (for deep frying)
sea salt

Deep fry the pork rind crumble at 210°C until puffed up, this should take approximately 15 seconds. Transfer to a clean j-cloth and season with salt. Allow to dry out in a warm environment.

Puffed Pork Skin

1 pork belly (all traces of meat removed from the underside)
vegetable oil (for deep frying)
sea salt (large pinch of)

(Prepare 4 days in advance)

Preheat the oven to 120°C.

Place the pork belly in a shallow tray and cover with cold water. Cover with tin foil and cook in the oven for 4 hours.

Drain off the water and, whilst still warm but not hot, scrape off any excess fat keeping the skin intact. Cut the skin into 8 even sized pieces.

Dehydrate on silicone paper in a dehydrator for 32 hours at its highest setting. Break the pork skin into random sized shards. Store in an uncovered container for a minimum of 48 hours.

Deep fry at 205°C so they are light and fluffy. Season with a pinch of salt.

Puff Pastry

225g strong flour
225g plain flour
¾ tsp sea salt
550g soft butter
3 tsp lemon juice
200ml cold water

Sieve both flours and salt together, then place into a large, metal mixing bowl.

Cut 200g of the butter into small slices and rub this through until it resembles fine breadcrumbs.

Add the lemon juice and water to the flour and lightly knead to form a smooth dough. Wrap the dough in cling film and refrigerate for 30 minutes.

Roll the pastry out on a lightly floured work surface to about 70cm x 40cm.

Slice the remaining butter and lay this over two-thirds of the dough. Fold the unbuttered dough third over the buttered one, then flip that over the remaining buttered third so that the butter is wrapped inside the dough.

Roll out the dough until it measures 35cm x 25cm. Refrigerate for 30 minutes.

Give the pastry what is known as 'one single turn'. Roll the pastry out towards the folds until it measures roughly 70cm x 40cm, then fold the pastry in by thirds again. Refrigerate for 30 minutes.

Give the pastry 3 more turns, refrigerating for 30 minutes between turns. Give the pastry one final turn and refrigerate for 1 hour. Remove from the fridge 10 minutes before using.

Raspberry Purée

1kg fresh raspberries
110g caster sugar
½ lime (zest and juice of)

Remove the stalks from the raspberries and discard.

Blend the sugar and raspberries together to a smooth consistency. Add the lime zest and juice, then pass through a fine chinois.

Saffron Mayonnaise

3 egg yolks
1 tsp Dijon mustard
2 tbsp sherry vinegar
saffron (large pinch of, soaked in 3 tbsp boiling water)
500ml rapeseed oil
sea salt (to taste)

Combine the egg yolks, mustard, vinegar, saffron and water in a bowl or the container of a food processor. Set the food processor on medium speed, or whisk by hand, and gradually drizzle in the oil while whisking or blending. When all the oil has been added, taste and season with salt.

Salt Baked Celeriac

250g plain flour
3 egg whites
150g rock salt
75ml water
1 celeriac

Mix the flour, egg whites and rock salt in a mixer for 4 minutes. Slowly add in the water until it becomes a tight dough. Keep mixing for a further 10 minutes.

Preheat the oven to 185°C.

Roll out the salt dough and encase the celeriac in the dough. Place the celeriac on a baking tray and bake for 1½ hours.

Allow to cool for 10 minutes, crack off and discard the salt dough. Peel the celeriac and use as required.

Stock Syrup

100g caster sugar
150ml water
½ vanilla pod
¼ stick cinnamon
1 star anise

Simmer all ingredients for 3-4 minutes. Store in an airtight container in the fridge until required. Strain before use.

Strawberry Purée

120g caster sugar
1kg fresh strawberries

Melt the sugar in a non-stick pan to create a light caramel. Add the strawberries and cook for 5-6 minutes to break down the fruit. Blend to a smooth purée, then pass through a fine chinois.

Sugar Ester

25g sugar ester
100ml cold water

Using a stick blender, blend the sugar ester through the water. Bring to a rapid boil, then blend again. Leave to cool. Once cold, use as required.

Sweetened Baby Capers

70g caster sugar
70ml water
400g mini capers

Boil the sugar and water, then allow to cool. Drain the capers of any liquid. Rinse well with cold water then dry. Pour the sugar syrup over the capers and leave to marinate for 2 hours. These will keep indefinitely in the fridge.

Tomato Ketchup

12 very ripe plum tomatoes (halved)
sea salt
1 clove garlic (peeled, sliced)
6 sprigs thyme
120g caster sugar
3 shallots (peeled, sliced)
400ml tomato juice
100ml cider vinegar

(Prepare ahead)

Place the tomatoes on an ovenproof tray and season generously with sea salt. Top with the garlic and thyme, then transfer to a dehydrator on the highest setting for 12 hours. Pour the caster sugar into a saucepan over a medium heat to make a dry caramel. This should be a light, golden brown colour.

Remove the garlic and thyme from the tomatoes. Add the tomatoes and shallots to the dry caramel, but do be cautious as this will spit. Pour in the tomato juice and vinegar, simmer for 10 minutes. Blend until a smooth consistency is achieved. Check the seasoning and pass the mixture through a fine chinois. Refrigerate until required.

Vanilla Salt

400g sea salt
5 vanilla pods (chopped)

Blend the vanilla pods with half of the salt in a spice blender. Pass through a fine sieve. Add the remaining salt, mix together well but do not blend. Store in an airtight container.

Continued: Basic Recipes

Veal Jus

5k veal knuckle bones
1½ bottles red wine
10 litres cold water

(Prepare ahead)

Place the veal bones in a large stockpot. Cover with enough cold water to come 10cm above the bones. Bring to the boil and skim off any impurities that come to the top.

Add a bottle of wine and bring back to the boil. Skim any impurities from the top of the stock again.

Simmer gently for 36 hours, skimming every couple of hours, topping up with a little more water so it always covers the bones.

Pass the stock through fine muslin cloth and discard the bones.

Refrigerate overnight or for 8 hours. Skim off any set fat from the stock.

Reduce the remaining half bottle of wine in a heavy-based pot until it is a thick, syrupy consistency. Add the stock and bring to a rapid boil. Skim the stock to remove any impurities.

Reduce the stock until you are left with 3 litres, skimming regularly.

Pass through fine muslin cloth twice.

Refrigerate until required, or store any excess jus in the freezer.

Vegetable Stock

1 onion
2 carrots
3 sticks celery
1 large leek
150ml white wine
parsley stalks, chervil stalks, thyme stalks
2 bay leaves
4 coriander seeds

(Prepare ahead)

Wash, peel and roughly dice all the vegetables and place into a stockpot.

Add the white wine and cover with enough cold water to come 20cm above the vegetables.

Bring to the boil and skim off any impurities from the top of the stock. Simmer gently for 1 hour, skimming every 20 minutes or so.

Add the herb stalks, bay leaves and coriander seeds then cover the pot with cling film and refrigerate overnight, or for 8 hours.

Pass the stock through fine muslin cloth and use as required.

Venison Stock

5kg venison ribs (chopped)
2kg venison leg bones and knuckles (chopped)
1 bottle red wine

Ask your butcher to chop up the bones for you so they fit in your largest stockpot.

(Prepare ahead)

Preheat the oven to 185°C.

Roast the venison ribs for 45 minutes, turning every 15 minutes, until an even golden brown colour is achieved.

Place the roasted ribs, the uncooked leg and knuckle bones into a large stockpot.

Cover with enough cold water to come 15cm above the bones. Bring to the boil and add the bottle of wine.

Skim any impurities from the top of the stock. Simmer gently for 9 hours, skimming every 20 minutes or so.

Pass the venison stock through fine muslin cloth. Refrigerate overnight or for 8 hours. Skim off any set fat from the stock and use as required.

Watercress Purée

150g butter
3 shallots (peeled, finely diced)
1 clove garlic (peeled, centre removed, crushed)
100ml milk
200ml double cream
100ml chicken stock
500g watercress
sea salt (pinch of)
50g spinach

Melt the butter and gently sweat off the shallots and garlic without colouring.

Add the milk, cream and chicken stock and reduce by three quarters.

Add half of the watercress and wilt down.

Season with a little salt. Stir in the other half of the watercress and the spinach and wilt down.

Pass through a sieve and transfer the watercress mix to a blender. Blend to a smooth purée, adding the liquid back in as required.

Pass through a fine chinois and adjust the seasoning to taste.

Terms | Meanings | Fancy Words

Abzorbit/Tapioca Maltodextrin
Derived from tapioca starch. Tapioca maltodextrin is often used to produce powders from oils or high fat based products such as chocolate or praline paste.

Acidulated Water
When an acid is added to water; lemon juice, lime juice or vinegar. This prevents skinned fruits or vegetables from browning.

Agar Agar
A gelling agent derived from seaweed, it produces a firm and brittle gel which will retain its structure up to a temperature of about 75°C.

Al Dente
Italian term used to describe a pasta or vegetable that is cooked until it offers a slight resistance to the bite.

Ascorbic Acid
A naturally occurring organic compound with antioxidant properties.

Bain-Marie
A pan or other container of hot water with a bowl placed on top of it. This allows the steam from the water to heat the bowl so ingredients can be gently heated or melted in the bowl.

Bake
To cook by dry heat, usually in the oven.

Baste
To moisten foods during cooking with pan drippings or foaming butter to add flavour and colour and to prevent drying out.

Beat
To mix rapidly in order to make a mixture smooth and light by incorporating as much air as possible.

Beurre Blanc
French translates as 'white butter'. A hot, emulsified butter sauce made with a reduction of vinegar and/or white wine (normally Muscadet) and diced shallots. Cold, whole butter is then whisked in, off the heat, to prevent separation or splitting.

Beurre Noisette
Unsalted butter is melted over a low heat until it begins to caramelise and brown. When it turns a nutty colour, it should be removed from the heat to stop it burning. Can be used as a base for butter sauces or added to cakes and batters.

Blanch
Boiling an ingredient before removing it and plunging it in ice cold water in order to stop the cooking process.

Braise
To cook meat, fish, or vegetables by sautéing in fat and then simmering slowly in very little liquid.

Brunoise
A culinary term where a knife is used in which the food item is first julienned, then turned a quarter turn and diced again, producing cubes of about 3mm or less on each side.

Calcium Chloride
A salt of calcium and chlorine, it is one of the primary ingredients in direct spherification. It is used in the setting bath to activate the sodium alginate.

Calcium Lactate
A calcium-rich product and is perfect for reverse spherification (dipped in sodium alginate bath) without adding any flavour at all to the end product.

Caramelise
To melt sugar in order to turn it brown and bring out the naturally occurring caramel flavours.

Carbon Black
Produced from carbonised vegetables, carbon black is used to produce a black or grey appearance in food.

Carrageenan Iota
Produces soft, elastic vegetarian gels, an ideal alternative to gelatine.

Carrageenans
Gelling agents derived from seaweed, often used in milk-based applications because they are effective at very low concentrations.

Cartouche
A piece of silicone or greaseproof paper that covers the surface of a stew, soup, stock or sauce to stop a skin forming.

Chiffonade
A chopping technique in which herbs or leafy green vegetables (such as spinach and basil) are cut into long, thin strips.

Chinois
A conical sieve with an extremely fine mesh.

Citrate
An alkaline powder which is used to lower high acidity levels in order to allow the gelling or stabilising to work effectively.

Clarified Butter
Milk fat rendered from butter to separate the milk solids and water from the butter fat.

Clarify
To separate and remove solids from a liquid, thus making it clear.

Compressed
The compression of food with the use of a vacuum pack machine to remove air.

Confit
A method of cooking where the ingredient is cooked and submerged in a liquid to add flavour. Often this liquid is rendered fat. Confit can also apply to fruits; fruit confits are cooked and preserved in sugar, the result is like candied fruits.

Court Bouillon
An aromatic stock made from adding onion, carrot, celery, sea salt, thyme, bay leaf, cloves, peppercorns, parsley and wine, lemon or vinegar to water and simmering for 30 minutes. It is usually prepared ahead of time, cooled and strained before using. Lemon or vinegar added to court bouillon preserves the colour of salmon.

Crackle Crystal
Carbonated sugar crystals which crackle and pop when placed in your mouth. Used as a topping or garnish to surprise and delight guests.

Cream
A baking term to soften butter by beating it at room temperature. Butter and sugar are often creamed together, making a smooth, soft paste.

Crépinette
Crépine is the French word for 'pig's caul' in which a crépinette is wrapped instead of a casing.

Crytex/Crisp Film
Acts as a protective barrier against oil, resulting in a really crispy and oil-free covering. It can be added to fruit or vegetable purées, which will then dry to a flexible, crisp glass-like texture.

Cure
To preserve meat or fish by drying and salting and/or smoking.

Dariole
A French term that refers to small, cylinder shaped moulds.

Dehydrate
Drying is a method of food preservation that works by removing water from the food. Food dehydrators are available in most cook shops.

Deglaze
To dissolve the thin glaze of juices and brown bits on the surface of a pan in which food has been fried, sautéed or roasted. To do this, add liquid, then stir and scrape over high heat, thereby adding flavour to the liquid for use as a sauce.

Dredge
To sprinkle or coat with flour or other fine substance.

Drizzle
To sprinkle drops of liquid lightly over food.

Dust
To sprinkle food with dry ingredients.

Emulsion/Emulsify
In the culinary arts, an emulsion is a mixture of two liquids that would ordinarily not mix together, like oil and vinegar.

Espuma Gun
A piece of equipment designed to encapsulate air into cold and warm preparations to create a very light foam.

Essential Oils
Oils from aromatic plants or spices obtained by distillation. Essential oils are highly concentrated and are used to add or intensify flavours across the menu.

Feuilletine
Crushed wafer pieces for added crunch.

Fillet
As a verb, to remove the bones from meat or fish. A fillet (or filet) is the piece of flesh after it has been boned.

Flake
To break lightly into small pieces.

Flavour Drops
Produced by distillation, these highly concentrated flavours can be added to just about anything to add or boost flavour profiles.

Fold
To incorporate a delicate substance, such as whipped cream or beaten egg whites, into another substance without releasing air bubbles. Cut down through the mixture with a spoon, whisk, or fork; go across bottom of bowl, up and over, close to surface. The process is repeated, while slowly rotating the bowl, until the ingredients are thoroughly blended.

French Meringue
Egg whites are beaten until soft peaks, at which point, sugar is slowly incorporated until the mixture has attained full volume.

French Trim
A method of preparing a rack of lamb by cutting the fat out around each bone down to the meat and scraping the bones of all sinew and fat. The lamb is then cut between the bones and through the eye of the lamb, leaving 1cm of meat still attached at the bottom.

Fry
To cook in hot fat. To cook in a fat is called pan-frying or sautéing; to cook in a one-to-two inch layer of hot fat is called shallow-fat frying; to cook in a deep layer of hot fat is called deep-fat frying.

Continued: Terms | Meanings | Fancy Words

Garnish
To decorate a dish both to enhance its appearance and to provide a flavourful foil. Parsley, lemon slices, raw vegetables, chopped chives and other herbs are all forms of garnishes.

Gellan Gum Type F
A vegetarian gelling agent produced by a bacterial fermentation. Gellan gum produces high heat resistant gels, fluid gels and heat stable sorbets that can be flamed at the table.

Gelatine
A translucent, colourless, flavourless food. It is commonly used as a gelling/setting agent. All gelatine in this book is bronze leaf gelatine.

Glaze
To cook with a thin sugar syrup cooked to crack stage; mixture may be thickened slightly. Also, to cover with a thin, glossy icing.

Gold Dust
Pure gold dust (24ct); this can be sprinkled over dishes as a garnish.

Gold Leaf
Pure gold leaf (24ct); used primarily as a garnish.

Gratin
From the French word for 'crust'. Term used to describe any oven-baked dish, usually cooked in a shallow oval dish, on which a golden brown crust of breadcrumbs, cheese or creamy sauce is formed.

Hickory Smoke Essence/Liquid Smoke Essence
Smoke flavoured liquid essence.

Hyfoamer
A natural whipping agent used to improve or replace the use of egg whites. Hyfoamer will not over whisk or crack like an egg white will; it is also heat and acid stable which will allow for the production of flavoured meringues, especially those with a strong citrus flavour and a low sugar content.

Isomalt
A natural sweetener, which has sugar-like physical properties and provides the taste, texture and half the calories of sugar. Isomalt is perfect for sugar pulling and casting of all your sweet decorations (flowers, leaves, ribbons, etc). It offers a higher resistance to humidity and stays flexible longer than regular sugar.

Italian Meringue
Made by beating egg whites until they reach soft, fluffy peaks, then slowly streaming in boiling sugar and beating the mixture until it is thick and glossy.

Julienne
A culinary knife cut in which the food item (vegetables, fruits or cheeses) is cut into long thin strips, similar to matchsticks.

Jus
The natural juices given off by the food. To prepare a natural jus, the cook may simply skim off the fat from the juices left after cooking and bring the remaining meat stock and water to the boil.

Knead
To work and press dough with the palms of the hands or mechanically, to develop the gluten in the flour.

Kuzu/Kudzu
A starch extracted from the kuzu plant from the mountains of Japan, used as a thickener.

Lecithin
Lecithin is an emulsifier (prevents oil and water from separating). It is found in plants such as soybeans, egg yolks and animal sources.

Liquid Glucose
A syrup which is generally used in addition to sugar. It prevents the recrystallisation of sugar and will influence texture, brilliance and the stability of flavours.

Liquor
The liquid that is left over from the cooking of meat or vegetables. Can be incorporated into sauces and gravy.

Macerated
Raw, dried or preserved fruit and vegetables soaked in a liquid to soften the food or to absorb the flavour.

Madagascan Bourbon Vanilla Beans
Dark brown, plump and moist beans with the naturally sweet aromatics of vanilla.

Maillard Reaction
A chemical reaction between amino acids and reducing sugars that gives browned foods their desirable flavour. It is sometimes called 'browning' and helps improve flavour significantly.

Mandoline
A cooking utensil used for slicing and for cutting juliennes. Slices can be very thin and be made very quickly. It ensures that all slices are uniform.

Marinate
To flavour and moisturise pieces of meat, poultry, seafood or vegetable by soaking them in or brushing them with a liquid mixture of seasonings known as a 'marinade'. Dry marinade mixtures composed of salt, pepper, herbs or spices may also be rubbed into meat, poultry or seafood.

Methylcellulose
Derived from cellulose. It is used to produce gels which gel when heated and will turn back to liquid when cooled.

Mirepoix
Combination of leeks, celery, onions and carrots.

Monte Au Beurre
Sauce finishing by adding small quantities of butter to thicken (emulsify) a sauce.

Pane
To coat with flour, beaten egg and breadcrumbs.

Panko
A Japanese-style breadcrumb.

Pâte A Bombe
A pâte à bombe is the French term for a mixture used as a base for making chocolate mousse and other mousse-like desserts.

Pectin
Naturally occurring in fruits, pectin is used primarily for setting jams and paté de fruits.

Pickle
To preserve meats, vegetables and fruits in brine.

Pinch
A pinch is the amount able to be held between a thumb and forefinger.

Pistoles
Originally this French word referred to gold coins in use in European countries until the late 19th century. Now, in the world of chocolate, pistole refers to the coin shaped pieces.

Plancha
A type of flattop grill used for cooking, which is composed of a thick plate of metal above the heating element to provide thermal mass and eliminate hotspots.

Poach
To cook very gently in hot liquid kept just below the boiling point.

Pork Rind Crumble
Uniform in size, this grade of pork rind will puff up to the size of puffed rice, ideal for use as a crumble topping or plate garnish.

Quenelle
A neat, three-sided oval (resembling a mini rugby ball) that is formed by gently smoothing the mixture between two dessertspoons.

Reduce
To boil down to reduce the volume.

Reduction
The process of thickening a liquid in order to intensify the flavour. This is done by evaporating the moisture in a liquid.

Refresh
To run cold water or pour ice over food that has been blanched in boiling water to stop the cooking process immediately.

Render
To make solid fat into liquid by melting it slowly.

Roast
To cook by dry heat in an oven.

Rocher
A one-handed quenelle, is a way to give a perfect oval shape using one spoon.

Sabayon
A sabayon is made by beating egg yolks with a liquid over simmering water until thickened and increased in volume. The liquid can be water, but Champagne or wine is often added.

Sauté
To cook and/or brown food in a small amount of hot fat.

Salt Baked
Refers to the method of baking an ingredient encased in a salt dough.

Scald
To bring to a temperature just below the boiling point.

Sear
To brown very quickly by intense heat. This method increases shrinkage but develops flavour and improves appearance.

Shred
To cut or tear in small, long, narrow pieces.

Shucked (Oysters)
Shucked oysters are those that have been removed from their shells.

Sift
To put one or more dry ingredients through a sieve.

Simmer
To cook slowly in liquid over low heat. The surface of the liquid should be barely moving, broken from time to time by slowly rising bubbles.

Skim
To remove impurities, whether scum or fat, from the surface of a liquid during cooking, thereby resulting in a clear, cleaner-tasting final produce.

Smoking Gun
A hand held cold smoker.

Sodium Alginate
Extracted from brown seaweed. Often used as a stabiliser, thickener or emulsifier. In the presence of calcium it forms gels. It is most commonly used with calcium lactate or calcium chloride in the spherification process.

Continued: Terms | Meanings | Fancy Words

Sodium Citrate
The sodium salt of citric acid. It is mainly used as a food additive, usually for flavour or as a preservative. It reduces the acidity of foods.

Sous Vide
French for 'under vacuum.' A method of cooking food sealed in airtight plastic bags in a water bath or in a temperature-controlled steam environment for longer than normal cooking times. The intention is to cook the item evenly, ensuring that the inside is properly cooked without overcooking the outside, and to retain moisture.

Spherification
A technique of making spheres with a very fine, thin membrane that is almost imperceptible in the mouth, allowing the sphere to burst in your mouth as if there were no solid substance between the liquid and your tongue.

Squid Ink
A dark pigment released into water by squid.

Steam
To cook in steam in a pressure cooker, deep well cooker, double boiler, or a steamer made by fitting a rack in a kettle with a tight cover. A small amount of boiling water is used, more water being added during steaming process, if necessary.

Sugar Ester
A very strong emulsifier used to create very light foams.

Swiss Meringue
Made by gently beating egg whites and sugar in a bain-marie. Once the sugar is completely dissolved, the mixture is pulled off the heat and beaten vigorously to increase and attain full volume and then at a lower speed until cool and very stiff.

Temper
A culinary term meaning to stabilise certain products, for example chocolate. Temper can also mean to bring food to the correct temperature.

Toss
To combine ingredients with a lifting motion.

Truss
To secure poultry with string or skewers, to hold its shape while cooking.

Ultratex
A corn starch which does not require heat to thicken liquids and sauces to the desired consistency. It adds a smooth creamy and glossy texture to liquids which can then be dried or frozen into a thin sheet for garnish. Ultratex has no aftertaste and will preserve the taste and colour of the original liquid. Designed for easy dispersion, it will not lump like other starches.

Whip
To beat rapidly to incorporate air and produce expansion, as in heavy (double) cream or egg whites.

Xanthan Gum
Made by bacterial fermentation, xanthan gum is widely used as a thickener and a stabiliser.

Thank You

Writing a cookbook is no easy undertaking, it is a monumental task. It is certainly more than I ever imagined, so that means I have a huge number of people to thank, not only for making the book possible but also for making me the chef that I am today and to be good enough to write a book in the first place.

My first massive thank you has to be to every boss, head chef or indeed work colleague I have ever worked with or for in the past. It is because of you I am where I am today, so thanks for pushing me further than I ever felt I could go. To the people I have worked for in the past, good and bad, thanks for either believing in me or making me want to prove you wrong, as it turns out you were either very right or very wrong.

To Nicola, my fiancée of 11 years, I promise we will walk down the aisle and it won't be during my split shift as I often joke, but properly. Thanks for the huge amount of support and belief over the years and indeed for helping me settle on the name of the book, as the saying goes behind every great man...

Emma Louise for sitting opposite me and organising and prioritising the book, and not to mention fixing my grammar, as at times I type like a drunk five-year-old. If not for you I would probably have missed every deadline that I was set.

To my current restaurant team, you are all awesome and I am sure individually will go on to great things. Thanks for putting up with me, I don't think I have been too difficult, but then again I would say that wouldn't I?

To my family, extended family and in-laws, you know that you mean the world to me and I can only apologise for missing out on so much and constantly putting my career first. Things are bound to slow down eventually, right?

To Paul for the photography, there really isn't anything I can say that the images on the page don't already.

To my publisher, Relish Publications, thanks for the belief that I was good enough to write the book in the first place and for putting up with my demands, endless changes and emails. I think we can say with great confidence that we have created a book we can all be proud of. So to Duncan, Teresa, Becky, Vicki and Val, a massive thank you.

To all the suppliers and producers, thank you for putting up with my perfecting demands, I like to think of them as requests but let's agree to disagree on that point. Thanks for your support, not only in the amazing produce you supply me with but also for understanding why I need the exacting produce you deliver. If it wasn't for your passion, mine wouldn't be possible. I have to single out the amazing Vicky from MSK for the panicked phone calls she constantly received some ten years ago when my experiments weren't exactly going to plan... has it really been ten years?

To my agent, Limelight Celebrity Management, thanks for the continued support over the last four years, it has been quite the journey so far, here's to many more adventures.

Finally I want to thank the most important people of all - my customers. Some have become lifelong friends and then there's my regulars. You are the reason the doors stay open because without amazing customers we would have no business. Thanks for putting up with our rickety chairs and lack of carpet when we first opened and for joining Nicola and me on what has been an exciting journey so far.

Photography

I first met Paul Johnston of Copper Mango through a mutual friend when I was on the search for an awesome food photographer for a column I was writing. Although photography was not Paul's first career choice, he has always been a hugely passionate photographer in his spare time. He spent almost 20 years of his working life in IT but, after voluntary redundancies were offered seven years ago at his workplace, he seized the opportunity to turn his passion into a career and so Copper Mango was born.

Paul and I have been working together for the past three years and during this time the style and quality of the images have grown in strength. So when discussions started around the possibility of my first book, only one name came to mind when it came to photography.

So often, a full team of food stylists and photographers are employed for a cookbook but for mine, it was just Paul and myself. For months on end, Wednesdays became photography day. We transformed the private dining room at the restaurant into a makeshift studio. I was the food stylist - I personally plated up every plate of food in this book and Paul took the images. His enthusiasm never faltered even as my suggestions got wackier along the way! He even travelled the length and breadth of the country to personally visit and photograph all my featured suppliers. I have never once approached Paul with an idea to be met with negativity. The passion he has for the outcome of his images is equal to the passion I feel for the plates leaving my kitchen.

For me the photography in the book had to be outstanding. Food is so visual; it is so often said that we eat with our eyes first. In the digital age, images of food are constant so I knew my food images needed to stand out. I had a very clear vision of how I wanted the book to feel however, what we achieved is something far beyond what I had even imagined at the time. From the get go, we thought outside the box; deciding on black and white backgrounds to really make the food 'pop'. We started experimenting with crockery and in many cases we went without crockery altogether, plating up dishes directly onto black and white surfaces. From sheets of Perspex to blocks of ice, we worked tirelessly to craft every image in a unique way. It was never the case of a quick snap will do. Each dish would be photographed from different angles. We would then review the images, decide on the best angle and work to perfect that shot. Patience was key - sometimes we would obtain the perfect image but I wouldn't be happy with the placing of one herb, for example, so it would mean taking the image again to ensure perfection. It was a real learning curve for us both but the excitement built and I always looked forward to receiving the folders of images for sign off. Paul's ability to capture my food still amazes me. To me, the images are stunning. For any chef, when creating a new dish, the quality of the ingredients is of utmost importance and for me, Paul has been a vital ingredient in the production of this book.

Just wait until I tell Paul about book number two...

Suppliers & Useful Contacts

Ardgay Venison
www.ardgaygame.co.uk
01863 766 162

Campbell Brothers
www.campbellbrothers.co.uk
0131 654 0050

Clarks Speciality Foods
www.clarksfoods.co.uk
0844 335 6908

Copper Mango
www.coppermango.com
07702 480 003

Creative Cookware
www.creativecookware.co.uk
0131 226 2117

Cyrenians Farm
www.cyrenians.scot
0131 333 5202

D R Collin & Son
www.drcollin.co.uk
01890 752 427

Edinburgh Tea & Coffee Company
www.edinburghteacoffee.co.uk
0131 669 9222

The Ethical Shellfish Company
www.ethicalshellfishcompany.co.uk
0845 116 2248

Gartmorn Farm
www.gartmornfarm.co.uk
01259 750 549

Hebridean Sea Salt
www.hebrideanseasalt.co.uk
01851 880 324

Instock
www.instockgroup.co.uk
0844 844 1563

Katy Rodger's Artisan Dairy
www.knockraich.com
01360 860 202

Lakeland
www.lakeland.co.uk
01539 488 100

Leadketty Farm
www.leadkettyfarm.co.uk
01764 684 532

MSK Ingredients
www.msk-ingredients.com
01246 412 211

Ochil Foods
www.ochilfoods.co.uk
01764 662 502

RR Spink & Sons
www.rrspink.co.uk
01241 872 023

Sapori Truffles
www.saporitruffles.co.uk
07711 319 768

Sous Vide Tools
www.sousvidetools.com
0800 678 5001

Thermomix
www.thermomix.vorwerk.co.uk
0330 660 0834

Markets

Edinburgh Farmers' Market
www.edinburghfarmersmarket.co.uk

Stockbridge Market
www.stockbridgemarket.com

Conversion Chart

Cooking Temperatures

Degrees Celsius	Fahrenheit	Gas Mark
140	275	1
150	300	2
160-170	325	3
180	350	4
190	375	5
200-210	400	6
220	425	7
230	450	8
240	475	9

*Temperatures for fan-assisted ovens are, as a general rule, normally about 20°C lower than regular oven temperature.

Volume Measurement Conversions

55ml	2 fl oz
150ml	¼ pt
275ml	½ pint
570ml	1 pt
1 litre	1¾ pt

Weight Measurement Conversions

1 teaspoon (5ml/5g)	¼ oz
1 tablespoon (15ml/15g)	¾ oz
10g	½ oz
25g	1oz
50g	2oz
75g	3oz
150g	5oz
200g	7oz
250g	9oz
350g	12oz
450g	1lb
1kg	2.2lb